THE COLOR OF CREATORSHIP

THE COLOR OF CREATORSHIP

Intellectual Property, Race, and the Making of Americans

Anjali Vats

STANFORD UNIVERSITY PRESS | STANFORD, CALIFORNIA

STANFORD UNIVERSITY PRESS
Stanford, California

Printed in the United States of America on acid-free, archival-quality paper

Library of Congress Cataloging-in-Publication Data
Names: Vats, Anjali, author.
Title: The color of creatorship : intellectual property, race, and the making of Americans / Anjali Vats.
Description: Stanford, California : Stanford University Press, 2020. | Includes bibliographical references and index.
Identifiers: LCCN 2019040803 (print) | LCCN 2019040804 (ebook) | ISBN 9781503603301 (cloth) | ISBN 9781503610958 (paperback) | ISBN 9781503610965 (ebook)
Subjects: LCSH: Intellectual property—Social aspects—United States. | Race discrimination—Law and legislation—United States.
Classification: LCC KF2979 .V38 2020 (print) | LCC KF2979 (ebook) | DDC 346.73048089—dc23
LC record available at https://lccn.loc.gov/2019040803
LC ebook record available at https://lccn.loc.gov/2019040804

Cover art: Nancy Y. Kim. *Bite of the Medusa* (detail), 2018. Acrylic Paint, Paper Cells, and Thread Embedded in Acrylic Paint Skin, T-Pins, 62×62 in.

Designed by Kevin Barrett Kane

Typeset at Stanford University Press in 10/14 Galliard Pro

For Jerrell Maurice Braden (1980–2012)
"hope you enjoy the spelling, i actually
paid attention, sort of this time."

TABLE OF CONTENTS

ACKNOWLEDGMENTS

Writing a book is a process, one that is often lonely, frustrating, fraught, and anxiety-producing. However, it is also a process that provides fertile ground for connection, collaboration, and joy. I am thankful that my experience has been more of the latter than the former, involving more personal and professional growth than I ever imagined possible.

I began this project more than a decade ago, though not in this form. My first engagement with intellectual property law came in 2004, during my second year of law school. After years of working on issues of race and gender, I found the thought of engaging with a body of law that did not seem to me at the time to interface with social justice to be an intriguing one. It was not until much later, after I had completed my LLM at the University of Washington and clerkship at the Supreme Court of Nevada that I seriously contemplated the potential for critical race engagement with intellectual property law.

By my first year of graduate school, in 2009, I had begun to think critically about representations of infringement, layering my studies of race and rhetoric atop those of law. In the intervening decade, this book came together as a project about the racial histories of intellectual properties, as well as the insights that Critical Race Theory could bring to even the most progressive understandings of copyright, patents, and trademarks. In short, while I did not know this book would be the endgame when I started the project, I am pleased that my path has brought me here. A great many people across periods of my life, academic disciplines, and geographic spaces have inspired, supported, mentored, and befriended me over the years. As I am told happens with first books, this project is a record of my journey with them as much as it is the product of my research and writing.

At Boston College, I have developed a network of wonderful and supportive colleagues and friends. In the Communication Department, thank you to Ann Marie Barry, Marcus Breen, Christine Caswell, Lisa Cuklanz, Leslie Douglas, Ashley Duggan, Ali Erol, Don Fishman, Kristin Hartnett, Lindsey Hogan, Brett Ingram, Ernesto Livon-Grosman, Kristin Peterson, Rita Rosenthal, Mike Serazio, Matt Sienkewicz, Tony Tran, and Celeste Wells. It continues to be a pleasure to work with all of you. I am particularly indebted to Lisa for being a tireless and dedicated advocate, mentor, and cheerleader to me in her role as department chair.

To my colleagues in African and African Diaspora Studies—Amey Victoria Adkins-Jones, M. Shawn Copeland, Allison Curseen, Kyrah Malika Daniels, Rhonda Frederick, Jonathan Howard, Régine Jean-Charles, C. Shawn McGuffey, Richard Paul, and Martin Summers—your brilliance, fierceness, warmth, humor, and undying commitment to social justice keep me going even in the toughest moments.

In Asian American Studies, I am grateful to Arissa Oh and Min Hyoung Song for building spaces to do the work that we do. In the law school, my thanks to Renee Jones, Vincent Rougeau, and Fred Yen for your enthusiastic commitment to this and other critical race studies projects that I have undertaken; your support has been integral to the completion of this project. Finally, to Provost David Quigley and Dean Greg Kalscheur—I cannot thank you enough for providing me with the space and latitude to take a year of research leave so that I could concentrate on completing this book; it is markedly better because I had that time.

One of the great pleasures and privileges that writing this book has afforded me is connecting with the Microsoft Research New England's intellectually vibrant Social Media Collective. Thank you to Nancy Baym, Tarleton Gillespie, and Mary Gray for embracing me as part of your community of scholars. I am also grateful to the many interlocutors with whom I had the opportunity to connect at SMC, including Kelly Buckley, Robyn

Caplan, Michaelanne Dye, Dan Greene, Sarah Hamid, Elena Maris, Dylan Mulvin, Chris Persaud, Bill Thies, and Penny Trieu.

Nearly a year of research leave spent at the University of California, Davis School of Law was also of considerable importance to the development of this project. My appreciation to Mario Biagioli, Anupam Chander, and Madhavi Sunder for inviting me to join King Hall's scholarly community. Thank you, as well, to Karima Bennoune, Jack Chin, Angela Harris, Jasmine Harris, Lisa Ikemoto, Rana Jafeel, Kevin Johnson, Peter Lee, and Donna Shetowsky for being generous scholars and fast friends. I also owe a debt of gratitude to the American Association for University Women for awarding me the postdoctoral fellowship that allowed me to spend immeasurably productive time in Davis finishing this book manuscript.

I was lucky enough to get a dream job at Indiana University the year after I graduated. The faculty I met in Bloomington—including Carolyn Calloway-Thomas, Steph deBoer, Liz Elcessor, Laura Foster, Ilana Gershon, Jane Goodman, Joan Hawkins, Mark Janis, Barb Klinger, John Lucaites, Radhika Parameswaran, Phaedra Pezzullo, Ryan Powell, Ted Striphas, Robert Terrill, and Greg Waller—provided guidance and friendship that have lasted far beyond my brief stopover in Indiana.

Much of this book was written in the Pacific Northwest, a place that never fails to nourish my soul. My gratitude to my PNW friends, colleagues, and mentors from across institutions who made and continue to make Seattle and Tacoma a scholarly home away from home: Herb Blau, Derek Buescher, Leah Ceccarelli, Maggie Chon, Lisa Coutu, David Domke, Justin Eckstein, Peter Ehrenhaus, Dexter Gordon, Christine Harold, Mako Hill, Jim Jasinski, Ralina Joseph, LeiLani Nishime, Sean O'Connor, Sue Owen, Zahr Said, Kathy Woodward, and Amy Young.

I owe special thanks to a few brilliant mentors, who continue to teach me to thrive in the academy and in life. Ralina and LeiLani, you are the best mentors, comrades, and friends that I can imagine. Dexter, you provided revelatory guidance when I didn't even know I needed it. And Maggie, your intellectual prowess coupled with gentleness of spirit have nourished my soul. Your conceptions of community and solidarity have inspired me as a young scholar. It is a privilege to do the racial justice work that each of you teaches and models on the West Coast here on the East Coast.

The Simpson Center for the Humanities provided a formative space for thinking through this project in its early versions. I am grateful still to have been part of a cohort of the Society of Scholars there, where we worked through the most difficult parts of our projects together. My deepest thanks to George Behlmer, Annie Dwyer, Benjamin Gardner, Gillian Harkins, Celia Lowe, Luisa Mackenzie, LeiLani Nishime, Maria Quintana, Christina Sunardi, and Patrick Zambianchi for your input on early versions of this project. Kathy Woodward, the fearless leader of the Simpson Center, is truly a model of humanistic intellectualism, collegiality, support, and class. I will never forget the enthusiasm with which she and Herb Blau invited me into not only their academic spaces but also their homes and hearts. Thank you as well to the Institute for Ethnic Studies in the United States (IESUS), at the University of Washington, for generously funding the research for parts of chapter 4.

Writing and accountability groups are a not insignificant component of completing projects such as these. I have had many iterations of both over the years. While all have been important, a few are particularly notable. Performing the Gap—comprised of Samer Al-Saber, Jacinthe Assaad, Raj Chetty, Amal Eqeiq, and Brian Gutierrez—gave me life as I pushed to finish the first version of this project. Finding a welcoming space full of committed, radical scholars of color turned lifelong friends was one of the best parts of grad school. I adore you all, and I am so pleased that we have found ways to stay together even as we have moved apart.

The Athens of America Rhetoric Reading Group (AARRG!) has offered support, feedback, and laughter that have gotten me through some of the most trying moments of this research. In particular, thank you to Jason Edwards, Michael Hoppman, Dale Herbeck, Odile Hobeika, Jamie Landau, Katie Lind, and Tom Nakayama; it has been a pleasure to have conversations with you about our work over the years.

Some colleagues and friends provided support, both tangible and intangible, that does not neatly fit into categories. Thank you to Jane Anderson, Angela Ards, Ann Bartow, Amit Basole, Vanessa Beasley, Jeff Bennett, André Brock, Caitlin Bruce, Dan Burk, Bernadette Calafell, Peter Campbell, Karma Chávez, Genevieve Clutario, Rosemary Coombe, Shilpa Dave, Shinsuke Eguchi, Lisa Flores, Nick Gozik, Debora Halbert, Doug Ishii, Nathan Johnson, Paul Johnson, Casey Kelly, Mark Lemley, John Lynch, Ashley Mack, Madhavi Mallapragada, Al Martin, Bryan McCann, Kembrew McLeod, Robert Meija, Chuck Morris, Lateef Mtima, Roopali Mukherjee, Kent Ono, Ersula Ore, Andy Owens, Minh-Ha T. Pham, Vincent Pham, Richard Pineda, Swarna

Rajagopalan, Sriri Ramasubramanian, Gil Rodman, Rich Schur, Hasit Shah, Dan Shalmon, Jessica Silbey, Claire Sisco-King, John Sloop, Kara Swanson, Siva Vaidhyanathan, Anghy Valdivia, Myra Washington, Isaac West, and Lesley Wexler—who have, at various moments, offered insight, guidance, wisdom, support, letters of recommendation, pep talks, writing groups, and comic relief. Rosemary Coombe deserves special mention for being an early and wholehearted supporter of my work since I met her in Osnabrück many years ago. Thank you as well to those scholars and activists who support Race + IP. If I have inadvertently omitted anyone here, it is not for lack of appreciation.

Research itself is only one part of my professional life. My students are a big part of the rest. A small army of graduate and undergraduate students and mentees has been closely involved with this project. Joshua Trey Barnett, Hamed Bayat, Caliesha Comley, Catalina deOnis, Nicolette Griot, Lily Nagengast, Titilayo Odelyeye, Anthony Smith, Bridget Sutherland, and Angelina Vallejo, thank you so much for all the effort you have put into helping me complete this project. It has been my pleasure to work with you and watch you find your own paths.

The run-up to finishing a book is quite the process. Maggie Chon, Lisa Corrigan, Don Fishman, and Angela Harris deserve a special note of appreciation for, among other things, serving as interlocutors at a daylong mini-conference focused on this project. While eight hours of feedback on a manuscript is by definition intense, they made the experience productive, supportive, fun, and delightfully lighthearted all at once.

To my editor Michelle Lipinski, you have truly made the process of writing a book a pleasure. Your excitement, investment, sense of humor, and astute insights have been invaluable in seeing this project through to completion. Thank you as well to Emily Smith and Nora Spiegel and to the rest of the team at Stanford University Press for their hard work, attention to detail, and patience in getting this project to press.

While most of the book is completely new material, Chapter One and Chapter Four are derived, in part, from an earlier essay, "Marking Disidentification: Race, Corporeality, and Resistance in Trademark Law," published in the *Southern Communication Journal* in 2016. Chapter Four is also derived, in part, from an earlier essay, "(Dis)owning Bikram: Decolonizing Vernacular and Dewesternizing Restructuring in the Yoga Wars," published in *Communication and Critical/Cultural Studies* in 2015. The pieces are cited in full in the bodies of those chapters. This book and the articles are better because of the rigorous engagement and generous support of the editors and reviewers at those journals.

Nancy Kim, whose art graces the cover, is a dear friend and collaborator. Nancy and I met in college, where our connection was strong and vibrant. We lost touch over the years, though, as we both traveled the world. In October 2018, we met again in a serendipitous moment. When I called Nancy a few months later asking if she'd be interested in being the cover artist for this book, she dubbed this our first collaboration. Thank you so much, Nancy, for sharing your art and this project with me.

The list of people whose friendship has gotten me through this project is far too long to include in full here. There are a few people whose names I simply cannot leave out, though. Sam Allen, Andrea Baldini, Eric Chalfant, Nate Cohn, Reynard Cross, Pete Gaulin, Jake Ginsbach, Aimi Hamraie, Allison Humble, Paul Kerr, Peter Klein, Liz Lemon, Michael Martin, Ben Meiches, Ali Na, Craig Schoen, Luke Stanford, and Phil Thompson—my gratitude and affection to each of you. For deep and abiding friendship, the kind that continually makes me a better person, I thank Phil Samuels, Deidré Keller, Pamela Pietrucci, and Lisa Corrigan. It means the world to me that you have each worn the hats of reader, interlocutor, cheerleader, consoler, and congratulator, with love, compassion, gentleness, humor, and enthusiasm.

Phill, I don't know what I'd do without your patience, acceptance, support, filthy dad jokes, and gift of song. Our conversations—about everything from critical race studies to comic book lore—make my life more joyful. Thank you for being you. To Pamela, my platonic life partner and rhetoric co-conspirator, I'm beginning to think it was more than luck that brought us together in Boston. I look forward to laughing, learning, and growing with your plant-loving punk ass for years to come. Deidré, I will always be eternally grateful for all that I've learned from you, as the family I choose and my intellectual soulmate. Sharing the ups and downs of my life and the project of Critical Race IP with you has been my honor. Lisa, I appreciate you more than you can ever know. You make me better intellectually, personally, and spiritually with your brilliance, generosity, wit, and labor. I love you all and cannot thank you enough for being on my side, unconditionally.

Last but not least, I am grateful to my family, near and far. These thank-yous are the most difficult because they require putting nearly forty years of unconditional love and support into a few short sentences. I am blessed to have a family, biological and chosen, that is unwaveringly dedicated to my education, growth, and well-being. To each and every member of my extended family, thank you for the role you've played in my life for all these years.

To Audrey Lynden, you and your family have been a steady beacon of light in my life. Words cannot express how much you all mean to me. To Naalti Chawla and Rohan Chawla, I'm so pleased to have you as my family—and to have the opportunity to plan shenanigans with the littlest member of the family. To Subodh and Shashi Vats, you've made me the person I am today. Without you and the lesson that there is no substitute for doing the work, none of this would have been possible. I love you all. And so it begins.

LIST OF ACRONYMS

A2K	Access to Knowledge
AYUSH	Ayurveda, Yoga and Naturopathy, Unani, Siddha, and Homeopathy
EFF	Electronic Frontier Foundation
EPO	European Patent Office
GATT	General Agreement on Trade and Tariffs
IPC	International Patent Classification
MPAA	Motion Picture Association of America
PMRC	Parents Music Resource Center
RIAA	Recording Industry Association of America
TDRA	Trademark Dilution Revision Act
TKDL	Traditional Knowledge Digital Library
TKRC	Traditional Knowledge Resource Classification
TRIPS	Trade-Related Aspects of Intellectual Property Rights
TTAB	Trademark Trial and Appeal Board
USPTO	United States Patent and Trademark Office
USTR	United States Trade Representative
WTO	World Trade Organization

THE COLOR OF CREATORSHIP

CREATING INTELLECTUAL PROPERTY, CREATING AMERICANS

Race enters writing, the making of art, as a structure of feeling, as something that structures feelings, that lays down tracks of affection and repulsion, rage and hurt, desire and ache. These tracks don't only occur in the making of art; they also occur (sometimes viciously, sometimes hazily) in the reception of creative work. Here we are again: we've made this thing and we've sent it out into the world for recognition—and because what we've made is in essence a field of human experience created for other humans, the field and its maker and its readers are thus subject all over again to race and its infiltrations. In that moment arise all sorts of possible hearings and mis-hearings, all kinds of address and redress.
—CLAUDIA RANKINE and BETH LOFFREDA,
"On Whiteness and the Racial Imaginary"

But you're a good girl!
The way you grab me
Must wanna get nasty
Go ahead, get at me
—ROBIN THICKE, PHARRELL WILLIAMS, AND T.I.,
"Blurred Lines"

INTELLECTUAL PROPERTY LAW, the body of legal doctrine and practice that governs the ownership of information, is animated by a dichotomy of creatorship and infringement. In the most often repeated narratives of creatorship/infringement in the United States, the former produces a social and economic good while the latter works against the production of that social and economic good. Creators, those individuals whose work is deemed protectable under copyright, patent, trademark, trade secret, and unfair competition law, create valuable products that contribute to economic growth and public knowledge. Infringers, those individuals who use the work of creators without their permission, steal those valuable products and act as drains on economic growth and public knowledge. These narratives, while comforting, are frequently oversimplified in public cultural conversations, in ways that center and elevate Westernness and whiteness and obscure and replicate histories of race and (neo)colonialism.

The Color of Creatorship is a book about the historical and continuing relationships between race and (neo)coloniality in intellectual property law. In it, I join a respected and growing group of scholars in contending that intellectual property law is a set of rhetorics about citizenship. However, unlike those who have previously written about the relationships between intellectual property and citizenship, I focus on the latter as a discourse through which race and coloniality continue to structure doctrinal practices in copyright, patent, and trademark law. Citizenship in the United States was and continues to be a raced concept. More specifically, it is a concept constructed by and through constantly evolving public cultural conceptions of Americanness, white masculinity, property, racial capitalism, and labor.

I use the term "intellectual property citizenship" as an anchoring analytic for understanding how intellectual property and citizenship have evolved—and continue to evolve—in deeply intertwined and raced ways. Through a periodic analysis of American legal cases, political speeches, and cultural practices, this book shows that copyright, patent, and trademark regimes are imagined through always already racialized notions of citizenship that purport to be free of racial bias. Citizenship, while presumed to be race neutral, is frequently defined via shifting normative claims about race, gender, and class and implicit definitions of "good citizens."[1]

This book is more specifically about the complex ways that whiteness and its attendant property interests structure intellectual property law, often in the guise of equality and race neutrality.[2] Racial inequality is a continuing and persistent problem in intellectual property law, not because of legal happenstance, economic motive, or racial accident but because copyright, patent, and trademark doctrines are fundamentally prefigured through raced conceptions of citizenship. Intellectual property citizenship, then, is a "grid of intelligibility"[3]—a framework for understanding how power is organized—that reveals the racializing and colonizing principles around which familiar and repeated doctrinal standards in copyright, patent, and trademark law were and are structured.

The codified racial discrimination that made intellectual property law the purview of whites in the 1800s did not disappear. It persisted through the continuing racialized entanglements of the principles of Euro-American citizenship with the principles of Euro-American creatorship. Because conceptions of Americanness were and are structured through a trenchant "racial episteme,"[4] a frame that a priori constrains possibilities for treating people of color as full persons, let alone full creators, the discourse of citizenship operates as a container for importing race into intellectual property law, even when the law itself purports to be colorblind. The continuing practice of thinking about copyright, patent, and trademark law through romanticized imaginings of American citizenship constrains the manner in which knowledge production/protection can be understood, managed, and adjudicated with respect to race. I do not claim that such racial investments explain the outcome in *all* intellectual property cases. However, I contend that intellectual property law is organized through a racial episteme that consistently protects the (intellectual) property interests of white people and devalues the (intellectual) property interests of people of color.

Tracing "racial scripts" is a tangible method for understanding America's racial episteme and how it informs citizenship and creatorship/infringement as discursive formations. Racial scripts are historically grounded and flexible racist logics about racial groups that can be accessed at any time to exclude the original or other people of color.[5] They operate as shorthand mechanisms for calling upon dominant American ideals of national identity, patriotism, political economy, and personhood without necessarily explicitly invoking racial categories or colonial logics. In this way, racial scripts can be baked into the seemingly colorblind ideals of American citizenship that, in turn, inform intellectual property law. Examining how intellectual property law operates as a space of racial formation in which the meaning of racial categories evolves over time is a prerequisite to undoing entrenched white privilege and democratizing knowledge production and ownership.[6]

Intellectual property law is also a "racial project,"[7] that reproduces particular racial orders, in which people of color are coded as lacking the capacity to create. Unspoken longings, fears, anxieties, and prejudices wrapped in economic and legal language move us to prefer certain intellectual property narratives over others, predictably to the detriment of people of color. When anti-racist, anti-colonial activists grapple with the racial episteme that structures intellectual property law, they can advocate for strategies that resist the underlying drivers of unjust copyright, patent, and trademark policies. While such resistive strategies may ultimately still provide only precarious and fleeting relief, as Derrick Bell famously argues, they confront the fears and anxieties that sustain racial and colonial knowledge hierarchies.[8]

This book contributes to a growing body of scholarship at the intersections of race and intellectual property law through its historically situated consideration of the links among race, coloniality, and knowledge governance.[9] It traces evolutions in the racial rhetorics around copyrights, patents, and trademarks that unfolded in parallel with the economic and political turns of the nation. Such an inquiry is useful in contextualizing the increasingly important legal regimes governing knowledge that mark some bodies as not only inherently incapable of creatorship but also inherently undeserving of citizenship. As the racial rhetorics of intellectual property law have changed over time, in ways that are consistent with post–civil rights era colorblindness, they have come to exclude people of color in new and different ways.

Accordingly, addressing intellectual property law's structural inequalities requires thinking about how these racial evolutions persist in a nation that claims to value all people equally. When marginalized groups are considered to be "aberrations from the ethnoclass of Man"[10] contra a white ideal, as Alexander Weheliye writes, they cannot fully occupy the space of creatorship or (intellectual) property ownership until the nation attends to the contours of inequality and exclusion. While Weheliye is commenting on anti-Blackness, his statement is true for all those people of color who are considered outside of the ethnoclass of Man. In the so-called information economy, intellectual property justice is racial justice.

Working through key moments in intellectual property history in the period between 1790 and 2016 reveals that even as American understandings of creatorship/infringement have seemingly evolved, they have actually remained remarkably racially conservative and consistent over time. This book will not provide an exhaustive account of race, coloniality, and intellectual property law during that period. Such a project is neither possible nor desirable. Instead, it focuses on reading some of the most important and notable historical touchstones in copyright, patent, and trademark law as examples of the continuity of racial scripts and colonial relations of domination in the context of knowledge production.

INTELLECTUAL PROPERTY CITIZENSHIP

Intellectual property law is a set of rhetorics that governs knowledge production. These rhetorics interface with larger cultural narratives about national identity, citizenship, personhood, and economic production.[11] Copyright law, the law of creative works, affords a limited monopoly to authors and artists who create literary, dramatic, musical, artistic, and other intellectual works that are "fixed in any tangible medium of expression."[12] Patent law, the law of inventions, affords a limited monopoly to inventors who create new and previously unknown technologies, which they disclose to the public. Trademark law, the law of identifying marks, affords a limited monopoly to trademark owners who use words, names, symbols, and designs to identify their goods and distinguish those goods from the goods of others.

These areas of law are distinct and different from one another, yet they are often lumped together in policy discussions because they govern knowledge production and knowledge protection. There is a strong argument for disentangling them when thinking about their respective cultural, economic, and political workings, as Richard Stallman argues.[13] Yet it is also useful to think across them, in a categorical sense, in order to identify their central stakes and metanarratives. In asserting that intellectual property law is a rhetorical enterprise, I mean that copyright, patent, and trademark law, like all other legal regimes, are discursive formations shaped by culture, identity, and power. They are not a set of universal or immanent rules about knowledge governance that originate with an infallible authority. They are negotiations of social values and ethical mores and their practical implementations. Rhetorical study can reveal where and how race, a socially constructed category, moves in intellectual property law, particularly over time.

Intellectual property citizenship, as I use the term here, points to the seemingly permanent nexus of copyright, patent, and trademark law and citizenship, a concept that necessarily implicates race, coloniality, racial capitalism, and personhood. It is an analytical tool for understanding the structural complexities of the legal regimes that define the mass noun "intellectual property" and a frame for rendering visible the power structures that prevent racially equitable outcomes in intellectual property contexts.

"Citizenship," a term that is often considered for its formal legal proper-ties, is also a culturally negotiated concept through which certain individu-als are included/excluded from the body politic. When it intersects with intellectual property discourse, as it has for hundreds of years, citizenship operates as a discursive vehicle for excluding racially marginalized groups from legal practices of knowledge production and ownership.[14]

As Jessica Silbey contends, intellectual property's narratives are really origin stories about the nation and its people, used to define and negotiate the boundaries of Americanness itself.[15] Collective myths around intellectual property citizenship reinforce and update Euro-American ideals of Romantic authorship/Romantic inventorship,[16] rendering them legible for the cul-tural politics of the era through evolving rhetorical constructions of hard work, innovation, ingenuity, and ruggedness. In the American imaginary, authors are creatives who produce valuable cultural works; inventors are geniuses who transform flashes of brilliance into practical inventions; trade-mark owners are producers of goods who protect hard-earned authenticity and quality.[17] Intellectual property citizenship is a mythical ideal defined in part through its relation to these characteristics of individuals who attain the American Dream. Further, it helps to show that intellectual property is a racialized concept, which obscures whiteness and racial power through the mobilization of national feelings of hope, optimism, and pride, as well as fear, anxiety, and protectiveness.

Silbey emphasizes the qualities of Americanness that underlie and ani-mate intellectual property in a mutually constitutive bond. However, she does not go so far as to unpack the *racial* meaning of such characteristics. Embedded in understandings of Romantic creatorship are intersectionally inflected racial and colonial presuppositions about the value of white male knowledge and the value of people of color knowledge.[18] Intellectual prop-erty law, as a rhetorical enterprise that shapes Americanness, also constitutes racial and colonial difference in ideological and material ways. Just as "[l]aw constructs race,"[19] intellectual property law constructs race.[20]

Copyright, patent, and trademark law define race by and through their racialized understandings of creatorship/infringement, which are funda-mentally linked to American conceptions of good citizenship/bad citizen-ship. In that sense, those court cases decided between the ratification of the Reconstruction Amendments and the civil rights movement that explic-itly defined race in refusing to extend citizenship rights to certain groups of people of color, which Ian Haney López calls the Prerequisite Cases, implicitly haunt intellectual property law.[21] Their racist and exclusionary articulations of citizenship undergird historical and contemporary legal understandings of who possesses the capacity to make intellectual property, which is in turn a central driver of the racialized American economy. As a result, anxieties about race, nation, and citizenship developed in ways that were mutually constitutive with anxieties about knowledge production, labor, and economics. Though contemporary colorblind rhetoric suggests that intellectual property has been delinked from such racial decision making, I argue otherwise. Intellectual property law is bound up with narratives of race, nation, and citizenship, as well as their attendant "structures of feeling," in Raymond Williams's parlance.[22] The relationship between intellectual property law and citizenship fuels understandings of creatorship that protect white interests in copyrights, patents, and trademarks.

Intellectual property citizenship is more than a description of the ties between intellectual property and citizenship discourse: it is a grid of intelligibility that reveals how the American racial episteme operates by and through the ideals of citizenship around which copyright, patent, and trademark law are imagined. For Foucault, a grid of intelligibility is a schema that helps to make sense of social orders.[23] In this context, intellectual property citizenship is a grid of intelligibility that aids in understanding how intellectual property and citizenship discourse coalesce to protect whiteness in copyright, patent, and trademark spaces. Thinking about citizenship as an ordering discursive formation through which intellectual property law is constructed reveals that race continues to be not just a superficial issue that determines the outcome of legal cases but an a priori racial ordering of the structures of knowledge production.

I argue that the outcome of individual legal cases involving creators of color is less important than how doctrinal standards were forged through epistemically raced conceptions of citizenship. The coalescence of intellectual property and citizenship produced doctrinal language that continues to systematically privilege whiteness even today. More specifically, America's racial episteme is "the strategic apparatus which permits separating out from among the statements which are possible those that will be acceptable within."[24] Understanding citizenship as a "strategic rhetoric of whiteness,"[25] in the words of Thomas Nakayama and Robert Krizek, transforms the object of study from the racial outcome in individual cases to the racial *logics* of doctrine itself. Though the race of the plaintiffs and defendants in intellectual property cases is helpful in locating moments of racial crisis, it is not dispositive in thinking about how race works in those moments.

The concept of intellectual property citizenship, as I have intimated through the binary of the good citizen/bad citizen, presupposes an actor, i.e., the intellectual property citizen. The remainder of the book contemplates how American public culture tends to imagine and implicitly invoke idealized intellectual property citizens as actors in narratives about the nation and its well-being. The good intellectual property citizen is shaped by invisible Euro-American norms of white masculinity and constructed in contrast to the bad intellectual property citizen. Familiar binaries of self/Other and good/evil transform intellectual property rhetoric into a tool for reinforcing structural inequality domestically and internationally.

Like the category of Romantic creatorship, the frame of the intellectual property citizen functions as flexible racial and (neo) colonial shorthand for determining, given the particular political and economic needs of the nation, who is categorized as creator. At one historical moment, as chapter 1 demonstrates, overtly racist restrictions on intellectual property ownership may be sufficient to protect whiteness as intellectual property. At another historical moment, as chapter 2 demonstrates, deploying colorblind understandings of creatorship may be useful in justifying racially exclusionary intellectual property practices. Within the narratives that structure intellectual property law, intellectual property citizens tend to move action forward, in familiar and predictable racial and (neo) colonial arcs.

Marouf Hasian uses the concept of "prudential characterizations"[26] to describe how law draws upon and constitutes cultural myths about nation and identity to navigate the facts of individual legal cases. While "prudence" is the ability to use reason to make a judgment in legal contexts,[27] prudential characterizations refer to the often enthymematic appeals to familiar myths and narratives to adjudicate cases. Hasian writes that characters in legal trials and legal narratives "provide us with enduring cultural exemplars that influence the ways in which we categorize trials, accept evidence, and apportion blame."[28] The Prerequisite Cases showcase how prudential characterizations operate in the context of citizenship, specifically by using race as a dispositive factor for predicting the work habits, integrity, and loyalty of prospective citizens. In doing so, the Prerequisite Cases employ familiar racial scripts as tools for marking the legal and ideological boundaries of citizenship.

In the context of intellectual property law, not only have courts and publics made similar prudential characterizations, but they have done so in ways that adhere to racial myths about creatorship, citizenship, and personhood. Intellectual property cases, then, do not simply mark the outcome of legal disputes over knowledge production and knowledge ownership; they also make explicit and implicit claims about, in the words of Benedict Anderson, the best ways to "think the nation."[29] Intellectual property's "imagined communities"[30] do not reflect America's melting-pot ideal but instead systematically protect whiteness as (intellectual) property. In this respect, citizenship is more than a legal term. It is also a discursive one that shapes and is shaped by overlapping and deeply racially biased bodies of law.

THE RACIAL SCRIPTS OF CREATORSHIP

Intellectual property law shapes and is shaped by citizenship. Citizenship, as a category, is prefigured by racial scripts in ways that normalize some people as citizens and others as non-citizens, which, in turn, circumscribes the outcome in intellectual property cases. Racial scripts describe "how racialization processes extend across time and space and affect racial groups even when they do not cross paths."[31] Understanding racist rhetorics in this way highlights the simultaneous *durability* and *flexibility* of language and sentiment about race, in a manner that is consistent with theorizations of racial formation. The play in the joints of racial scripts protects white supremacy, often by racializing people of color using one or more sets of racist stereotypes in ways that provoke strong racial feelings. Historical uses of racial scripts prime audiences for accepting them again, in different contexts.

According to Vincent Pham, racial scripts are "anchored in history"[32] and "reoccur, interact, and work concomitantly to constitute our ideas about some racial groups in relation to other racial groups."[33] These racial scripts also often "reinforce a cultural logic of race as the basis of national belonging [and] legitimate citizenship."[34] As critical race studies scholars have consistently demonstrated, though formal equality may be a reality in contemporary American law, including intellectual property law, informal racism seeps into legal doctrine and the practice of law. Pinpointing the language that intellectual property law uses to invoke conceptions of citizenship and related racial scripts, particularly as they code for who has the capacity to create/infringe, reveals an underlying racial episteme, calcified in precedentially trenchant judicial decisions.

In following the movement of race and citizenship through legal cases over time, I show that intellectual property citizens are collectively constituted as creatives who exhibit "true imagination" in the context of copyright law, contributors to "human progress" in the context of patent law, and participants in the "consumer gaze" in the context of trademark law. These familiar clusters of intellectual property rhetorics are consistently articulated through the racialized language of citizenship, which is, in turn, linked to the myth of the American Dream. As Stuart Hall explains, "articulation"[35] is the construction of chains of meaning that reinforce unspoken racist assumptions about particular groups, frequently inferentially.

Imagination is articulated with such characteristics as creativity and originality, which identify those worthy of accessing the American Dream. Imagination is racialized through the invocation of racial scripts that label people of color as imitators who presumptively lack the capacity for groundbreaking thought. Similarly, human progress is articulated with such characteristics as innovation and ingenuity, which are defining characteristics of the American Dream. Human progress is racialized through repeated racial scripts that label people of color as lazy thieves who are capable only of rote reproduction. The consumer gaze is articulated with such characteristics as authenticity and quality, which are also attached to the American Dream. The consumer gaze is racialized through racial scripts that label people of color as objects, not subjects, of consumption and therefore neither the producers nor the consumers that trademark law was intended to protect. Focusing on these categories over time shows how intellectual property doctrine is connected to larger, racialized themes about nation and citizenship. The notion that intellectual property law has become equitable, then, is a dangerous one that ignores the relative stability of the orientations of copyright, patent, and trademark law to whiteness/racial difference.

The three conceptual trajectories connected with intellectual property law and citizenship that I identify here are evident over time in doctrinal evolution. True imagination, which emerged in the United States in the 1700s, is anchored by a binary of originality/unoriginality. That binary is legible in the racialized "transformativeness" debates around sampling in the 1990s and the (neo)colonial management of the public domain in the 2000s. Human progress, which also emerged in the United States in the 1700s, is anchored by a binary of nature/science. That binary is legible in justifications for protecting products of "human ingenuity" in the 1990s and the (neo)colonial claim to the products of that concept in the 2000s. The consumer gaze, which emerged in the 1800s in the United States, is anchored by a binary of consumer/consumed, legible in the management of "dilution" in the 1990s and the repeal of protections for "disparaging and scandalous" trademarks in the 2000s.

True imagination, human progress, and the consumer gaze invoke and reinvent the binary distinctions that undergird them and the relationship of those binaries to citizenship and, accordingly, to race. While race and intellectual property scholars have explored parts of these legal doctrines and binaries, they have rarely considered them collectively in historical trajectories over time, particularly with respect to their connectedness and evolution. I demonstrate how the racial inequalities in copyright, patent, and trademark law are interlinked and ongoing through their organizing racial scripts and (neo)colonial implications.

Racial scripts as reading practice

Racial scripts, because they can be traced over time, function as method for understanding how race moves and evolves while also staying constant. In researching this book, I did not begin by using racial scripts as method but rather came to them while mapping intellectual property's racial histories. In assembling an archive for study, I took a broad view of intellectual property law, politics, and culture as sites for the negotiation of race. I was initially concerned with comprehensively surveying intellectual property law's most important turning points, which are familiar to copyright, patent, and trademark scholars. Once I identified those historical and doctrinal moments that fundamentally shaped intellectual property law, I began to systematically map related cases, political speeches, and popular cultural texts that implicated race and (neo)coloniality.

It soon became clear that questions of citizenship are not merely incidental to the intersections of race and intellectual property discourse but central to them. Reading their intersections through additional methods derived from Critical Race Theory (CRT), ethnic studies, and rhetoric helped me to recognize that the moments of racial and (neo)colonial conflict that I pinpointed were not singular events but related moments in larger cultural processes of racial formation.[36]

These moments also shaped core themes in copyright, patent, and trademark law. I accordingly chose the case studies in this book on the basis of their relationships to one another and their representativeness in demonstrating how race, intellectual property, nation, and citizenship have been coded and racialized together over the past two hundred years, using through lines of true imagination, human progress, and the consumer gaze. The concept of intellectual property citizenship brings these insights together and offers a schema for considering the racial connections between historical and contemporary copyright, patent, and trademark rhetorics.

My approach to racial scripts draws upon rhetorical study, specifically the transdisciplinary method that Michael Lacy and Kent Ono call "critical rhetorics of race."[37] Critical rhetoric, a project that originates with Raymie McKerrow's 1989 essay of the same name, urges rhetorical scholars to ask how power is constructed through and shaped by public cultural rhetorics in ways that produce domination and freedom.[38] Critical rhetorics of race urge rhetorical scholars to do the same with respect to racial and (neo)colonial power. As Lacy and Ono put it, "A critical apparatus that can expose and interrogate racialized discourse as it changes and adapts to new cultural conditions is necessary."[39] This project applies and develops critical rhetorics of race in the context of intellectual property law by focusing on identifying and tracing discursive markers of racial and (neo)colonial power in public culture, particularly legal cases, political speeches, and popular culture, over time.

While lawyers read legal cases as documents that shape and develop doctrine and policy, scholars of legal rhetoric read them as markers and makers of culture and identity. Legal cases are conduits for race because they offer and shape often racialized rhetorical resources for the negotiation of legal outcomes. As Haney López contends, racial categories evolve over time, through overt and implicit invocations in legal cases.[40] Like Pham, I construct a "discursive field"[41] that puts race and intellectual property in conversation with each other as a means of theorizing racial struggle, using case studies grounded in legal, political, and popular texts.[42]

I have divided intellectual property history from the 1700s to the 2000s into three distinct periods, which I have defined using the predominant racial zeitgeist of the era. In the first period, intellectual property law and citizenship were de jure linked through codified discrimination; in the second, they were de facto linked through the ideology of racial liberalism; and in the third, they were projected internationally while maintaining the fiction of the postracial domestically. The final selection of case studies here, when read together in their larger political and cultural context, offers a theoretical approach for understanding how rhetorical continuities around race are deeply intertwined with intellectual property's structural exclusion and racist representations.

I have, with Deidré Keller, previously written about Critical Race Intellectual Property (Critical Race IP) as a theory and method for producing scholarship at the intersections of intellectual property and race. Most significantly, Critical Race IP is a tool for bringing CRT and Critical Intellectual Property (Critical IP) together in multidisciplinary ways that highlight how intellectual property law protects whiteness as property. *The Color of Creatorship* embraces Critical Race IP, "the interdisciplinary movement of scholars connected by their focus on the racial and (neo)colonial non-neutrality of the laws of copyright, patent, trademark, right of publicity, trade secret[s], and unfair competition using principles informed by CRT."[43] By engaging in rhetorical study of racial scripts in intellectual property law, the project employs the practices of CRT while simultaneously constituting a burgeoning area of scholarly and activist inquiry.

Because the struggle over creatorship is fundamentally connected with narratives of white memory, white guilt, and white fragility, Critical Race IP scholars can benefit from thinking alongside critical race studies scholars and employing all available tools to think through race and (neo)coloniality. This book provides a model for how new Critical Race IP scholarship can build new theories and methods to dismantle knowledge inequality and unveil intellectual property law's connections to the nation's racial episteme. While a rich and rapidly growing body of scholarship exists at the intersections of race and intellectual property law, there is much more work to be done, theoretically and practically.

Intellectual property as racialized mass noun

Understanding the racial scripts embedded in intellectual property law requires treating the legal regime as both a collection of individual bodies of law and a mass noun. While Richard Stallman is correct that intellectual property is a "seductive mirage"[44] through which policy differences between copyrights, trademarks, and patents are obscured, the term "intellectual property" has rhetorical properties that when used in public culture require study, especially with respect to race. Discursive deployments of intellectual property as a single concept facilitate the creation of a homogeneous and racialized category of creatorship as well as the mobilization of public feelings about knowledge production. Moving between intellectual property law as a mass noun and as a collection of bodies of law is useful in teasing out the structural and rhetorical implications of the racialized practices through which racial hierarchy is sustained.

With the exception of a few works, such as Madhavi Sunder's *From Goods to a Good Life: Intellectual Property and Global Justice*, scholarship on intellectual property and race tends to address case studies within individual bodies of law. This approach is important and valuable, as it investigates in depth the racial implications of particular intellectual property policies. However, as Silbey argues, "[t]he origin stories that circulate about intellectual property protection span all three forms. The repetition of these stories of consent through the case law, the litigation that becomes case law, and the statutory and constitutional history behind the law, serves to further reinforce the message of consent."[45]

Intellectual property law's narratives about race span all three forms of law as well. In the colonial period, knowledge production was structured through overt racism, with whites presuming they had superior capacity to create and know. That overt racism evolved over time. With the rise of corporate content ownership and neoliberalism, types of intellectual property became increasingly blurred. This blurring also facilitated the securitization of intellectual property, by linking infringement and counterfeiting with national security threats, such as terrorism and organized crime. From the late 1970s onward, Jack Valenti, former president of the Motion Picture Association of America (MPAA), came to be known for associating intellectual property infringement with terrorism, comparing it to rape and sexual assault, and racializing its perpetrators.[46] Valenti's rhetorical moves facilitate the treatment of intellectual property protection as a racialized mass noun. His discursive strategies, which others in the film and music industry have modeled, deploy intellectual property strategically in ways that are legible only through study of the term's use to describe and read across multiple bodies of law.

Because, in the context of law and public culture, all forms of knowledge production are often treated *together*, as a chain of creation, marketing, and circulation—particularly under the streamlined economic model of neoliberalism—narratives of race move across the permeable boundaries of copyright, patent, and trademark law. Different types of intellectual property protection operate in tandem with one another, racially and rhetorically, with copyrights and patents forming the basis for the production of valuable commodities, which circulate through global economies, licitly or illicitly.

Here, Stallman's argument proves the theoretical need to study the rhetorics deployed in discussions about copyrights, patents, and trademarks together. He argues that legislative debates and lobbying around intellectual property always already appeal to "creativity" and "innovation" even though those ideas do not operate across areas of law.[47] Studying intellectual property's racial scripts demonstrates that ideals of ingenuity are not only consistently invoked concepts used in copyright, trademark, and patent discourses, among others, but also serve as rhetorical shorthand for constructing a white male knowledge citizenry.[48] While important and valuable in thinking through the policy implications of copyrights, patents, and trademarks, Stallman's insistence that we consider each area of law separately encourages us to elide the implications of race. The full strategic benefits of flattening of knowledge policy, particularly vis-à-vis race, are legible only as we consider racial scripts and racial capitalism *across* types of intellectual property, while attending in detail to the structures of feeling underlying copyright, patent, and trademark law.

Law and (racial) economics

In responding to arguments about race, intellectual property scholars often appeal to economics as an explanatory framework for the outcomes in question. Despite Zahr Said's optimistic observation that critiques to it are flourishing,[49] law and economics has and continues to be the predominant lens for theorizing intellectual property law. Often, as Mitu Gulati and Devon Carbado argue,[50] Critical Race Theory and law and economics go so far as to offer competing instead of complementary explanations for macro and micro institutional practices that produce inequality. Yet investigating the relationships among (intellectual) property, citizenship, national identity, and personhood calls for considering how race and capitalism are coproduced, particularly in a world in which former attorney general Michael

Mukasey referred to intellectual properties as America's most "precious commodities."[51]

Racial capitalism, as Cedric Robinson conceptualizes it, points us to the complex relationships between capitalism, race, and (neo)colonialism.[52] Jodi Melamed characterizes the scholarship that flows from Robinson's work—which describes this book as well—writing: "A thread of emergent critical understanding, proceeding from the recognition that procedures of racialization and capitalism are ultimately never separable from each other, seeks to comprehend the complex recursivity between material and epistemic forms of racialized violence, which are executed in and by core capitalist states with seemingly infinite creativity (beyond phenotype and in assemblages)."[53]

Read through the lens of racial capitalism, intellectual property rhetorics and structures are revealed to be part of a larger system of race and political economy that is "fully saturated by racialized violence."[54] The economic value of devaluing the creatorship of people of color intersects with the economic value of legally, structurally, and ideologically overvaluing white creatorship in ways that reinforce the exclusion of people of color from that same category. Intellectual property outcomes, which mediate conflicts around already heavily circulated and valued cultural objects, are never produced in line with rational, race neutral economics, if such a thing even exists.

Robinson's formulations of racial capitalism, a concept that Melamed aptly refers to as an "activist hermeneutic,"[55] critiqued Marxism's presumption that capitalism would do away with racism in its development. Instead, "antinomies of accumulation require loss, disposability, and the unequal differentiation of human value, and racism enshrines the inequalities that capitalism requires."[56] Knowledge production, an activity that, like property ownership, consistently structurally privileges the creatorship of white persons on the basis of their "superior" mental capacities, is a racialized form of capitalist production. Histories of appropriation of Black blues and jazz music,[57] commodification of indigenous knowledge,[58] and circulation of derogatory brands,[59] for example, demonstrate the many ways in which intellectual property has worked by and through the (racially) capitalist exploitation of people of color.

Notably, racial capitalism, like the relationship between intellectual property, race, and citizenship, has evolved over time. Significantly, the development of the term intellectual property and the conflation of copyrights, patents, and trademarks aid in ensuring the smooth operation of capitalism, in part by maintaining a racially unequal terrain of creatorship. Reading across types of intellectual property renders visible the manner in which individual bodies of law are mobilized rhetorically in order to justify systems that have racialized impacts. In this sense, intellectual property law is doubly inflected by race, first as a space for the negotiation of racial desire and second in the implementation of policies and proposals that further entrench systems of racial capitalism.

More importantly, the case studies in *The Color of Creatorship* demonstrate that economic arguments flatten out the racial complexities of intellectual property law in ways that make it appear that people of color are "winning" despite doing so within a system that is ideologically rigged in favor of whiteness. Scholars who continue to argue for economic explanations for outcomes in intellectual property cases without analyzing race and (neo)coloniality miss the forest for the trees. Even the important critiques of unequal contract negotiations, doctrinal insufficiency, and colonial power differentials that scholars like Kevin J. Greene, Lateef Mtima, Peter Drahos, and Olufunmilayo Arewa make shy away from offering historically and ideologically situated explanations of how and why economics fails to produce equity and inclusion in the intellectual property context.

THE "BLURRED LINES" OF RACIAL CREATORSHIP/INFRINGEMENT

The controversy around the hit R&B single "Blurred Lines," by Robin Thicke, featuring Pharrell and T.I., is a useful entrée into the discussion about race, intellectual property rights, and citizenship. With lines like "I know you want it,"[60] the lyrics (re)sparked national and international discussions about the role of popular music in shaping cultural norms around rape culture, toxic masculinity, consent, and nostalgia. Yet gender was only one topic about which the song and the musicians who performed it received pushback. In 2015, the trio surprised audiences by filing a preemptive copyright lawsuit requesting a judgment that their song did *not* infringe upon Marvin Gaye's hit "Got to Give It Up." After they filed their complaint, Gaye's estate countersued, claiming copyright infringement.[61]

The jury ultimately awarded Gaye's estate $7.4 million, an outcome that "sent shockwaves through the music industry,"[62] but the Ninth Circuit nonetheless upheld the decision.[63] Debate over the case continued well past

2015 and focused as much on race as it did on gender. The central question in the case that ensued around "Blurred Lines" was whether Thicke, Pharrell, and T.I. produced a piece of music that was "substantially similar"[64] to copyrightable and protectable *expression*, not uncopyrightable and unprotectable *ideas*, in Gaye's sheet music, not in his performed song. While Thicke, Pharrell, and T.I. claimed that they had copied only the unprotectable "feel" of Gaye's composition, and in fact only part of that,[65] the jury determined that "Gotta Give It Up" and "Blurred Lines" were, indeed, substantially similar based on the musical notations of the two songs.[66]

Gaye's talent and stylistic innovation, the markers of his exemplary creatorship, provided justification for the seemingly racially reparative outcome in *Williams v. Bridgeport Music, Inc.* (2015) (hereinafter *Williams*), a case that purportedly protected a well-known Black artist from the (white) vultures in the music industry.[67] In some instances, this narrative moved into the realm of racial fantasy of reparation,[68] imagining the case as a remedy to hundreds of years of exploitation of Black artists. In other instances, the framing was more pragmatically focused on the evolution of legal doctrine as a practical means of protecting previously unprotectable Black musical practices.[69] If Thicke and Pharrell had been more sympathetic plaintiffs, narratives about the case may have painted Gaye in a less flattering light.

One set of critics of the verdict, who take a largely mainstream law and economics approach to copyright law, contended that Gaye's estate was the beneficiary of overprotection because the ambient sound of "Blurred Lines" is not copyrightable expression. They further contended that *Williams* is a decision that will, at best, impoverish the public domain and, at worst, bring about the death of music as we know it. Whether maintaining that the astronomical jury verdict resulted from misleading jury instructions,[70] protecting material that was "not original or not relevant,"[71] marked a moment of "emulation"[72] instead of infringement or impoverished the public domain, those critics in this category are united by their desire to advocate for what they perceive as a fair and accurate balance of copyright protection.

Another set of critics of the verdict argued that the decision did a disservice to the goal of radical racial equality in copyright, in part because one remedial outcome cannot repair a history of racial injustice, particularly when it ignores the consequences of the verdict for appropriative styles, such as hip hop, and doubles down on an exploitative system of racial capitalism.[73] Those in this camp pushed back against the notion, familiar to critical race scholars and Black feminists, that tinkering with law itself can ever really repair a copyright system that is racist to the core, particularly without fueling intraracial and interracial acrimony.

Perhaps the most curious aspect of the dispute over *Williams*, a case with successful and well-known Black artists on *both* sides, is that it largely became a rallying cry for racial justice activists on *one* side, specifically vis-à-vis the need to protect Gaye's music from Thicke's exploitation. The appeal of such a narrative is not difficult to discern. Thicke, the son of beloved Canadian comic Alan Thicke, appeared clueless at best and unhinged at worst as the lawsuit came to a head. Thicke's responses to the outcry, alternately defended the song as respectful to women and disclaimed responsibility for writing the lyrics, marked him as both immature and out of touch.[74] The song's music video confirmed his seemingly toxic persona. Thicke's hashtagged name is visually front and center in the four-minute montage, despite the fact that the video features two famous Black musicians. Like the scantily clad women Thicke engages with, Pharrell and T.I. act as props to Thicke's uncomfortable playful/predatory sexual fantasy. Even when they do get screen time, it is with a feel of minstrelsy, as they dance across the screen with naked (or nearly naked) women while seemingly mimicking Thicke. The video's imagined racial and gender hierarchy is clear: Thicke is at the top, Pharrell and T.I. are next, and the women, who mostly appear to lack sexual agency except as sex objects, are at the bottom.

The unrated version of the spectacular affirmation of toxic white masculinity ends with the words ROBIN THICKE HAS A BIG DICK in silver balloons on the screen. At a moment in which (white) feminists were vocally protesting rape culture, Thicke became an easy target, because of his unsavory politics. His white masculinity and erratic antics made him both a saleable artist and a compelling villain, particularly with Motown legend Gaye on the other side.

After Thicke admitted that he was so high as to be incapacitated while writing "Blurred Lines," it became clear that Pharrell, the successful, Black, rap music producer who received only co-writing credit, was the primary author of the song.[75] This important fact begs the question of why narratives about Pharrell's authorship and positionality were not more prominent in the media coverage of the case.[76] Thinking about the narratives that did or might have come to the fore in the media is an important exercise because it highlights how and why copyright law—and intellectual property law more generally—is shaped. One explanation for the media coverage in the case is that Gaye is a particularly compelling intellectual property citizen, given his groundbreaking work in R&B during and after his association with Motown Records. The effort to blame Thicke for copying Gaye's music while erasing Pharrell as the sole author of "Blurred Lines" appears rooted, at least partially, in the desire to protect those who work hard and innovate in ways that square with the American Dream. While such a conclusion is linked to the narrative of the Romantic author, it also exceeds that myth, through its relation to the politics of race, citizenship, property, and labor, particularly in the music industry.

The racial justice conclusion that audiences ought to draw from the dispute over "Blurred Lines" is not that *more* copyright can protect people of color but that *different* copyright is necessary to push back against the underlying values and ideologies that shape copyright law.[77] Here, the failure of Thicke's white masculinity becomes a spectacle that overshadows the racial identities of his coauthors. Thicke so epitomizes the image of the "bad white"[78] that Richard Dyer describes that he cannot claim his position as a Romantic author, especially given demands for gender equity. Read opposite the younger Thicke, Gaye's "Gotta Give It Up" is, in Gerald Early's words, a "nostalgic memoir"[79] of Motown, a place and sound in which older Black and white generations achieved the mythic American Dream and appeared to triumph over racism.

Pharrell's authorship, which may have been complicated in the public imaginary by his embrace of the much-criticized language of the "new Black man,"[80] is lost in the tidal waves of Thicke's escapades and Gaye's talent. Moreover, Pharrell stands for a genre of authorship that, for many Americans, still represents the urban decay and threatening Black masculinity that politicians demonized from the 1980s through the 2000s. Gaye, though associated with an era of national tumult, offered a classic musical style that the media and the public seemed to romanticize, particularly for its connection to American notions of creative genius and even civil rights triumph. Although Gaye's estate was represented by Bridgeport Music, a one-man-dominated "sample troll"[81] that leveraged George Clinton's widely used music as a means of capitalizing on violations of copyright licensing requirements, responses to the verdict often criticized those who "can't really do anything original"[82] and who "steal the swagger."[83] In other words, even though Bridgeport Music is a villain in the eyes of many music fans, Thicke,

Pharrell, and T.I. are no heroes. Some scholars certainly expressed concern that the outcome in *Williams* would threaten the integrity of songwriting, but ultimately they were few and far between. The calls to protect Gaye and his musical contributions by protecting his music were much louder than fears that doing so was actually quite a fraught move.

Mark Lemley has argued that Boyle's understanding of the Romantic creator is a simplistic one that misses the role of economics in copyright cases.[84] *Williams* showcases, in a contemporary example, how creatorship, race, citizenship, nation, labor, and property are tied up with economics. Romantic creatorship, when read in the larger context of intellectual property citizenship, prefigures economics itself. James Boyle, Jennifer Jenkins, and Keith Aoki lay the groundwork for such an argument in their comic *Theft! A History of Music*.[85] At a metalevel, *Williams* was a dispute about two genres of music, soul and hip hop, which were and are the sites of racial and generational conflict. Despite the fact that *The Root* interviewed three copyright experts who observed that "Blurred Lines" contains no samples, the publication nevertheless went on to call Pharrell a "sampling artist."[86] That word choice, while true of Pharrell in other instances, muddies the waters of this case by invoking specters of theft.

A reading of "Blurred Lines" as a complex negotiation among Black and white publics from the soul and post-soul generations,[87] (white) feminists and antiracists, a zealous corporation (Bridgeport Music), and a legal system that consistently disenfranchises Black creators starts to unveil how whiteness works through imaginings of good creatorship, sentimental divide-and-conquer politics, economic calculations, and purportedly race neutral legal appeals. Individuals invested in social justice outcomes in the case, for instance, had a seemingly forced choice between embracing nostalgia and reparation for Gaye, who was arguably a better creator than Pharrell but certainly no better a feminist than Thicke, or a commitment to the musical innovation of hip hop and an interpretation of the public domain that had historically disenfranchised Black artists. Neither choice is optimal and both illustrate how structural racism, racial scripts, and racial feelings calcify over time into layers that produce divisive cases such as this one.

I argue that the lose-lose situation that seemingly coincidentally reappears in intellectual property cases involving people of color is a feature, not a bug, of knowledge protection regimes. A legal system that is invested in Euro-American conceptions of creatorship and offers people of color only tools that pit them against one another in oppositional ways is structured not to produce racial justice but to shore up protection for *whiteness* itself as (intellectual) property.

Williams is an example of how Alan Freeman's critique that civil rights law operates from a "perpetrator perspective"[88] that treats racism as exceptional rather than quotidian applies to copyright law. Pharrell's disenfranchisement results partly from the need to produce and protect a particular vision of nation, one in which civil rights succeeded and racism ended. The postracial veneer on *Williams* enables the denial of Pharrell's racial personhood while centering racial capitalism. Only by grappling with America's underlying racial episteme, through practices of decolonization, can antiracist activists get to the heart of intellectual property's race problem.

Decolonization, which I turn to in the conclusion as a method that complements and overlaps with CRT and critical rhetorics of race, is a reorientation of the racial episteme, because it dismantles the racist and (neo)colonial binaries that underpin copyright, patent, and trademark law. More specifically, decolonial approaches to intellectual property law are central to combating the "hidden agenda of modernity"[89] that endorses oppression through embrace of the "*logics* of progress, enlightenment, development, and democracy which made the domination of Other peoples a thinkable option."[90] Decolonial strategies, above all else, emphasize the need for a multiplicity of visions of creatorship, as opposed to specifically Euro-American understandings of how creation does and should unfold. Decolonial theory is a particularly useful framework for Critical Race IP scholars because it aids in building the nuanced vocabulary and methods necessary to engage the structural and cultural complexities that undergird intellectual property inequity.

CHAPTER PRÉCIS

The remaining chapters of the *Color of Creatorship* work through the history of intellectual property citizenship as it developed in tandem with the nation's racial histories. Broadly speaking, the book moves from considering the nation's practices of formal exclusion to the emergence of a racial liberalism and finally to postraciality. It also examines how creators of color reimagine intellectual property citizenship, particularly by pushing back against racial scripts. The conclusion returns to Critical Race IP and decoloniality as practical starting points for thinking about how to undo the links among race, coloniality, and intellectual property law. I do not mark precise years for these eras of racial formation but rather offer schema for mapping intellectual property histories and racial histories together. The beginning and ending of racial liberalism, for instance, are not only debatable but also not central to identifying and examining the trends presented here.

Chapter 1 lays out the history of formal exclusion in the context of intellectual property law and names the primary racial scripts through which that exclusion was articulated. It makes a case for the formation of the nation's intellectual property citizenship as raced. In the context of copyright law, true imagination emerged as a racialized standard for separating white creativity from people of color creativity. The anti-Blackness directed at Phillis Wheatley, the nation's first published Black poet, is traceable through the copyright doctrine of the period, including in cases such as *Chaplin v. Amador* (1928) and *Supreme Records v. Decca Records* (1950).

In the context of patent law, human progress developed into a means of normalizing the separation of white intelligence from people of color intelligence. Enshrined in the Constitution, the seemingly innocuous term came to be embodied in the exhibitions at the nation's World's Fairs and art that imagined nation and citizenry. (White) human progress operated as a mechanism for excluding people of color from the very imaginary of inventorship.

Finally, in the context of trademark law, the emergence of the consumer gaze produced a structural legal distinction between producers/consumers of goods and goods for circulation. People of color, as demonstrated by cases such as *Aunt Jemima Mills Co. v. Rigney & Co.* (1917) and *Gardella v. Log Cabin Products* (1937), became racialized objects, not collaborative subjects, of the consumer gaze. Together, these articulations of intellectual property law set the stage for future implicit bias enacted in purportedly race neutral ways.

Chapter 2 grapples with creatorship/infringement in the period of racial liberalism. With the turn to racial liberalism, intellectual property citizenship remained a racialized category, though in forms now circumscribed by liberal ideology. In the context of copyright law, the standard of true imagination reemerged in disputes over sampling and parody. Copyright cases such as *Grand Upright Music, Ltd. v. Warner Bros. Records, Inc.* (1991),

Campbell v. Acuff-Rose Music (1994), and *Suntrust Bank v. Houghton Mifflin Co.* (2001) demonstrate how racial anxieties about Blackness were displaced onto legal categories of "originality" and "transformativeness." Though they seem like victories, these cases ghettoized Black creatorship by protecting only the most exceptional artists and relegating all others to the category of copyright thugs.

Patent law replicated the nature/science binaries that underpinned the category of human progress through the articulation of the standard of human ingenuity. This category, while again seemingly race neutral, propertized people of color and prevented them from protecting their own works of creatorship, particularly in cases such as *Diamond v. Chakrabarty* (1980) and *Moore v. Regents of the University of California* (1990).

Finally, trademark law reinforced the notion of whiteness as property by expanding the scope and explicitness of the consumer gaze in managing social relations. Dilution law functions, racially speaking, as a mechanism for mediating the white racial anxieties of the time, particularly around "mixing," in its artistic and identity forms. These examples render visible the racialized hierarchy of intellectual property citizenship and the failures of colorblindness.

Chapter 3 examines how the domestic move toward postracial creatorship mobilized white and nationalist intellectual property sentiments and directed them at foreign Others. Once again, intellectual property citizenship remained raced, though through nationalist unity reminiscent of early copyright laws. Examining cases in which the United States demonized foreign nations illustrates how race and (neo)coloniality operate in tandem to protect whiteness as (intellectual) property, frequently through racial capitalism. Domestically, *Matal v. Tam* (2017) signals the victory of philosophies of postraciality and racial libertarianism with respect to race, nation, and free speech. Here, the "foreign" nation is Indian Country, a land that is erased and disenfranchised through the Supreme Court's embrace of a vision of trademark law that puts people of color, not whites, in charge of managing the acts of discrimination against them.

Similarly, while patent cases such as *Assn. for Molecular Pathology v. Myriad* (2013) and *Bowman v. Monsanto* (2012), even as they seem to maintain—or even narrow—the scope of patentable subject matter, reinforced the binary of nature/science and thus white gatekeeping of the category of human progress. *Novartis v. Union of India and Others* (2013), a case decided by the Supreme Court of India, illustrates that postracial creatorship worked in opposition to hyperracial infringement, with the United States demonizing countries like India for refusing to abide by (neo)colonial and racist international intellectual property agreements.

Finally, the seemingly postracial and progressive copyright decision in *Golan v. Holder* (2012) actually constructs and expands a white nationalist public domain, by marking domestic copyright interests as more important than international ones. The Supreme Court's decision to allow Congress to manage the public domain at will is a colonizing act that, consistent with the nation's originary narrative of true imagination, refuses the equality of foreign—often non-white—nations. Reading these examples intertextually shows how purportedly postracial rhetorics do not eliminate race discrimination or (neo)colonialism but relocate them geographically by erasing structural equality domestically and projecting it internationally under the guise of ushering in a new era of legal harmonization. It also demonstrates the permeable boundaries of racism and (neo)coloniality, which though they refer to different practices and processes are fundamentally linked through logics of racial capitalism.

Chapter 4 considers resistance to the racialized category of the intellectual property citizen. Three case studies show how people of color use radical performative politics to resist racist and (neo)colonial practices in copyright, patent, and trademark spaces. In a refusal of copyright law's imaginings of intellectual property citizenship, Prince changed his name to ♀ (hereinafter Love Symbol). By culture jamming copyright law, he asserted that he was a creator, not slaveable property, and refused notions of Black people as primitive copiers.

In order to contest Western commodification of yoga, Indians and Indian Americans developed a new language of creatorship, one that transformed technical intellectual property rhetoric into a tool for claiming ownership in cultural property. Similarly, the Indian government created a digital database, the Traditional Knowledge Digital Library (TKDL), as a means of decolonizing Euro-American patent regimes.

In a move that refused trademark law's objectification and propertization of people of color, Marshawn Lynch claimed property rights in his own Black bestial body through the Beast Mode® clothing line. Lynch simultaneously embraced, refused, and monetized the stereotype of the Black beast in order to assert his rights to full intellectual property citizenship and bodily autonomy.

The Conclusion uses these case studies as a means of returning to the practical questions of how scholars and anti-racist activists can engage the histories set forth in this book as well as Critical Race IP and decolonial theory to rescript intellectual property law. In concluding, it returns to *Williams* and develops more fully one Critical Race IP reading of that case.

CHAPTER ONE

THE INTELLECTUAL PROPERTY CITIZEN

> Imagination! who can sing thy force?
> Or who describe the swiftness of thy course?
> Soaring through air to find the bright abode,
> Th' empyreal palace of the thund'ring God,
> We on thy pinions can surpass the wind,
> And leave the rolling universe behind:
> From star to star the mental optics rove,
> Measure the skies, and range the realms above.
> There in one view we grasp the mighty whole,
> Or with new worlds amaze th' unbounded soul.
> —PHILLIS WHEATLEY, "On Imagination"

WITH THE PASSAGE OF THE first federal intellectual property and naturalization statutes in the United States in the late 1700s, creatorship, citizenship, and whiteness came to be formally linked. Knowledge production, which had always functioned as a racialized practice, came to mark the boundaries of Americanness and the ideals of citizenship, in part through the rhetorical inclusion of whites and the rhetorical exclusion of people of color from those respective categories.[1] As the overtly racist purposes and ideologies of intellectual property law came to be constituted with national identity and race, they set the stage for future doctrinal approaches to repeat and rewrite their logics. Racial scripts that emerged before or coextensively with nation building also shaped copyright, patent, and trademark law, and the legal boundaries of citizenship. "Common sense" and "scientific" understandings of the intersections among race, creativity, innovation, hard work, and intelligence enshrined in law and popular culture became important heuristics through which intellectual property developed.[2] Doctrinal standards that, absent formal exclusions, would appear to be race neutral operated as mechanisms for shoring up white Americanness through production, ownership, and management of knowledge.

Significantly, the racial scripts that came to be intertwined with intellectual property doctrine in this era did not disappear but remained, in rhetorical and ideological "fragments," in the words of Michael McGee,[3] scattered through copyright, patent, and trademark doctrine, for centuries. This is not to say that race was or is always a dispositive factor in the outcome of intellectual property cases. Rather, it is to say that while markets could theoretically operate in race neutral ways, given the trajectories of racial capitalism and intellectual property law, they did not and do not do so. It is therefore imperative to study when and how racial exclusions from this era remain embedded in intellectual property law, as "sediments"[4] built into theory and practice.

This chapter examines how, historically and through formal exclusion, race, intellectual property law, and citizenship came to be consistently intertwined and racial scripts about the unimaginativeness, intelligence, laziness, disloyalty, hypersexuality, and dangerousness of people of color became central to defining who was and was not American. Between the 1700s and the mid-1900s, creatorship and citizenship were coproduced, with both of them drawing from the broader "rhetorical culture"[5] around race to articulate their core principles. The citizen creator was the idealized maker, the Romantic creator who comported with the fetishization of imagination, human progress, and consumer desire. Even as the nation's racial politics became more progressive, or at least less formally racist, intellectual property discourses and policies consistently returned to the rhetorical and structural resources through which creatorship was cast as fundamentally white.

Citizenship was explicitly juridically marked for "whites only" through a litany of governmental actions from Fugitive Slave Laws to the Chinese Exclusion Act. Each of these domestic moves signaled a desire to build an American nation in which only whites were citizens and national expansion, economic protectionism, and indigenous industry were federal priorities. The often protectionist sentiments that were embedded in discussions of intellectual property policy, for instance in disputes over protection of foreign copyrights,[6] drew upon larger conversations about citizenship's whiteness, sometimes consciously through the invocation of familiar racial scripts and sometimes unconsciously through the mobilization of racist sentiments. Overtly and inferentially racist claims in public culture shaped the nation's understandings of who ought to be protected by intellectual property law and who ought to have access to the American Dream, which in turn shaped copyrights, patents, and trademarks.[7]

Charles Mills refers to the "first period of de jure white supremacy,"[8] which he characterizes as being marked by an explicit racial contract. Periodizing intellectual property's racial commitments in a similar manner reveals how formal exclusions related to property and personhood were articulated and reinforced through contemporaneous articulations of citizenship—and therefore Americanness—to keep people of color from enjoying equality of protection of creative works, inventions, and identifying marks.

I am less interested in demarcating specific changes in the period from the late 1700s to the mid-1900s with respect to race, citizenship, and intellectual property law than I am in establishing that despite the considerable racial democratization of creatorship that occurred from the 1830s onward, the "inner energy," in Eva Illouz's words,[9] of intellectual property law and political economy remained white and continuously racially exclusionary. The production and articulation of the concepts of true imagination, human progress, and the consumer gaze during this period created legal doctrinal containers for racial scripts embedded in discourses of citizenship to haunt contemporary copyright, patent, and trademark law. Copyright discourse treated creativity as a raced endeavor through the continual invocation and bounding of the concept of imagination. Patent discourse treated innovation in the same way through its raced conceptions of human progress. And trademark discourse, which increased rapidly as the nation's industrial economy grew, supported intellectual property law as racial project by protecting racist images as product identifiers.

Together, these practices marked whites as producers/consumers of intellectual property in a system of racial capitalism and people of color as objects of production/consumption. In this sense, intellectual property actively contributed to the white supremacist projects of slavery, settler colonialism, and imperial expansion—which critical race theorist Andrea Smith identifies as linked to anti-Blackness, anti-Indigeneity, and anti-Asianness, respectively—by allowing whites to own not only the physical labor of people of color but also their intellectual labor and likenesses.[10] "White supremacy," as I use the term here, refers to a system of structural power in which "whites overwhelmingly control power and resources" and "ideas of white superiority and entitlement are widespread."[11]

By the time the contemporary information economy had begun to emerge in the mid-1900s, copyrights, patents, and trademarks had established doctrinal standards that were intertwined with all three of the pillars of white supremacy and citizenship that Smith identifies. Racial scripts facilitated legal doctrinal moves that reinforced white supremacy across racial groups. Further, these doctrinal standards were part of a larger system of "emotional capitalism,"[12] with which public feelings around race, (neo) colonialism, citizenship, nation, and economy in intellectual property law were interwoven to produce (white) citizen creators.

INTELLECTUAL PROPERTY AND THE ARTICULATION OF A PROPER (WHITE) CITIZENRY

Copyright and patent law created a raced system of protection through triangulation with legal definitions of personhood and citizenship. While copyright and whiteness were legally linked through state restrictions on property ownership and citizenship well before the first federal copyright legislation,[13] the Copyright Act of 1790 formalized those connections by explicitly affording copyright protection to any author in the United States "being a citizen or citizens thereof, or resident within."[14] Given that under the Three-Fifths Compromise, enslaved persons were not treated as whole people, they were not afforded the basic rights of citizens or even persons. The so-called Citizenship Clause in the Copyright Act of 1790—and subsequently the Copyright Act of 1836—ensured that predominantly whites were granted copyright protection, and even when people of color were able to secure such rights, it was only through successful negotiation of white gatekeeping.[15] Because the Supreme Court's infamous decision in *Dred Scott v. Sandford* (1857) was not overturned until 1868, with the passage of the Fourteenth Amendment, Black people continued to be denied basic citizenship rights long into the nineteenth century.

Karla Mari McKanders uses the phrase "tiered personhood"[16] to describe the system in which the rights afforded to all individuals, regardless of citizenship status, are "bypassed . . . by defining certain groups as nonpersons based on differences between dominant and subordinate groups."[17] For instance, even when copyright law's formal racial restrictions ended, the nation's racist attitudes persisted. Jim Crow, which violently pushed back against the rights afforded by the Fourteenth Amendment, was only one manifestation of such tiered personhood and the systematic racial subordination that supported it.

Formal citizenship requirements for copyright registration eventually ended with the International Copyright Act of 1891, a statute that, in theory, extended copyright protection to all individuals in the United States.[18] However, the International Copyright Act of 1891 neither ended the nation's desire to associate American citizenship with whiteness nor prevented the de facto racial discrimination that followed from legal articulations of copyrightability. Lauren Berlant describes sentimental approaches to citizenship, which posit the citizen not as political subject but rather as "someone with attachments and intentions and pain capacities—for example, as a *subject of feelings*—who longs for what everybody is said to long for, a world that allows access to vague belonging, a sense of unanxious general social membership that ought to be protected by the institutions that bind power to ordinary life."[19]

In Berlant's reading, the formal legal language of citizenship, which scholars and lawyers often emphasize as the site of rights and entitlements, can be separated from its informal rhetorical and affective ones. Doing this shows how exclusion works through the association of some bodies with nation and citizenship and the exclusion of other bodies from those same categories. As Sara Ahmed puts it, shared feelings are what bring individuals together and "bind the imagined white subject and nation together."[20] Shared feelings among white men about how intellectual property law should work and who should benefit from its legal determinations were wrapped up with racial ideals of citizenship and national identity, in a manner that coalesced to produce apparently race neutral legal decisions and economic policies.

More specifically, the concept of true imagination operated as a vehicle for making raced judgments about the nature of creativity. Even when authors of color won their copyright cases, they were doing so through a doctrinal lens implicated by citizenship that prefigured them as lacking creative capacity. The revelation that true imagination became a tool for excluding Black people from access to authorship is well established.[21] The connection between that phrase and citizenship, however, is far less thought out.

Copyright's protectionist tendencies can be read as moves to police belonging, particularly through xenophobic attachment to whiteness. *Yuengling v. Schile* (1882), a copyright case that contemplated the boundaries of domestic protections for foreign authors suing in U.S. courts, articulated the prevailing nationalist and protectionist aims of using copyright law to protect (white) domestic industry. The decision noted that "the prohibition against an extension of the copyright to alien authors was as broad as the section authorizing copyright in favor of resident authors,"[22] thus reading the denial of copyright protection to foreign authors broadly and in a manner consistent with the sentiments of the young nation. In shoring up the nation's protectionist posture in the area of copyright law, *Yuengling* also reaffirmed that intellectual property law could and should be motivated by a desire to unify white men in the nation against the racial and economic threats of immigrants, particularly of color.

Michael Perelman and Lateef Mtima note that protectionist motives were evident across areas of intellectual property law, as were understandings that white plunder was an acceptable means of securing Manifest Destiny, global power, economic might, and domestic labor.[23] Mtima further contextualizes this argument vis-à-vis national identity, writing "America's leaders and populace were not overly concerned with the trivialities of foreign rights in intangible property, especially if such rights stood in the way of nation building . . . the misappropriation of a few stories and songs was hardly an affront to the national conscience."[24] In a time period when the Chinese were identified as part of a barbaric, machinistic, "Oriental" nation whose values were "incompatible with the United States and threatened to corrupt the nation,"[25] and other racial groups were scripted in similarly racist ways, intellectual property's legal and economic decisions were inseparable from whiteness itself. Despite formal equality, copyright law and conceptions of citizenship constructed a domestic and racialized version of Americanness, which privileged white intellectual properties using familiar and established racial scripts.

The story of race and citizenship in patent law is analogous to the story of race and citizenship in copyright law. The Patent Act of 1790, which was amended in 1793, afforded patent protection "upon the petition of any person or persons . . . setting forth that he, she, or they hath or have invented or discovered any useful art, manufacture, engine, machine, or device, or any improvement therein not before known or used."[26] As previously discussed, the architectures of slavery and racial hierarchy, including the Three-Fifths Compromise, formally dictated that slaves were not persons under U.S. law. While some white women and men of color, such as Thomas Jennings, managed to secure patents under the Patent Act of 1790,[27] only white men were guaranteed full rights as citizens and persons under the law. The Patent Act of 1836 retained the word "persons,"[28] and accordingly the overt and inferential inequalities that came with it.

Into the 1900s, structural disadvantages coupled with deeply rooted prejudices continued to intersect with intellectual property formalities to prevent people of color from protecting their inventions in systematic ways, though once again not completely. As Rayvon Fouché and Sharra Vostral argue, "[E]ven into the mid-twentieth century, racial segregationists and women's rights opponents used the paucity of patents by women and people of color as evidence of their inability to think creatively and contribute to an evolving technological nation."[29] This catch-22 severely and cruelly constrained the manner in which people of color could push for equal rights in the area of intellectual property and demonstrate their capacity to create. Those who had not shown themselves to be a historical part of human progress according to white yardsticks and legal regimes could not effectively demonstrate that they could be part of human progress in the future.

Like copyright law, patent law is more than simply a legal construct. It is instead a rhetorical and cultural formation through which national identity and citizenship were and are constituted. The relationship of inventing to the developing nation's very idea of itself and the American Dream points to the importance of patenting in mediating culture. As Dan Burk and Jessica Reyman contend, "patents play an important *social* role in industrialized societies."[30] Patents are certainly artifacts of *technological* society. They are also—as Fouché and Vostral, among others—demonstrate, artifacts of a *racialized* society. Brian Frye's recent essay "Invention of a Slave" notes how decisions to patent or not to patent the inventions of enslaved persons implicated larger conversations about slavery, abolition, and territoriality in the nation.[31] For instance, protecting the inventions of enslaved persons could be read as an endorsement of abolition, upsetting the balance between slave states and free states in the young nation.

That patents were explicit and implicit mediators of national conversations about citizenship, personhood, and slavery should not be surprising, particularly given America's desire to articulate its identity around work ethic, ingenuity, discovery, and progress. The concept of "discovery," as used here, has both material and immaterial implications. With respect to the latter, the nation's quest for knowledge was part of a larger investment in Enlightenment narratives of linear progress. With respect to the former, the nation's commitment to inventiveness was driven by and contributed to territorial expansion. Manifest Destiny relied on invention, specifically technologies that could make it possible to traverse the new nation. As such, "the idealism of Manifest Destiny would become entwined with America's growing obsession with technological progress . . . whenever progress was invoked, technology was its basis."[32] In these respects, patents are sociolegal constructions with significant racial implications. Not only were many people of color denied the right to protect their inventions, they were viewed as obstacles to the nation's inherent mission of advancing progress and civilizing the uncivilized.

TRUE IMAGINATION IN THE CONSTRUCTION OF RACIAL PERSONHOOD

The concept of true imagination, which became an important doctrinal standard for determining whether creative works were protectable from the 1700s on, functioned as an important mechanism for linking copyright law with race. Copyright was the vehicle that American Republicans used to unify the nation around a rapidly developing print culture as well as one that embraced whiteness as a prerequisite for authorship.[33] Because the nation's citizens were by definition white, not of color, American copyright formally and informally imagined and incorporated a national identity that excluded people of color from its rights and privileges.

Yet the understanding of people of color as being outside the boundaries of creatorship and citizenship persisted long after copyright's formal exclusions ended. The ideological continuity of conceptions of true imagination lasted well into the mid-1900s, before evolving yet again. In the late 1700s, the trial of Phillis Wheatley, the first Black woman to publish a book of poetry in the United States, and Thomas Jefferson's subsequent commentary on that trial formalized beliefs that Black women—and, by extension, other people of color—lacked the capacity to imagine, in part because they were not whole persons. Though primarily formed around anti-Black racial scripts, the framework of true imagination reared its head again in subsequent disputes involving Latinx and Black authors. Even as pushes against formal racism began to succeed, legal cases continued to perpetuate the racial double standards that Jefferson articulated in Wheatley's trial. The underlying racial scripts that were determinative in these cases—i.e., that Black people lack the creativity, work ethic, and intelligence to imagine in a manner consistent with copyright law—operated to denigrate Latinx authors. In other words, racial scripts of anti-Blackness became vehicles for dehumanizing other people of color as well.[34]

The racial double standard of Phillis Wheatley (1790)

All evidence suggests that the young Phillis Wheatley did not set out to become the first African American to publish a book of poetry in 1790. Publishing the book was no small feat, and it happened only with the encouragement of her owner, Susanna Wheatley.[35] In order to receive copyright protection for her work, Wheatley was forced to prove to eighteen white men, who declared themselves the "most respectable characters in Boston,"[36] that she indeed possessed the creative capacity to write the poems that she claimed as her own. While Wheatley ultimately convinced those men that she had produced copyrightable poetry, she did so at great cost, both personal and racial.[37] Wheatley's continuing difficulties highlight the extent to which her struggle was not simply about the quality of her work; it also had to do with the racial scripts and racist sentiments around Blackness at the time. Despite the complex legal negotiations over the vocabulary of copyright, specifically the standard of originality, that emerged in the 1820s, there does not appear to be any white analogue to Wheatley's trial.

Proving originality, a legal doctrinal standard that became more restrictive in the early and mid-1800s before becoming more liberal, nonetheless would not likely have given rise to suspicions about an *inherent* lack of capacity to imagine, as it did with Wheatley.[38] Instead, as Wheatley's trial demonstrates, the presumptions against Black creatorship were unique and ingrained in American culture. For centuries after the trial, African American writers and artists sought to refute the claim that Black people lack imagination and, therefore, the ability to create with originality. Moreover, the anti-Black spectacle of Wheatley's trial mobilized racial scripts that could be applied to other groups, such as Indigenous peoples and Latinx persons, thereby articulating and amplifying racist and colonialist sentiments about their incapacity to create.

In 1781, Thomas Jefferson, who had never met Phillis Wheatley, described her as lacking the capacity for true imagination. Jefferson's racialized proclamations about the capacity to create and the definition of true imagination, with analogues to "imitation," came to be embedded in copyright law's originality standard as continuing justification for racism. In essence, true imagination and imitation evolved into shorthand for racial scripts about Black creatorship. At a time when the violence of Jim Crow operated as a structural barrier to full equality for African Americans in the South, the phrase worked to demarcate white creativity from Black creativity. Jefferson, who crafted a secondhand racist and sexist account of Wheatley, commented in *Notes on the State of Virginia*:

> Misery is often the parent of the most affecting touches in poetry. Among the Blacks is misery enough, God knows, but not poetry. Love is the peculiar oestrum of the poet. Their love is ardent, but it kindles the senses only, *not the imagination*. Religion, indeed, has produced a Phillis Wheatley; but it could not produce a poet. The compositions published under her name are *below the dignity of criticism*.[39]

Jefferson's assessment sets up personhood, particularly of the mind, as a prerequisite for creatorship, arguing that Wheatley's lack of imagination stems from her inhumanity. He constructs her work as not only unprotectable but also unworthy of criticism. His racism runs through this section of the text, reaffirming that Black people lack higher imaginative capacity despite a talent for music. Jefferson goes on to rhetorically construct a distinction between labor of the mind and labor of the body, identifying whites as superior in both and Black people as capable only of the latter. Incapacity for labor of the mind is justification for excluding enslaved persons from citizenship. Jefferson observes of African Americans:

> They seem to require less sleep. A black after hard labour through the day, will be induced by the slightest amusements to sit up till midnight, or later, though knowing he must be out with the first dawn of the morning . . . They are more ardent after their female: but love seems with them to be more an eager desire, than a tender delicate mixture of sentiment and sensation. Their griefs are transient. Those numberless afflictions, which render it doubtful whether heaven has given life to us in mercy or in wrath, are less felt, and sooner forgotten with them. In general, their existence appears to participate more of sensation than reflection. To this must be ascribed their disposition to sleep when abstracted from their diversions, and unemployed in labour. An animal whose body is at rest, and who does not reflect, must be disposed to sleep of course. Comparing them by their faculties of memory, reason, and imagination, it appears to me, that in memory they are equal to the whites; in reason much inferior, as I think one could scarcely be found capable of tracing and comprehending the

investigations of Euclid; and that in imagination they are dull, taste-less, and anomalous.[40]

Jefferson invokes typical racial scripts of anti-Blackness here, highlighting unintelligence, laziness, irresponsibility, uncontrollable desire, lack of complex emotion, inability to experience pain, and bestiality as reasons that African Americans could not possibly produce intellectual properties.[41] These racial scripts do not comport with collective white male understandings of Americanness and citizenship, which emphasize ingenuity, hard work, grit, discipline, thoughtfulness, depth of feeling, and measured civic engagement.

Jefferson's racist rant sets a high bar for Black creators as compared to white creators, who were held only to statutory requirements of showing "proof of the labor of the mind,"[42] which evolved into the modern-day standard of "a modicum of creativity."[43] Jefferson's widely read passage also uses the strangely sentimental and notably feminine benchmark of capacity to feel emotion to prove his point. Inability to *feel* with depth and breadth is a sign of the inhumanity of Blackness and a racial script that is redeployed in intellectual property law in similar ways across racial groups throughout the twentieth century. Capacity to feel with depth and breadth is a marker of the humanity of white men, though their expression of emotion is always measured.

Jefferson goes on: "Why not retain and incorporate the blacks into the state, and thus save the expence of supplying . . . the vacancies they will leave?"[44] In response, he writes, "To these objections, which are political, may be added others, which are physical and moral."[45] In addition to evidencing the racism that marked America's early understandings of creativity as fundamentally linked to whiteness, Jefferson's comments forge a connection between imagined (in)capacity to create, capacity to feel, and worthiness for the right to citizenship. In his tautological argument, Jefferson defines African Americans as lacking the capacity to feel and therefore create, which makes them ineligible for citizenship.

In addition to advancing a racist and specious argument about Black creatorship, Jefferson trades in racial feelings. There is no objective standard for true imagination; there is only a racialized one, which is based on Jefferson's individual sentiments projected onto the conceptual category of Black creativity. Through *Notes on the State of Virginia*, these personal assessments come to be public feelings, which sentimentalize and racialize creatorship, citizenship, and creativity. In a move that exemplifies emotional capitalism and anti-Blackness, Jefferson not only made it acceptable to link race, creatorship, and public feelings; he made it intuitive and compulsory.

The sentimentalization of true imagination is amplified by what Stephen Best describes as a "two body problem."[46] As Anthony Farley argues, enslaved persons were "the apogee of the commodity,"[47] insofar as the labor and bodies of enslaved persons were monetized and violently mobilized to produce more enslaved persons. In Best's reading, the commodity form meant a separation of physical labor from intangible labor, with whites claiming ownership in both. The orientation of white to Black was one of human to object. That relationship did not yield on the basis of Black creatorship. Rather, the concept of "living property"[48] undid the original Marxist commodity form in favor of a new one. Because their physical labor and intangible labor were propertized, Black creators could not, conceptually speaking, easily or effectively propertize the fruits of their own labors.

This Lockean double bind created a property relation that facilitated the projection of white feelings about creatorship onto Black bodies, without regard for the personhood of Black creators. Black creators, because of the overtly racist premise that they did not engage in (human) "sweat of the brow,"[49] were largely not allowed to own the fruits of their labors. In a moment when intellectual properties, national identity, and emotional capitalism were developing simultaneously, that double bind shaped the country's very understanding of copyrights, patents, and trademarks in a manner mediated by race. Cases in this period demonstrate that, though not explicitly invoked, Jefferson's understanding of true imagination continued to persist in copyright law.

Imaginative snowflake language is not only recurrent in nineteenth- and twentieth-century copyright cases, it marks copyright law's racial commitments.[50] True imagination,[51] a standard derived from the Enlightenment, reinscribes ideals of a white, Romantic creator. As Silbey puts it, in exploring the origin myths of intellectual property law, "[c]opyright returns to the hierarchical distinctions that value art more highly if it 'results from the true imagination rather than mere application.'"[52]

In the decades after Jefferson wrote *Notes on the State of Virginia*, the Jacksonian Indian Wars, Manifest Destiny, and the Great Depression shaped the American consciousness. By 1933, policies such as the Buy American

Act used protectionist rhetorics to justify xenophobic hatred and anti-immigrant sentiments, often against East Asians, who were routinely racially scripted as unassimilable "forever foreigners"[53] and "yellow perils"[54] who arrived from nations with populations so large and technologically skilled as to threaten to overrun the United States. William Hearst's Buy American propaganda proclaimed that "[c]heap foreign goods"[55] caused the Great Depression and "[a]lien manufacturers and merchants have practically wrestled the American market away from us and appropriated it to themselves."[56]

The divisive racial scripts and racial sentiments about labor and economy that Hearst and others invoked aggressively counseled Americans to purchase domestically crafted products. In this way, race and making came to be connected, in a way that systematically devalued people of color and their labor. The racialized commitment to true imagination continued long past the Great Depression, in a manner associated with rugged individualism and a desire to possess,[57] and coalesced with other intellectual property tropes. Two cases— *Chaplin v. Amador* (1928) and *Supreme Records v. Decca Records* (1950)— exemplify how true imagination emerged in copyright law, in racialized ways.[58]

Latinx imitation in Chaplin v. Amador (1928)

In the case of *Chaplin v. Amador* (1928) (hereinafter *Chaplin*) "imitation," also Wheatley's purported transgression, became a vehicle for marking Charlie Chaplin's performance of a Tramp character as distinctly more original than the performance of a competing Tramp. The latter was played by a Mexican man, by the name of Charles Amador. Yet as Siva Vaidhyanathan has observed, the very decision to focus on the imagination/imitation binary is an arbitrary and raced one that inconsistently privileges some types of creation over others. The same language used to justify placing blues and jazz in the public domain functioned to protect Chaplin's representation of a generic character from competition.[59]

More specifically, the famous comic sued an alleged impersonator, who performed the character Charlie Aplin in a film titled *The Race Track*, for unfair competition.[60] Amador lost the suit on the grounds that he was "imitating the plaintiff in such a way as will deceive and defraud the public."[61] Chaplin, on the other hand, the presiding judge H. L. Preston noted, had "perfected"[62] the genre of character. As Preston writes, "[t]his character, and the manner of dress, has been used and portrayed by

Charles Chaplin for so long and with such artistry, that he has become well known . . . to such an extent that a display of his picture . . . even with no name at all, has come to mean the plaintiff."[63] In fact, Chaplin was neither the originator nor the sole user of the comedic Tramp character; the court's construction of him as a "perfect" version of the character was based in romanticized understandings of comic critiques of the age of mechanical reproduction.[64]

Chaplin may have been a comedic pioneer, but he was also invested with a racialized mythic significance as "the last vestige of romantic authenticity" that extended far beyond his actual talent or inventiveness.[65] As Peter Decherney documents in detail, Chaplin himself was an imitator of a classic vaudeville vagabond trope, who though lauded by critics, was copied by hordes of aspiring comics. Indeed, Chaplin even glibly commented, in a move that doubly supported and cut against his originality, "the whole world wears pants."[66] As Preston crafts a narrative about Chaplin's uniqueness, he also invokes familiar racial scripts about Latino men as thieves, which are leveraged when politically expedient.[67] This argument also demonstrates how racial scripts about Black people—i.e., that Wheatley lacked the capacity for imagination—can subsequently be applied to Latinx people, across time and legal cases. Read in this context, *Chaplin* is a case that has the effect, even if it lacked the intent, of racially circumscribing creativity through imitation.

Preston offers little reason other than ethnocentric sentimentality to show that Chaplin is "the best" in a sea of Tramps and ought to receive protection. Read alongside *Stowe v. Thomas* (1857) (hereinafter *Stowe*), a case in which Harriet Beecher Stowe attempted and failed to prevent German copyright infringement of her book *Uncle Tom's Cabin*, *Chaplin* showcases the racialized inconsistencies and power dynamics in copyright and unfair competition decisions invoking true imagination/imitation. Whereas Robert Grier, the judge in *Stowe*, narrowly reads copyright law to refuse to protect Stowe's popular and expertly crafted tale of an escaped slave because he determined there were no grounds to do so, Preston, broadly protects the comic's popular and expertly crafted performance of a common character who was himself an imitator.

Chaplin and *Stowe* are very different cases. Chaplin involves allegations of imitation by an individual while *Stowe* involves claims of infringement by a foreign state. In the moment that *Stowe* was decided, the latter fact was an important one because the nation was still determining the scope of authorial protections. However, as Vaidhyanathan contends, Grier crafted a particularly strict understanding of the distinctions between protectable and unprotectable expression that echoed Thomas Jefferson's thoughts on copyright. Just over a decade later, authors had made considerable strides in protecting their copyrighted works and intellectual property law was expanding in scope at an exponential rate.[68]

In a young nation that was crafting its copyright futures, *Stowe*, which became a lightning rod for stronger rights for authors, is more of a historical outlier than it might initially seem. At the very least, the anti-racist short-comings and power politics of these two cases, especially in contrast to one another and later copyright expansions, are notable. Race was a potent and persistent undercurrent in battles over the scope of copyright law.

Stowe and, later, Chaplin, both of whom are white plaintiffs, were granted access to qualities of imaginativeness, creativity, and uniqueness, while Amador was not.[69] Chaplin, whose work was read as a radical critique of the political economy of the moment, was perceived as genius while Amador was treated as mere copier. Not only are such findings historically consistent with the Wheatley episode, but they also draw upon and apply familiar racial scripts about people of color across racial groups. To delink Preston's argument from its racial and economic backdrop is to overlook an important means of reconciling the contradictory outcomes in these cases. *Stowe* and *Chaplin* show how property rights in expressions formed along lines that used true imagination/imitation as a flexible tool for expanding and contracting copyright and unfair competition to protect, albeit inconsistently, white creators who comported with ideals of Romantic creatorship and their attendant economic gains.[70]

As Chaplin's vaudeville-derived Tramp style became a prime target for imitation by thousands of other comics, he and his lawyer sought to crack down on the Tramp explosion.[71] However, Chaplin lost his first case in a decision that only emboldened imitators.[72] Because there was, as Decherney notes, "no indication . . . that the existence of counterfeit Chaplins injured the original, at least not by deceiving his audience into misspending their ticket money,"[73] Preston's Romantic investment in Chaplin as "the best" entrenches the relationship between whiteness and (intellectual) property without economic justification. Chaplin persuaded Preston that he was a special snowflake and deserved unprecedented monopoly rights in his character, even as Chaplin himself was sued twice for copyright infringement during the wait for the appeal in *Amador*.[74] In a set of legal battles between comics that lasted for years —Chaplin even tried to settle with Amador for three of them—*Amador* is notable.[75]

In the years between *Stowe* and *Chaplin*, the United States experienced significant racial and economic turmoil. Emancipation fundamentally altered the nation's relationship to race as the South struggled to rebuild itself after a devastating conflict. Railroads, telephones, and flight dramatically changed the landscape of communication in the country, while World War I and the Great Depression created tumult of a different kind. Though the United States had won the Mexican-American War, U.S. economic growth and the Mexican Revolution prompted an influx of immigrants from Mexico. Against this backdrop, Latinx bodies, particularly Mexican ones, became sites for the projection of racial scripts and racial feelings, including anxieties about lack of jobs, economic stability, and racial purity. In moments of crisis, Latinx immigrants, who flowed into the nation without restrictions or quotas during the Great Depression, were coded in public culture as inherently criminal, with innate proclivities toward theft and drug dealing. As Steven Bender writes, during the 1920s silent films went from representing ruthless and violent rural Mexican banditos to representing urban Mexican drug dealers and gang members, who were no more flattering.[76] Like their Black counterparts, Latinx persons were understood to be lazy and unimaginative, with little intelligence. It is unsurprising, then, that Amador, particularly when read in contrast with Chaplin, was treated as thief and scoundrel.

Race offers a compelling explanation for why Chaplin, who represented for the Frankfurt School the pinnacle of white resistance to the evils of industrialization, capitalism, and mass production was distinguishable from Amador. By the 1910s, Chaplin impersonators were ubiquitous. Chaplin look-alike competitions were common, and one Chaplin-style performer, Billy West, had already made fifty films.[77] However, while the courts did not protect Chaplin from white artists, Judge Preston invoked familiar racial scripts and racial feelings around deception and fraud, which were typically applied liberally and flexibly to Latinx, Black, and Asian individuals, in making his decision. Like Grier, Preston never mentions race; he implicitly invokes it to protect the work of a white and much beloved comic. His finding that Amador engaged in fraudulent imitation necessarily contrasts with Chaplin's whiteness and points to all the impersonators who were *not* sued for copyright infringement. Practically speaking, only Black and Brown mimesis is adjudicated as threatening theft.[78]

As Olufunmilayo Arewa argues, racial whiteness determines the boundaries of creativity, in ways that *"assume* that copying of existing texts reflects a lack of creativity or originality."[79] Chaplin is the keeper of "perfection," while Amador exists as imitator extraordinaire, the *singular* Tramp whose works offer justification for expansion of copyright law via unfair competition protection. Placing a limit on "imitation" operates as the vehicle for this expansion, in a manner that entrenches familiar white attachment and control over the imaginings of Romantic authorship.

Amador worked as a vehicle to protect Chaplin's reputation and star status, not simply his originality.[80] This monetization of his image was a reputational expansion of whiteness as (intellectual) property, one that Amador could not access by virtue of his racial identity and the purported innate unoriginality of his ideas. Arewa thus gets to some—but not all—of the problem here. Amador is subject to both provincial and racialized notions about the way creativity operates and to troubling racial scripts and racial feelings about Mexicanness. But Chaplin's victory demonstrates that copying can result in uniquely original works, if only brought into being by the right—or white—author. The racial double standard of copying is one that was also materially produced, as Kembrew McLeod notes, as part of the systematic refusal to allow Black people to access education and raced understandings of mimicry.[81]

The decision's omission is as damning as its commission. Amador's Mexicanness appears to preclude him from status as a Romantic author, because he is presumed to lack the theoretical prowess that Chaplin possesses and his Mexican protégés are illegible to the court, particularly in an era when racial feelings of fear of Mexicans as devious, lazy, unintelligent thieves were commonplace. Reading backward and forward historically— all the way back to *Wheatley* and forward to *Supreme Records*—shows that racial scripts regarding purported lack of imaginativeness among people of color rear their heads when white artists enforce their rights.

Yet Amador's representations of Chaplin were anything but projections of these racial stereotypes. Instead, they were part of a larger patchwork of Chaplinesque performances that unfolded in Latin America. As Jason Borge writes, Latin American appropriations of Chaplin offered "an elastic trope through which to re-articulate local and national identities in ways that highlight both their intimate links with and their alienation from metropolitan models."[82] While he points out that the sparse historical record around Amador makes it difficult to make the case in the context of *Amador*, the Mexican artist is nonetheless part of a larger landscape of creative expression that was illegible to American courts.

Specifically, the outcome of *Amador* is consistent with the treatment of Amador as criminally brown—as Borge puts it, "In the 1920s, thanks largely to the legal actions of such comedians, the courts 'shifted from addressing imitation and borrowing as natural forms of cultural development to seeing them as theft'"[83]—and inconsistent with the recognition of people of color creativity. Like *Stowe*, the case trades on white racial feelings, this time a sentimental adoration for Chaplin and the myth of his uniqueness and authenticity. *Chaplin* accordingly operates to reinforce racial scripts applied to multiple groups while further reproducing a Romantic and nostalgic attachment to creators like Chaplin.

White "distinctiveness" in Supreme Records v. Decca Records (1950)

Supreme Records v. Decca Records (1950) (hereinafter *Supreme Records*) replicated the problem of *Amador* through its characterization of the creativity of Black jazz musician Paula Watson. In it, the court invoked racial scripts of Black people as lacking in creativity, intelligence, and uniqueness under the guise of protecting "imagination and skill." Watson, who recorded the song "A Little Bird Told Me," sought to protect her work against the cover of white musician Evelyn Knight, recorded for Decca Records. While the case is a procedurally thorny one in which the composer owned the copyright and the arranger was attempting to claim protection for her arrangement,[84] the opinion nonetheless makes a number of racially problematic statements about imagination/imitation in line with those of the past cases engaging those concepts.

At the time, artists generally did *not* have rights in musical compositions that they performed.[85] However, there were exceptions to that rule, analogous to *Chaplin*. As Judge Leon Yankwich wrote in response to Watson's unfair-competition claim: "[B]efore a musical arrangement may be protected as a right against a competitor, it must have a *distinctive characteristic*, aside from the composition itself, of such character that any person hearing it played would become aware of the distinctiveness of the arrangement."[86] Knight's version of the song, Yankwich reasoned, did not infringe on Watson's purported arrangement of the song because the former involved "intelligence, imagination, or skill"[87] and the latter did not. Reasoning that *Chaplin* was evidence of the distinctiveness principle, Yankwich determined that Watson's version of the song *lacked* the uniqueness to be protectable.[88] Yankwich further concluded that Decca Records did not engage in "palming off"[89] of the unoriginal work, so there was no actionable unfair competition.

While technically consistent with the law of the time around arrangements, read in the historical context of *Wheatley, Stowe*, and *Amador* and the subsequent line of cases in which courts found distinctiveness to exist, Yankwich's decision is a judgment on Black/white artistry itself, one that calls upon Jefferson's proclamation that Black people were biologically incapable of exhibiting the characteristic of true imagination that would be evident in a bona fide (white) American creator and exemplary American citizen but not in one who was merely copying. Watson was not only an unoriginal musician; she was an implicitly bad intellectual property citizen, who could not live up to the ideals of Americanness.

Yankwich writes, "There is a line of cases which holds that what we may call generically by the French word representation—which means to perform, act, impersonate, characterize, and is broader than the corresponding English word—is not copyrightable or subject to any right recognized under the law of unfair competition."[90] He went on to make a series of racially troubling claims about the unprotectability of Watson's recording. There are three ways in which his opinion racialized creatorship: it left Black artists who could not read unprotected at equity or at law, it continued the trend of overvaluing white creatorship over Black creatorship, and it contributed to the racial common sense that artists of color created nothing of value because they were mere imitators.

As to the first, Yankwich noted that "musique a faire,"[91] including hand-clapping, rhythm, and beat, is not protectable because it is "well known in the art."[92] As the recent "Blurred Lines" controversy shows, elements such as rhythm are distinctive and protectable, though U.S. copyright law has repeatedly *chosen* not to protect them.[93] Yankwich also clearly had an aesthetic preference for Knight's rendition of the song, which he called "rich, against a musically colorful background . . . full, meaty, polished" with "more precise, complex and better organized orchestral background."[94] On the other hand, he described Watson's rendition as "mechanical, lacking inspiration, containing just the usual accompaniments and the usual intonations one would find in any common recording."[95] Yankwich's own racial scripts and racial feelings, which are traceable from Jefferson through *Stowe* and *Amador*, inform his purportedly objective test about the distinctiveness of the compositions. Watson's (Black) jazz style is lost on him, because he is drawn to aesthetic qualities of Knight's (white) artistry.

Yankwich's decision makes visible the double standards to which Black creators were historically held, across media forms, through seemingly race neutral legal language that was tied up in sentimental understandings of American creatorship and American citizenship. This is particularly true when reading the cases that followed *Chaplin* and *Supreme Records*. In *Goldin v. Clarion Photoplays* (1922) (hereinafter *Goldin*), for instance, the court found that a white magician could prevent a motion picture company from producing a film about sawing a woman in half. Even though Goldin was not the first artist to saw a woman in half, the court held that perfecting the illusion was "the result of [Goldin's] ingenuity and skill."[96] The binary of imagination/imitation, as articulated in *Goldin* was certainly doctrinally different from that in earlier cases. However, it continued to use that binary as a litmus test for understanding when and where protectable authorship existed. Cases such as the ones I have traced here were instrumental in refusals to protect the creative works of people of color and, in later years, portray them as bad intellectual property citizens.

Though the line of distinctiveness cases identified here sometimes protected characters and not individual musical works, that line of cases was neither clear nor fixed prior to *Supreme Records*. Yankwich had considerable discretion in deciding whether to protect Watson and, even in doing so, he could have used different language. Notably, *Supreme Records* was decided in 1950, just years before Emmett Till's murder provided a spark for the civil rights movement. In 1957, Yankwich penned a law review article titled "Legal Protection of Ideas: A Judge's Approach." In it he writes that "[o]riginality refers to expression and authorship and not the novelty of the subject matter."[97] "Expression, style, and idiom," he maintains, are hallmarks of originality of authorship; they are the litmus tests for copyrightability.[98] The test for originality, Yankwich concludes, can be consistent and "universally accepted."[99] Though Yankwich may have believed that statement, it is widely theoretically disputed.

Regardless of his intent, however, Yankwich advances a vision of originality that renders his racial proclivities invisible and wraps them in a cloak of objectivity. "Expression, style, and idiom," as *Supreme Records* demonstrates, are anything but objective. As scholars of public feelings contend, much of the negotiation of affect occurs unconsciously, without explicit engagement with others. *Supreme Records*, a case about which very little has been written in the context of race, exemplifies this view. While skeptics will argue against reading race into a situation in which legal constraints prevent racially equitable outcomes, the history of consistent use of the phrase true imagination in racialized ways suggests that it is necessary to carefully attend to underlying justifications for such outcomes. Copyright law is not, as Yankwich argues, made up of "universally accepted" legal standards; it is shaped by racial scripts and racial feelings used to make economic decisions about extending limited monopolies and affording lucrative copyright and unfair competition protections to creators. As such, it is not only structured by racial scripts and racial feelings but also structures the very landscape of capitalism in which creative works created by people of color are valued and exchanged.

"THE PROGRESS OF SCIENCE AND THE USEFUL ARTS" AS ENTHYMEMATIC WHITENESS

Patent law in the United States has always been structured as a story of human progress. Indeed, the constitutional mandate for the protection of patents states that the U.S. federal government should "promote the progress of science and useful arts, by securing to authors and inventors the exclusive right to their respective writings and discoveries."[100] Patent law in the United States has also always been a story of Romantic inventorship. As Kara Swanson writes, "[An] inventor was a romantic author who did not write."[101] Inventors were imagined as lone (white) geniuses who created new and valuable inventions through their own hard work and determination. The story of patenting was intertwined with and co-produced the nation's stories of race, national identity, citizenship, and economic prosperity.

People of color, because they were understood and treated as nonpersons who were capable only of physical labor, definitionally could not contribute to the progress of the nation. William Thornton, a former superintendent of the Patent Office, held a deeply racialized fear that the "barbarians at the gates"[102] would destroy the repository for America's great works of genius, an attitude that marked a long tradition of understanding human progress as tied to whiteness, particularly in the context of inventorship.

The notion of human progress functioned as a "rhetoric of exclusion,"[103] which necessarily included only those who were regarded as civilized and human. That rhetoric of exclusion became a central organizing theme of patent law, an area of jurisprudence that also defined the nation. The racial scripts that patent law invoked were similar to those of copyright law, while racial feelings of pride and confidence coupled with anxiety and resentment were more constructed around Jefferson's explicitly white understandings of national identity, citizenship, and economic prosperity.

Commissioner of Patents Edmund Burke wrote in 1846:

> The fruits of [the inventor's] genius . . . are constantly liable to be wrested from him by the *unscrupulous and dishonest*, who . . . are apt to regard the rights of the inventor as the *fruits of a monopoly* which it is a merit instead of a wrong to break down and destroy . . . The right of the inventor to his invention, in the judgment of all enlightened minds, cannot but be viewed as far more sacred than mere things of property. It is a mental creation, or rather the discovery of a principle or thing never before known to the world, and may be . . . productive of countless blessing to the human family, affecting their destinies as individuals and as communities through all time. When the wonderful discoveries of a Watt, a Fulton, a Whitney, and an Arkwright, and the great results to the individuals and to nations which have followed from them, are contemplated, it is not difficult to realize the value of the splendid gifts which science . . . has bestowed upon man, nor to estimate the claims which the true inventor has upon society. He may truly be called *the pioneer of civilization, the explorer of the unknown* world of science and art. And yet how many of those truly great benefactors to their race have fallen victims to *ingratitude and wrong*, and gone down to their graves in *penury and sorrow*.[104]

Burke, in making an argument for patent law, calls upon Romantic imaginings of creatorship, economic metaphors, and public feelings. Inventors are threatened by the "unscrupulous and dishonest" but are protected by "enlightened minds." Inventorship protects humanity and shapes the destinies of individuals. Inventors are pioneers, explorers, and civilizers and bring progress to society. Patents are their tools for protecting the economic gains owed to them, gains that are threatened by those who do not support patents and those who show "ingratitude and wrong" and accordingly doom inventors to "penury and sorrow." Burke constructs an inventor whom the public can imagine as honorable and deserving, one who is put upon by those who object to patent laws. Inventions are hallmarks of a great civilization, inspiring pride and underpinning prosperity. The colonial metaphors of pioneering, exploring, and civilizing are also undoubtedly raced and gendered ones, which when coupled with the Patent Office's 1857 declaration that enslaved persons could not own patents, underscore the white nationalist sentiments of the passage.[105]

The National Portrait Gallery at the Smithsonian Institution in Washington, DC, houses the 1862 painting *Men of Progress*, which also reflects this narrative. The artwork depicts nineteen white men gathered around a table amid a sea of inventions and drawings. The image highlights America's consistent narrative of imagined progress through invention and its (white) agents. The website for the piece reads:

> Throughout the 1800s, homegrown American scientists and inventors were a source of pride for the fledgling republic . . . The period also coincided with the peak of the Romantic Period in art, music, and literature. Accordingly, a host of contemporary children's books, fawning biographies, and sentimental paintings like Christian Schussele's *Men of Progress* lionized American inventors by portraying them as heroic figures.[106]

According to the story of the image and echoing Burke's words, Jordan Mott, the inventor of the coal-burning stove, commissioned a painting of American scientists and inventors who "had altered the course of contemporary civilization."[107] Among those pictured were industrial giants including Samuel Colt, Cyrus Hall McCormick, Charles Goodyear, and Elias Howe.[108] While the group of individuals never met, the image demonstrates the whiteness of creatorship in the American imagination at the time, despite the reality that people of color were inventing important technologies as well.[109] In the painting, invention, progress, and whiteness were linked in the national imaginary, so much so that the image that Schussele created still hangs in the Smithsonian, as a tribute to its days as the nation's first home for the Patent Office. The image trades in

sentimental pride and patriotism, which, when coupled with nationalist statements, anchor pro-patent arguments and define America and its
citizens.[110]

Schussele was reflecting sentiments that had accompanied imaginaries of
inventorship for a century. During the War of 1812, as Thornton reportedly said to the British, who had already destroyed the nation's Capitol:

> Are you Englishmen or only Goths and Vandals? This is the Pat-
> ent Office, a depository of the ingenuity of the American Nation, in
> which the whole civilized world is interested. Would you destroy it? If
> so, fire away, and let the charge pass through my body . . . the effect
> is said to have been magical upon the soldiers, and to have saved the
> Patent Office from destruction.[111]

Thornton's statement is an often-repeated example of the importance of
the Patent Office to American identity. In Thornton's formulation, the willingness of the British to destroy the Patent Office made them uncivilized,
like the Goths and Vandals, "the corrupters and destroyers of the culture
of the Romans,"[112] who were often described as part of a "rude northern
race."[113] Though the Goths and Vandals eventually epitomized whiteness,
as "barbarians" they embody the disorder and chaos of racial Otherness to
the human progress associated with the Roman Empire. This same narrative
reappears in the context of US-Indo relations dressed in the guise of civility, as I show in chapter 3. In Thornton's portrayal, America becomes the
site for and steward of the knowledge that ensures linear human progress.
As James Boyle puts it, "We are driven to confer property rights in information on those who come closest to the image of the romantic author,
those whose contributions to information production are most easily seen
as original and transformative."[114] Through this period, those persons were
imagined to be white. Giants such as Thomas Jefferson, Benjamin Franklin,
Thomas Edison, and Henry Ford—all of whom have checkered histories of
inventorship—became the exemplars through which the ideal of the good
citizen creator/the bad non-citizen imitator were built.

John Gast's 1872 painting *American Progress* tells a similarly racialized
story. In it, settler colonists move westward, toward a herd of buffalo and
a group of seemingly fearful Indians. The landscape is dotted with technologies of transportation—horses, covered wagons, stagecoaches, and
trains—that echo the narrative of human progress that Burke, Schussele,

and Thornton tell. Invention is not only an act of human progress but also an act of whiteness. Native Americans appear in visual contrast to the white settler colonists, who farm the land and explore the waterways. The image connects Manifest Destiny to invention and patents, as well as feelings of pride and triumph about settler colonialism. The painting also recalls the legal doctrines that facilitated settler colonialism, specifically the Doctrine of Discovery set forth in *Johnson v. M'Intosh* (1823) and the broken promises enshrined in treaties that the United States largely did not honor.[115] A woman floats above the scene, holding a schoolbook in one hand and wearing a white gown and a star on her forehead. She presides over colonial expansion, as if to bless it with the knowledge of human progress.

At best, these visual narratives perpetuate the notion that people of color could offer only knowledge that was as yet unrefined, as Aoki puts it in a riff on Claude Levi-Strauss, "raw v. cooked knowledge."[116] White ideals of inventorship thus anchored the nation's mythologies of knowledge production and economic prosperity. People of color, in this imagining that reinforced racist understandings of the "Vanishing Indian,"[117] who was a barbaric and uncivilized nonperson that could not join the civilized world,[118] had no place in the pantheon of human development. Here, the lines between anti-Blackness and anti-Indigeneity are blurred, as the racial scripts of uncivilization are applied to Black people and indigenous peoples. Though mixed race Native Americans may not have experienced the "social death"[119] that Afropessimists contend marks Blackness, they were systematically exterminated, erased from view, and treated as nonpersons who were close to nature. In short, the visual narratives of human progress affirmed white supremacy.

Because the values of patent law and human progress also underpin understandings of the American Dream, the latter is laced with racialized understandings of meritocratic achievement.[120] The figure of the citizen creator was not an incidental or identity-neutral element of the American narrative but an essential and raced one. Inventorship, the American Dream, and economic prosperity were mythically co-created, in order to shape and manage the desires and anxieties of the nation and its citizens. The values of the American Dream—inventiveness, rugged individualism, self-reliance, hard work, honesty, and perseverance—were associated with a particular kind of whiteness, that was intertwined with masculinity, progress, and nation-building. Inventorship thus became the exclusive domain of white men, who were imagined to be the economic and technological engines of the nation.

For James Truslow Adams, who in 1931 became the first to invoke the phrase, "[t]hat American dream of a better, richer, and happier life for all our citizens of every rank, which is the greatest contribution we have made to the thought and welfare of the world"[121] was one of the most important unifying ideologies of the United States. The American Dream is just that, though, an ideology. It is a myth of nation and citizenship grounded in ambiguity and uncertainty—and therefore anxiety.[122] Agency, Adams continues, is "the idea that individuals have control over the course of their lives . . . the bedrock premise upon which all else depends."[123] Agency renders that ambiguity, uncertainty, and anxiety, as well as human life, bearable. Robert Rowland and John Jones describe the American Dream as "a progressive myth in which the heroes are ordinary, rather than extraordinary."[124]

Those who best embody the American Dream, however, are the people who already benefit from its meritocratically allocated spoils. Those who do not succeed never possessed the skill to do so—and more importantly, they are an existential threat to those who do. The American Dream is, accordingly, a powerful ideological tool that serves "axiological, epistemological, and identity functions,"[125] particularly around race. The American Dream unavoidably made and makes, in George Lipsitz's terms, a "possessive investment in whiteness,"[126] while coding those who are not white as threats to the desires of (white) American citizens. Even when people of color are narrativized as having achieved the American Dream, their success is frequently linked with their exceptional hard work and assimilation into the greatest nation in the world, not with the capacity for knowledge production and full membership in the nation.[127]

Within this context, articulations of "progress and the useful arts" functioned as a means of creating and confirming an imagined trajectory of *white* development, including using the language of the American Dream.[128] The concept of scientific progress implicitly set up a narrative of race in which white persons performed the heroic task of civilizing non-white nonpersons.[129] In the syllogistic logic that developed around invention, patented inventions contributed to human progress, progress was the domain of inventive (white) persons, and therefore inventive (white) persons could create progress. This set up, as countless scholars have demonstrated, an organizing schema for what could be "discovered" and transformed into scientific progress and who could do the "discovering." This organizing schema, subsequently evolved into the complex technological nature/science distinctions of later eras.

More specifically, the continuity of racial scripts about nature/science over time created an enthymematic whiteness in which the identity category could be unstated yet always inferred. In short, the narrative of progress as white is an "argument . . . drawn from premises that do not need to be stated 'since the hearer supplies them.'"[130] Racial scripts about the American Dream and human progress operated as stand-ins for language about race. They were deeply associated with the racializing ideologies of this era but modernized in ways that came to be coded as colorblind and postracial. Neither conceptions of human progress nor the American Dream became more racially inclusive over time, despite the nation's deeply held beliefs to the contrary.

Perhaps no spaces better exemplified the promise and peril of the American Dream, as well as its connections to inventorship, citizenship, and economic prosperity, than the nation's World's Fairs.[131] From 1851 to 1940, the World's Fairs became "'great new rituals of self-congratulation,' celebrating economic and industrial triumphs."[132] These monuments to American innovativeness showcased white masculine creatorship while Otherizing people of color in ways that reinforced settler colonialist narratives of inventorship. The World's Fairs represented racist taxonomic classifications, with "a neat ordering of the world according to classes, types, and hierarchies—a system inherited from the Enlightenment."[133] Further, the World's Fairs in the United States operated as platforms for scientizing racism itself, through the work of racist anthropologists, sociologists, evolutionary biologists, and eugenicists invested in American Empire.

More often than not, groundbreaking technologies were displayed alongside "exotic" humans in a manner that reinforced binary distinctions between creators and non-creators, civilized and uncivilized cultures, and citizens and non-citizens of the United States. These narratives operated through the heroic depictions of white male invention.[134] Yet the ambient feelings of the World's Fairs—that is to say the atmospheric sentiments that flowed through the event—were excitement, triumph, and possibility, for the nation's (white) citizens.

Notably, the 1893 World's Columbian Exposition in Chicago held a "Negro Day,"[135] which represented Black people as savages who were incapable of participation in the inventional showcase. Negro Day unfolded

against the backdrop of a series of exhibits that contrasted the White City
with the living arrangements and cultures of groups of racial Others. Black
civil rights activists responded to the racism of the Columbian Exposition
by protesting the lack of a respectful African American exhibit. They contended, in part, that the absence of Black people excluded them from access and inclusion in the civilized and inventional worlds. Quite simply, in
the World's Fairs, Black people were denied personhood.

In a pamphlet titled "The Reason Why the Colored American is Not
in the World's Columbian Exposition" ("The Reason Why"), Frederick
Douglass, Ida B. Wells, and others expressed their views on the exclusion
of Black people from narratives of inventorship and human progress:

> The exhibit of the progress made by a race in 25 years of freedom
> as against 250 years of slavery, would have been the greatest tribute
> to the greatness and progressiveness of American institutions which
> could have been shown the world . . . The wealth created by [the
> industry of the colored people of the United States] has afforded to
> the white people of this country the leisure essential to their great
> progress.[136]

This counterpoint to the predominant racial scripts and racial feelings of the
era demonstrates that intellectual property discourses and inventorship narratives are neither static nor uncontested. Instead, they are part of hegemonic
negotiations over the right to be seen as a creator, a citizen, and a person.

These hegemonic encounters persisted, particularly in the context of patent law, as people of color attempted to push back against the stereotypes
and sentiments that hindered their ability to take part in the unfolding of
human progress. Yet despite these attempts, by the 1900s, representations
of people of color as outside the category of inventorship seemed cemented
in the American unconscious.[137] Even in the face of continued pressure
for racial justice, the remaining two World's Fairs of the era, in Chicago in
1933 and New York in 1940, entrenched the same binaries of creatorship/
non-creatorship and savagery/civilization that previous World's Fairs had
employed. African Americans were simply not represented as part of the
theme of Century of Progress.[138] Returning to Fouché and Vostral serves as
a reminder that the omission of people of color—particularly Black, Asian,
Native, and Latinx individuals—from the narrative of human progress created a double bind that reaffirmed the conviction that they could not invent.

That narrative persisted over the years, even as the nation embraced color-blindness and postraciality.

CONSUMER CONFUSION AND
THE CONSUMER GAZE

Trademark law, which existed at only a state level until the mid-1900s,[139] both amplified and quelled national desires and anxieties associated with race, national identity, citizenship, and economic prosperity. Passed in 1946, the nation's first federal trademark statute, the Lanham Act,[140] played a central role in perpetuating and reinforcing the whiteness of U.S. citizenship as well as racial hierarchies from the Antebellum Era that Emancipation disrupted.[141] Yet unlike copyright and patent law, trademark law did not explicitly exclude certain groups from protection. Instead, it produced a legal framework through which racial hierarchies could be normalized and managed visually, in consumer spaces.

Along with a precipitous rise in U.S. trademark registrations in the 1900s, "product consciousness had become so crucial a part of national history and popular self-identity that the public's relation to business took on a patriotic value."[142] Rosemary Coombe, citing Michael Warner, notes that trademarks are "constitutive parts of a public sphere—constructing a common discourse to bind the subject to the nation and to its markets,"[143] while Richard Schur comments that "[c]irculation of racial imagery is not simply an accidental effect of the current trademark system but a fundamental element of its logic."[144]

America's trademarks effectively and affectively traded on nostalgia and desire for particular racial orders, thereby simultaneously managing white fears about the end of slavery and offering reassurances about racial futures. They did so by structurally and doctrinally affirming particular subject positions, specifically those of the white, heterosexual male. Trademark law developed around a largely white and male consumer gaze that, through legal doctrine and images, objectified and commodified women and people of color, often through the invocation of familiar racial scripts. Because the consumer gaze operated both legally and culturally, it is traceable through legal cases and trademarks themselves, as both explicitly and implicitly reified the consumer authority of white heterosexual masculinity.

Trademarks entrenched a flexible but nonetheless consistent triangular relationship among individual, product, and nation, which played an important role in the construction of a sentimental and anxious national identity in two important respects.[145] First, they represented race and racialized labor in ways that offered a soothing balm for whites after the national trauma of the Civil War. Exaggerated, sexualized, and mocking trademarks from Little Black Sambo to Chiquita Banana promoted the ideas that people of color were nonpersons, who were incapable of producing valuable knowledge, best suited for unskilled and service labor, and were not full and participating members of the national body politic. These representations built upon familiar racial scripts of people of color as unintelligent, lazy, incapable, devious, and primitive. Perhaps more importantly, these representational practices demarcated white Americans—with white, heterosexual men having particular authority—as *producers* and *consumers* of people of color instead of as persons existing in equal relationality with them. The white male consumer gaze dictated the language and trajectories of legal doctrine and specified which visual images had value.

Second, these ideas and values came to be embedded within trademark doctrine, by empowering some to consume and marking others for consumption. That distinction, of course, humanized some individuals and dehumanized others. The Doctrine of Consumer Confusion, the test for determining whether and when the "reasonable consumer"[146] is duped by a "confusingly similar"[147] trademark, embraced racial scripts and racial feelings that prevailed at the time. Defined by an implicit male consumer gaze grounded in the structural realities of a white male judiciary and white male property holders, consumer confusion naturalized white masculinity as the default legal standard for seeing and judging trademark infringement.[148] In doing so, the Doctrine of Consumer Confusion created a form of particularly American emotional racial capitalism in which racial identity, citizenship, and personhood collided in the marketplace, in the specific forms of trademarks and trademark doctrine.

The pervasive use of derogatory images of people of color as trademarks created a "scopic regime,"[149] an unspoken but accepted visual order of things, which reflected white, male, settler colonialist understandings of the world. In Judith Butler's definition of the term, "[t]he visual field is not neutral to the question of race; it is itself a racial formation."[150] Seeing unfolds within a set of ideological constraints, which limit the very possibilities of radical seeing. Trademark's racialized scopic regime resulted from the creation and reproduction of a white male consumer gaze,[151] that was produced by and reproduced white men as consumers. In a nation in which white men held most positions of power and most economic assets—including property rights, lawmaking authority, permission to govern, and industrial production—trademarks visually reflected and constituted their understandings of the world, even when women and people of color were doing the producing/consuming.

Put differently, a scopic regime shaped by the male consumer gaze in the late 1800s and early 1900s was one that necessarily objectified people of color and presented them as commodified trophies of colonial conquest. Conceptually speaking, those individuals who were afforded political, cultural, and economic authority made the world in their image, as a means of retaining power.[152] Moreover, they created conditions that produced more white male consumers like themselves, who validated the racial hierarchies that trademarks imagined in a self-reproducing cycle.

Returning to Berlant, trademarks identified communities of belonging and non-belonging, particularly by unifying whites around their objectification and consumption of people of color. (White) consumers were implicitly joined together by the joy of purchasing commodified forms of Otherness, of "eating the Other."[153] Imagistic representations of racial scripts transformed racial common sense into visual vernacular while simultaneously calling upon (white) American citizens to come together to form strong and resilient capitalist markets. These images, in turn, normalized the feelings of antipathy toward non-white citizens that continued to circulate. While some racially exaggerated, sexualized, and mocking images of white persons—for instance, the Fighting Irish—certainly exist, they are relatively more rare and considerably less damaging than analogous images of people of color.[154] For a young nation articulating its racial hierarchies, understandings of labor, and economic investments, demeaning images of people of color served as potent vehicles for entrenching a range of racial scripts and racial feelings as well as shaping understandings of nation and citizenship. Indeed, they ensured that whiteness and power were intertwined.

Aunt Jemima provides one example of how the nation's racial scripts around the (white) consumer gaze coalesced in concise, visual, economic forms in trademarks. The loyal homemaker was emotional racial capitalism personified. Her image demarcated a community of individuals who were sentimentally intertwined with the Old South from which she emerged.

The mammy, Patricia Hill Collins explains, is a "controlling image,"[155] a stereotype specifically of the "faithful, obedient domestic servant."[156] Because of her maternal caretaking, the mammy represents an idealized relationship to white masculinity, and necessarily replicates, biologically and culturally, the very racial hierarchy and structures of power that result in widespread anti-Black oppression.[157] As her image circulated in trademark form, so did the ideologies of race and gender that she implicitly represented and perpetuated.

Aunt Jemima represented a modernization, not a mere replica, of the mammy: the humble pancake-maker conveyed the message that even in post-Emancipation America, Black women were happy, even jubilant, to remain obedient caretakers, confined to the kitchen, looking after children other than their own. Aunt Jemima insidiously normalized the domestication and subservience of Black women in the anti-slave North even as African Americans were advocating for progressive racial politics.[158] Transforming Aunt Jemima into a trademark not only visually reified anti-Black racial scripts but implicitly suggested that Black people were not the ones looking at or even buying consumer products. Consumption was crafted by white men for the visual pleasure of white men and white women, in order to confirm and maintain their power, identity, and authority.

America's most well-known mammy, Aunt Jemima gained widespread appeal in the late 1800s, after the mammy figure had been popularized through cultural works like *Uncle Tom's Cabin* (1852), *The Clansman* (1905), *Imitation of Life* (1933), and *Gone with the Wind* (1936). With the possible exception of *Uncle Tom's Cabin*, those works endorsed the oppression of Black people by cultivating fear of racial violence, miscegenation, and racial feelings of white superiority. They also perpetuated racial scripts about Black women as unintelligent, unimaginative, and servile, characteristics that prevented their recognition as citizens or persons.

Aunt Jemima was initially introduced as a minstrel character, derived from Billy Kersands's song "Old Aunt Jemima."[159] Beginning in 1875, she became a staple of minstrel shows around the nation, which, as Eric Lott demonstrates, were sites for the production of profound racial hatred and racial desire.[160] Lott's understanding of racial desire manifests in the context of Black women who take care of white children and develop a filial bond that benefits them at the expense of Black families. Aunt Jemima was and remains an important symbol of this familial relationship and its central role in maintaining and, indeed, replicating systems of white supremacy after the end of slavery in the United States.

The R. T. Davis Milling Co.—which became the Aunt Jemima Mills Co. in 1890—called upon Kersands's figure in designing the trademark for its pancake mix. In 1893, at the World's Columbian Exposition, the new Aunt Jemima Mills Co. hired Nancy Green to play a real-life Aunt Jemima. She continued to do so until her death in 1923.[161] In 1937, Quaker Oats registered the Aunt Jemima trademark and hired Anna Short Harrington to play the character, which she did until her death in 1952.[162] While Quaker Oats still uses the trademark to sell pancake mix today, the image of Aunt Jemima has evolved considerably, from the overtly racist images of the late 1800s to the inferentially racist images of the 1990s and 2000s. Nonetheless, Aunt Jemima retains her role as a servant and caretaker in a system of white patriarchy, a throwback to post-Emancipation servitude and racial hierarchy who still appears in ad campaigns surrounded by white families.[163]

Aunt Jemima is not, however, significant only as a trademark. Rather, two pieces of litigation demonstrate how trademark law dealt in racial scripts and racial feelings that not only normalized anti-Blackness but also structured the nation's economy. In *Aunt Jemima Mills Co. v. Rigney & Co.* (1917) (hereinafter *Aunt Jemima Mills*), at the height of America's fascination with World's Fairs and in the midst of the Great Migration, Aunt Jemima Mills sued Rigney & Co., a competitor that had also been using an Aunt Jemima trademark to sell pancake mix. The Second Circuit found for Aunt Jemima Mills Co., concluding:

> To use precisely the same mark . . . is, in our opinion, evidence of intention to make something out of it—either to get the benefit of the complainant's reputation or of its advertisement or to forestall the extension of its trade. There is no other conceivable reason why they should have appropriated this precise mark.[164]

This passage echoes the copyright and unfair competition cases of the period, particularly in its discussion of intentionality and reputation. The project of establishing and protecting reputational identity was central to the growth of the American nation. As with *Chaplin* and its progeny, *Aunt Jemima Mills Co.* involved the articulation of a right to exclusive use of a character—here a trademarked one. While Aunt Jemima became a resistive trope through which Black women contested the management of their bodies,[165] the trade in and circulation of derogatory images of Black women as well as the construction of value through a (white) consumer gaze persists even today. Aunt Jemima gained cultural significance post-Emancipation because of those who were complicit in a particular gendered racial hierarchy.

The dispute over the similarity of the Rigney & Co. trademark to the Aunt Jemima Mills Co. trademark was a negotiation between two white male owners who claimed property rights in the image of a Black woman and the racial feelings that the image inspired. The court concluded that Rigney & Co. must have been attempting to free ride on Aunt Jemima Mills Co.'s reputation, which was built almost completely on Nancy Green's reputation. Green's image, which she had little capacity to control given the limited forms of work and legal rights available to Black women at the time, became the object of the struggle between the two companies.[166] Imitation—the same word that anchors the outcomes in *Chaplin* and *Supreme Records*—takes on new meaning as the human inspirations for Quaker Oats's commodified character are erased from the history of the trademark.

When Harrington's family attempted to claim property rights in the trademark that Quaker Oats had benefited from for years, Quaker Oats appealed to racial feelings that have their roots in the Antebellum Era, writing: "The image symbolizes a sense of caring, warmth, hospitality and comfort, and is neither based on, nor meant to depict any one person."[167] The sentiments that the company evoked to cast doubt on Harrington's claim originate in the racial scripts of Black mammies as symbols of loyal caretaking and appeal to white supremacy in implicit ways. They are also in direct tension with the antecedent case, in which the Aunt Jemima Mills Co. asserted its property rights in a trademarked image built primarily on the performances of one woman, not the cultural sentiments of the time.

On the one hand, Quaker Oats claimed that Aunt Jemima was a generically "caring," "warm," "hospitable," and "comfortable" figure. This defense of the appropriation of Black womanhood was an appeal to nostalgic and fantastical racist sentiment about the Antebellum South. Though no Black domestic servant would have intentionally chosen the status of an enslaved person, Quaker Oats ignored that reality, choosing instead to resort to saccharine imagistic racial scripts and racial feelings as alibis for continuing racism. On the other hand, Green transformed Aunt Jemima from a cartoon into a real person. She was so closely associated with the trademark that upon her death in 1923, a newspaper declared "'Aunt Jemima,' of Pancake

Fame, Dead."[168] Though Harrington was a later iteration of Aunt Jemima, the sentiment that Quaker Oats expressed—that the character was not built on real people—was a disingenuous one that erased the history of actual humans in producing the mammy stereotype. In short, Quaker Oats managed to have its pancakes and eat them too.

The example of Aunt Jemima demonstrates how trademarks can generate racialized surplus emotional value,[169] which transforms uncompensated likenesses and objectifications of people of color into lucrative properties, largely for the benefit, convenience, and comfort of white persons. The image of Aunt Jemima, in particular, mediates American racial feelings about whiteness, slavery, and consumerism in a legalized form of identity theft. Even if the litigants had standing, it is likely that they would have lost the case, because of the long legal history underlying these sentiments and the national pride that they engender.

Gardella v. Log Cabin Products (1937) (hereinafter *Gardella*) showcases this complex relationship, specifically highlighting how trademark law operates as a space for normalizing whiteness as property. Tess Gardella, the Italian woman who played Aunt Jemima in the Broadway production of *Showboat*, sued Log Cabin Products and Quaker Oats for unfair competition and violations of civil rights. She alleged that the companies had appropriated the character in which she had "acquired certain rights."[170]

In finding against Gardella, the Second Circuit determined that Aunt Jemima, a character still owned by Quaker Oats, had "unique significance"[171] that prevented Gardella from claiming that the two companies had unjustly imitated her version of the character. In its decision, the court called upon the distinctiveness claims used to protect predominantly white men in the long line of imitation cases, including and after *Chaplin*. The court went on to explain that if Quaker Oats did not already hold property rights in Aunt Jemima, the two companies "would have no right to trade upon [Gardella's] reputation or to pass off an imitation of her singing or form of entertainment either of which caused deception."[172] Nonetheless, because Gardella came to Aunt Jemima after Quaker Oats and the company did not attempt to appropriate her version of the character, she had no cause of action.[173] As in past copyright and unfair competition cases that used claims of distinctiveness to disenfranchise people of color, *Gardella* protected the property rights of companies that had built their value on the objectification of the bodies and creativity of racial Others. Yet given the facts of the case, there are no clear heroes or villains here, only doctrinal trends.

Gardella is a deeply troubling case because it involves a dispute between a white woman who performed in Blackface and a white-owned company over the rights to the image of a deceased Black woman. In addition to highlighting how whites claimed property rights in Black bodies, and white performances of Black characters, it demonstrates how trademark law transforms whiteness into property. Both Gardella and Quaker Oats used their whiteness to assert property rights through intellectual property law, in ways that individuals such as Green and Harrington could neither structurally access nor practically contest. The case thus highlights the racial double standards that apply in intellectual property cases and the manner in which trademark law operates to create and protect (white) property rights in racial scripts and racial feelings. Not only is Green disenfranchised but so too is the rest of the nation, which is largely constrained from reimagining or recommodifying Aunt Jemima in the trademark context.

Under *Gardella*, like *Chaplin* and *Supreme Records*, whites are accorded property rights in the imitative likeliness of others even when people of color are not accorded those same rights. As Jane Gaines argues, it was the "'imprint of profit' on the spoken word that produced the voice of Aunt Jemima as commercially appropriable."[174] Yet that is only part of the story. Aunt Jemima was also commercially appropriable because of the racist and nationalist sentiments she represented for whites—including unity, safety, prosperity, pleasure, comfort, and joy—and the racial scripts she implied. Aunt Jemima clarified for the nation its racial identities and the economic future that would bring stability. As the dispute over *Gone With the Wind* and *The Wind Done Gone* discussed in chapter 2 illustrates, ownership over mammy images is an important point of contention across types of intellectual property law and American history.

Aunt Jemima, like many other trademarks of the period, was intended to help heal the (white) nation's racial wounds. As such, she served as a visual vehicle through which the nation could claim to own people of color, particularly Black women. Aunt Jemima also served a practical trademark value by protecting consumers from the potential confusion between items that are produced by different companies but bear the same or similar trademarks. The Doctrine of Consumer Confusion was and is a legal doctrinal means of ensuring that companies do not use trademarks that are "confusingly similar"[175] to existing trademarks, thereby protecting consumers and trademark owners. The consumer in trademark cases was judged in relation to the "reasonable consumer."[176] That is, in order to determine whether trademark infringement occurred, courts asked whether a reasonable consumer would have been confused as to the source of the competing product under the circumstances of the case.

Schur contends that the Doctrine of Consumer Confusion is not only legal doctrine but also a metaphor for understanding the intersecting relationships among the reasonable consumer, national identity, and racial feelings. He writes of trademarks such as Aunt Jemima that they "might relieve some (white) consumers of any remaining confusion they may possess about race relations or their place in the racial hierarchy."[177] Theorizing cases involving "consumer confusion" through this lens makes visible the ways in which they, like copyright and patent cases, reinscribed racial scripts and conducted racial feelings, because they were crafted by white propertied men and they protected largely white male consumer bases from the harm of buying competitors' goods.

At a basic level, the Doctrine of Consumer Confusion evolved in the context of racial capitalism in the United States. In the 1920s, as Fordism was taking root in the nation with the production of the assembly line, capitalism remained fundamentally racialized. Manning Marable observes that at the heart of economic prosperity in the United States was a fundamental anti-Blackness, one that ensured the systematic underdevelopment of Black communities.[178] Similar arguments can be made of Native American and Latinx peoples, who were objects, not the subjects, of capitalist growth. In this context, trademark law developed to protect the real property interests of a new class of capitalist producers and consumers, who were never contemplated to be people of color.

In trademark law, the "reasonable consumer" is the analogue to the "reasonable person" of civil and criminal law. As feminist legal scholars contend, he—not the feminine "she" or the gender-neutral "they"[179]—is imagined as the sometimes hapless and often unsophisticated victim of attempts to pirate and counterfeit name-brand items and free ride on the reputation of an established brand. Yet because in the 1900s, the Doctrine of Consumer Confusion and trademarks themselves rhetorically interpellated people of color as property for citizens to consume and not as the ones acquiring property, the (white) reasonable consumer was an economically important citizen buyer whom companies sought to protect from deception and deceit. As such, trademark doctrine itself participated in the formulation of an ideal citizenry, with trademarks serving as vehicles for doing so.[180] As with the reasonable person, the consumer who is confused by similar products was and remains largely by default imagined to be part of the generalizable white majority, not a minoritarian group.

Take, for instance, an early Maryland case that aimed to protect "ordinary purchasers purchasing with ordinary caution."[181] This early description of the "reasonable consumer," in 1879, was likely to describe the white men, not women, people of color, or the intersections thereof. While it is difficult to prove the race of the parties in consumer confusion cases, the beliefs of the time suggest that there was nothing "ordinary" about people of color in the late 1800s and that the level of caution they exercised, given the repeated racial scripts of the era, was unlikely to rise to the level of "ordinary caution" even in the best of circumstances. The same case speaks of "fraudulent or colorable imitation,"[182] a legal standard that in cases like *Chaplin* and *Supreme Records* was often heavily racially biased against people of color and continued to be so well into the mid-1900s.

Over the years, the legal standard for defining the "reasonable consumer" evolved to include those who were "paying ordinary attention."[183] While that turn of phrase was more spacious than previous legal standards, it was still based on the court's imagining of "ordinariness," a term that, given beliefs about the desired racial composition of the nation, the boundaries of citizenship, and racialized imaginings of intelligence and sophistication, was unlikely to center the perspectives of people of color. By the mid-1900s, trademark law had developed nuanced tests for considering whether "consumer confusion" had occurred. However, as feminist intellectual property scholars demonstrate, even those tests were applied by a predominantly white, male, middle-class judiciary whose politics in the pre–civil rights era were historically unlikely to align with those of people of color.[184] Given the scopic regime that informed trademark law, the manner in which "reasonable consumer" and "imitation" were defined, and the identity of the judiciary suggest that "consumer confusion" was raced white in ways that supported and upheld an economy built on whiteness as property and racial capitalism not equity and inclusion.

Imagining the consumer in this way created a particular and narrow vision of confusion, one that did not take into account the needs of people of color or even their potential role as consumers in the rapidly growing American economy.[185] Moreover, it resulted in the formation of a consumer market in the United States that was based on an implicit theory of white domination and white fragility. While litigants of color could likely make some limited claims for trademark infringement, they nonetheless faced a number of structural barriers to winning. Laura Heymann notes that both the "reasonable person" and the "reasonable consumer" are "more like a rule than a standard" and that in order to ensure consistency in precedent and the marketplace, "there is a tendency—in fact, a need—to treat this person as monolithic."[186] The homogeneity of the "reasonable consumer" coupled with the inability of people of color to file claims allowed the Doctrine of Consumer Confusion to become a vehicle for protecting white supremacy and whiteness, even through race neutral language. Coupled with the images that trademark law circulated, trademark law played an important role in constructing American citizenship as a category intended to protect whiteness as property, by way of a male consumer gaze.

CHAPTER TWO

THE RACE LIBERAL INTELLECTUAL PROPERTY CITIZEN

You need to shave that stuff
[Big hairy woman] You know, I bet it's tough
[Big hairy woman] All that hair, it ain't legi-i-it
['Cause you look like Cousin I-I-I-I-It]
[Big hairy woman]
　　—THE 2 LIVE CREW, "Pretty Woman"

AS THE FORMAL RACISM and overt violence of the Jim Crow era gradually evolved into the informal racial exclusion and unconscious bias of the
post–civil rights era, the language of colorblindness and universalism became increasingly common in the United States. By midcentury, *Brown v.
Board of Education* (1954) had removed formal obstacles to integration,
though not the racial animus that fueled them. The civil rights struggles
that followed *Brown*, hastened by Emmett Till's brutal murder, resulted
in a renewed wave of national legislation, including President Dwight D.
Eisenhower's Civil Rights Act of 1960, President John F. Kennedy's Civil
Rights Act of 1964, passed after his assassination, and President Lyndon
B. Johnson's Voting Rights Act of 1965.

While overt racism was becoming increasingly unpalatable to Americans, it was not morality that prompted the radical civil rights reforms of
the 1960s. Instead, as Mary Dudziak shows, the United States could not
legitimately promote democracy in the Cold War while managing race
through the framework of "separate but equal."[1] Accordingly, post–World
War II movements advocating for civil rights and decolonization came at
a price, specifically the development of seemingly race neutral rhetorics of
racism and systems of global racial capitalism. Domestically, the language
of colorblindness supplanted that of overt racism while internationally,

rhetorics of trade liberalization replaced those of explicit colonialism. These larger historical trends manifested in the context of intellectual property law in two ways: the use of race neutral legal doctrine to engage in racial discrimination at home and the use of international intellectual property regimes to perpetuate a system of knowledge colonialism abroad.

These trends accelerated in 1948, with the entry into force of the General Agreement on Tariffs and Trade (GATT), and culminated in the creation of the World Trade Organization (WTO) in 1995. Together, these evolutions produced an era of race liberal creatorship, in which racist conceptions of intellectual property citizenship from the pre-Emancipation era persisted despite seemingly progressive liberalism.

Unsurprisingly, laws, policies, and discourses that "did not see race" did not remedy the persistent structural inequalities that had resulted from centuries of racism and dispossession. They only created an appearance of equality that operated as a perpetual alibi to claims of race discrimination. In part, as Jodi Melamed argues, racial liberalism refers to the transition from "mesmerizing narratives of the white man's burden"[2] that informed openly racist and colonial policymaking to "liberal antiracisms—of reform, of colorblindness, of diversity in a postracial world—that explained (away) the inequalities of a still-racialized capitalism"[3] as official state policy. No longer did the management of race entail grappling with structural racism. Instead, anti-racism required citizens, policymakers, and lawmakers to adopt colorblind universalism, a form of thinking that identified racism and the effects of racism as individual matters, not structural ones, and emphasized individual rights and formal equality as the paths to racial justice.

The effect of the turn toward racial liberalism was to protect white supremacy in novel and less-overt ways, often through the mobilization of coded language that could not be easily discredited. Racial liberalism "instantiated a new worldwide racial project that completely supplemented and displaced its predecessor: a formally anti-racist, liberal-capitalist modernity articulated under conditions of US global ascendancy."[4] Nikhil Pal Singh's understanding of race in the world of racial liberalism, as a set of "historic repertoires and cultural and signifying systems that stigmatize and depreciate one form of humanity for the purposes of another's health, development, safety, profit or pleasure,"[5] gestures toward the importance of racial scripts in sustaining racial inequality even in a world of purported colorblind universalism. Even as the United States moved toward desegregation and equality, national conservatism around race and capitalism entrenched systematic oppression, albeit in ways that were less overt than in previous eras.

This chapter examines how intellectual property law continued to construct racialized understandings of creatorship through the language of citizenship and personhood in the post–civil rights era. Intellectual property rhetorics were not immune from the ideologies and discourses of racial liberalism—in fact, the former and latter were deeply intertwined. After the civil rights movement, copyright, trademark, and patent law, which had in previous eras formally excluded people of color from protection, modernized and coproduced age-old racial scripts alongside racially liberalized but persistently white discourses of citizenship and nation. Yet the political, cultural, and doctrinal language of intellectual property law often escaped scrutiny. Instead, it continued to normalize white knowledge production at the expense of the creatorship of people of color and used purportedly race neutral legal language to maintain systems of racial capitalism.

The race liberal creator was a white male genius—a Romantic creator modernized through the language of racial liberalism—whose success was deserved because of his commitment to hard work, ingenuity, and creativity. Race liberal creatorship operated as a tool for fueling purportedly colorblind American nationalism while demonizing people of color and eliding explicit engagement with the debates about racial equality, including those that followed the collapse of Johnson's Great Society and the assassinations of Dr. Martin Luther King Jr. and Robert Kennedy. From the 1960s on, creatorship evolved into an increasingly important imagined engine for national growth, one that also stoked the fires of economic protectionism, xenophobic nationalism, military adventurism, and neocolonial extraction. Copyright, trademark, and patent law evolved not in the spirit of radical equality espoused by the civil rights movement but from a perpetrator perspective, which protected white property interests in knowledge while disciplining people of color for their creatorship.

Three sets of racial scripts organized intellectual property law and racial feelings about the role of copyrighted works, trademarks, and inventions in the race liberal era. First, developing understandings of expertise as the primary domain of Western science updated familiar, raced conceptions of human progress and cemented understandings of knowledge as white property. While such negotiations unfolded primarily in the area of patent law, the Sampling Wars of the 1990s also normalized whiteness and the performance of white practices of knowledge making as central to expertise and thus property ownership. Second, the criminalization of non-white creatorship—through anti-Black tropes of hip hop artists as obscene, thieving copyright thugs—mobilized not only familiar racial scripts as a means of discrediting people of color creatorship but also anxieties about crime, economic growth, and jobs in America. This process invoked raced definitions of true imagination that had run through earlier copyright jurisprudence. Third, white resentment about racial mixing and power persisted after the Supreme Court's decision in *Loving v. Virginia* (1967), which found anti-miscegenation statutes to be unconstitutional. These anxieties about racial purity manifested in the context of trademark law, specifically the periodic embrace of trademark dilution. The resurgence of jurisprudence and legislation around trademark tarnishment and trademark blurring, subsets of trademark dilution, refashioned the consumer gaze to reflect national sentiments about white marginalization, specifically via economic language about expansive brand protection.

In these ways, copyrights, patents, and trademarks continued to operate as sites for the projection and production of anxieties about the state of the nation and its (white) citizenry, just as they had in past eras. Indeed, the presumption that the racial ideologies of knowledge production somehow shifted is counterintuitive, given the persistence of racist ideologies in other areas of culture and politics. Reading intellectual property citizenship through the lens of racial liberalism is thus a productive means of rendering these increasingly hidden racial investments visible and identifying the contours of the ideal race liberal creator.

PRODUCING A RACE LIBERAL CREATORSHIP

In the new phase of globalization that emerged from the post–World War II international order, the United States took a commanding role in managing trade and tariffs and legally defining copyrights, trademarks, and patents, both domestically and internationally. With the expansion of GATT and the eventual creation of the WTO, it became clear that evolving intellectual property rights regimes, like their civil rights counterparts, "excluded radical or fundamental challenges to status quo institutional practices in American society by treating the exercise of racial power as *rare and aberrational* rather than as *systemic and ingrained*."[6] A general lack of reflectiveness—or perhaps lack of interest—with respect to intellectual property's effects on systemic racial inequality combined with discourses about Black criminality, obscenity, originality, expertise, citizenship, and national identity in ways that entrenched white supremacist regimes of knowledge ownership.

The year 1966 marked an important turn in intellectual property's commitments to racial liberalism. That year, Jack Valenti, former aide to President Lyndon Johnson, became president of the Motion Picture Association of America (MPAA). Valenti's tenure was notable not only because it brought politics and the film industry together but also because it heralded the beginning of important policy and rhetorical changes in regulating intellectual properties, many of which were deeply racialized and sentimentalized in the service of economic nationalism.

The beginning of Valenti's tenure coincided with a number of evolutions in political economy and intellectual property rights. As the United States shifted away from Fordist models of economic production, it gradually became a net exporter of intellectual property rights.[7] As the nation's relationship to intellectual properties evolved, so too did the economic, political, and rhetorical value of copyrighted works, trademarked goods and services, and patented inventions.[8] While nationalist xenophobia persisted, the once protectionist impulses of those protecting intellectual property law evolved into a desire to profit from the export of domestic products, through intellectual property maximalism. Valenti was one of the first and most vocal in post–World War II America who not only preached the value of U.S.-produced intellectual properties but also exploited the idea of them in the construction of a predominantly white national identity and associated racial scripts and racial feelings.

Citizenship is, as Robert Asen contends, a discursive practice comprising "fluid, multimodal, and quotidian enactments."[9] It is also a fundamentally lived practice, which can be formed and re-formed through individual acts. Ian Haney López, in writing about the Prerequisite Cases, observes that some citizenship restrictions are simply fiated. This is, in essence, because courts can "do things with words."[10] In this way, the legal and the rhetorical meet in the space of the judiciary, in a manner that makes individual performances into law. In the context of intellectual property law in the race liberal era, the formal racial requirements of earlier years evolved into informal judicial pronouncements about good intellectual property citizens and bad intellectual property citizens disguised as Black letter law.

Intellectual property cases developed their own "grammar of race,"[11] which drew upon familiar racial scripts of Black, Native, Brown, and Asian peoples. "Racial common sense,"[12] a legal standard that was consistently invoked in order to define people of color as not white in the Prerequisite Cases, is legible in intellectual property cases as well. While intellectual property's racial common sense is not explicitly named, cases of the post–civil rights era consistently repeat familiar racial scripts, which disproportionately affect people of color. In the context of patent law, racial common sense dictated that Indigenous peoples lacked the know-how to turn their wisdom into science, that they remained objects, not subjects, of progress. In the context of copyright law, racial common sense dictated that Black artists who sampled were simply stealing. In the context of trademark law, racial common sense dictated that trademarks had to be protected from dilution in order to mollify white anxieties about racial intermixing. Through the lens of racial liberalism, intellectual property law operated as a space in which "race-based exclusions . . . *result from deep social habits such as where people live, who they know socially, what private organizations they belong to, and so on.*"[13] Claims that America had entered an era of colorblindness did not halt the racialization or (neo)colonization of knowledge production.[14]

Charles Mills's understanding of the "racial contract"[15] is particularly useful for thinking about intellectual property in the time of racial liberalism. John Locke, along with Immanuel Kant and Thomas Hobbes, offered theories of individual rights, democratic governance, and statehood that imagined that citizens of a state received a set of rights and entitlements in exchange for protection. Locke's understanding of property as produced through the mixture of labor with nature is one that underpins copyright and patent law.[16] Yet as Mills contends, the white and idealized understanding of the social contract that Locke, Kant, and Hobbes advanced fails to account for race in theorizing of personhood, which ensures that "the contract . . . has really been a racial one, an agreement among white contractors to subordinate and exploit non-white noncontractors for white benefit."[17] Without critical attention to who has access to the category of humanness that underpins rights-based equality, continued racial discrimination is inevitable and indeed desirable under liberalism.

The narrative of individual self-determination as the most important factor in success, which became prevalent after Daniel Patrick Moynihan wrote of the need for "benign neglect,"[18] negated racism as a cause of poverty, instead allocating blame to individual bad actors and cultures of poverty. Still, raced beliefs about the nature of personhood and citizenship persisted as racism evolved into a battle for individual rights, ensuring that even as people of color received formal equality, they could not achieve lived equity. The turn toward colorblind universalism emboldened America's commitment to meritocracy and fairness, enabling the belief that those who did not succeed simply did not work hard enough. Thus, while the 1960s and 1970s saw formal civil rights gains, those gains were quickly reversed through regressive decisions about busing and affirmative action.

Similar trends were evident in intellectual property law, whose gatekeeping maintained white supremacy domestically and internationally.[19] Racial liberalism, then, brought formal equality and even considerable economic gains for people of color. However, it did so while failing to repudiate the belief that people of color cannot produce knowledge and embracing structural commitments to economic liberalization.[20] The latter, though it had the potential to be race neutral, entrenched existing divisions because it operated from a place of racial capitalism, not distributive justice.

(WHITE) EXPERTISE AS PROPERTY

Race liberal understandings of creatorship in the area of patent law worked through the modernization of the association of scientific expertise—and thus the definition of human progress and who could advance it—with whiteness. Though seemingly race neutral in its valuation of scientific and technological knowledge, expertise is a cultural construct,[21] a racial formation through which certain knowledges are valued and others are not. Anticolonial scholars have consistently demonstrated that settler colonists objectified Otherness and projected European understandings of knowledge and expertise onto colonized peoples as a means of claiming power. In the race liberal era, expertise and whiteness remained linked through the construction of distinctions between manufactured "real" knowledge from unrefined "traditional" knowledge and who had the capacity to produce the former.

This is not to say that the material advances of science and technology were not tangible and important or even that people of color were and are not overrepresented in some fields of expertise. Rather, it is to argue that from the 1960s on, expertise in the areas of science and technology was increasingly necessary to produce commercially valuable intellectual properties and that these forms of expertise were constructed around Euro-American ideals at the expense of people of color. Defining the category of expertise in the race liberal era worked to identify a category of *non-experts*, including people of color who were producing traditional knowledge.[22] Patent law socially constructs value in certain kinds of (intellectual) property and in certain kinds of imagined intellectual property citizens, specifically those who can make scientific knowledge that is legible in increasingly internationalized systems of Western patent law in ways that are consistent with raced and colonial conceptions of xenophobic nationalism.[23]

Accordingly, the argument that some scholars make that patents derived from traditional knowledge do not foreclose traditional uses of knowledge misses the point.[24] Whiteness remains racially scripted as superior to nonwhiteness in ways that facilitate white ownership of property and accumulation of wealth. Access to value creation results from the perception that people of color are outside of the scientized regime of knowledge production and, indeed, the categories of citizenship and personhood themselves. Access to the theoretical capacity to contribute to human progress remained limited and constrained by the racial scripts ascribed to people of color and the structural limitations of intellectual property, created by conceptions of nature/culture and development.

Public cultural deployments of expertise evolved in response to rapid scientific and biotechnological development and the concomitant need to reconstruct the relationships between whiteness and property and (neo)coloniality and property. In an age of biotechnology, whiteness, in Cheryl Harris's words, remained "a prerequisite to the exercise of enforceable property rights,"[25] here in the context of expertise. However, the precise landscape of (white) expertise took on new forms. As Zoltan Majdik and William Keith write, "[D]elimiting who can be an expert and whose decisions come from a place of expertise to the provenance of epistemic principles limits our ability to act as experts."[26] The epistemic distinction between nature and science that emerged as overt and extractive racism in the colonial era also became a de facto racial division in the race liberal era. That updated distinction facilitated the understanding of certain kinds of raced knowledge—and the persons who created it—as less valuable than others. Because whiteness and expertise remained linked in race liberalism's racial episteme, those producing traditional knowledge were often constructed as less than whole people without the capacity to invent.[27]

Whiteness continued to operate as a priori evidence of access to expertise or potential to expertise while non-whiteness worked as a marker of non-expertness and suspectness about potential to expertise. Moreover, because values such as hard work and ingenuity continued to hold a special place in the American imaginary, those who comported with those values were deemed good intellectual property citizens. People of color largely produced raw materials, which were "purified" and "refined" in the science-industrial complex for sale in the global economy. They did not do the hard scientific labor, in part because they simply could not do it, that merited valuable patent protection. Unconscious racial and (neo)colonial judgments about expertise, built into the racial episteme of the nation, thus delineated between nature/culture and expertise/non-expertise, and reified fundamentally raced hierarchies of knowledge production.

Two cases, *Diamond v. Chakrabarty* (1980) (hereinafter *Chakrabarty*) and *Moore v. Regents of the University of California* (1990) (hereinafter *Moore*), were central to the development of the nature/culture distinction and its attendant use of raced hierarchies of expertise. The nature/culture distinction also formed an important foundation for bioprospecting, an extractive and (neo)colonial practice of using traditional knowledge as a basis for developing patented inventions that emerged, in the face of much criticism, in the 1990s and 2000s.[28]

Chakrabarty involved a patent dispute over a bacterium that Indian microbiologist Ananda Mohan Chakrabarty had genetically engineered. At issue was whether the bacterium was patentable under 35 U.S.C. § 101 of the Patent Act, which applies to "any new and useful process, machine, manufacture, or composition of matter, or any new and useful improvement thereof." After the USPTO and the Patent Office Board of Appeals denied Chakrabarty's patent application, the U.S. Court of Customs and Patent Appeals—and subsequently the Supreme Court—reversed.[29] In deciding the case, the Supreme Court considered whether gene patents fit in the unpatentable category of "the laws of nature, physical phenomena, and abstract ideas,"[30] which are "manifestations of . . . nature, free to all men and reserved exclusively to none"[31] or a "product of human ingenuity," which is "a nonnaturally occurring manufacture or composition of matter."[32] In ruling that they were the latter, the Supreme Court invoked Jefferson's proscription that "ingenuity should receive a liberal encouragement"[33] in reading § 101. It observed of Chakrabarty's invention: "His discovery is not nature's handiwork, but his own."[34]

Despite controversy over the outcome of the case and its broad grant of protection for "anything under the sun that is made by man,"[35] subsequent decisions interpreted *Chakrabarty* as expansively protecting biotechnologies in the service of racial capitalism. The case is notable not simply because of the decision but because of the manner in which it definitionally excluded certain, often marginalized, forms of knowledge by casting them "as subversive, inherently dangerous, oppositional, and always already guilty."[36] As Shobita Parthasarathy shows by tracing through the amicus briefs and court rulings in *Chakrabarty*, "patent policy insiders tried to keep out any novel forms of knowledge or reasoning that would have challenged their power and the established ways of thinking about patent policymaking."[37] Patent power, which was and is intertwined with corporate power, was thus also racialized power, which delegitimized knowledge produced outside of the Global North by condescendingly categorizing it as mere "traditional knowledge."[38]

While *Chakrabarty* involves the Supreme Court's recognition of an Indian man's "human ingenuity" in a way that is contrary to the history of racialized creatorship, it does so around a narrow conception of human progress, which closes conceptual space in which people of color can be imagined as inventors. The affective construction of a community of "diverse" experts bound together by their adherence to the American Dream's characterizations of innovativeness does not remedy the ideological investments of an intellectual property system that commodifies the knowledge that people of color hold via whiteness. The Amicus Brief of the Pharmaceutical Manufacturers Association, for instance, buys into the familiar metaphor of human progress, contending that Chakrabarty is entitled to a patent by virtue of his "discovery."[39]

Indeed, "discovery, development, and manufacture"[40] in the "promising field"[41] of biotechnology drive the (neo)colonial language of the amicus brief's argument. The goal of the organization is to promote "this country's progress" through "technological innovation." It is not so much that these concepts are shocking as that they reinforce colonial distinctions between nature and culture in ways that render modes of knowledge production that do not conform to these ideals valueless. They further highlight the linkages between idealized American citizenship, the American Dream, and patent law. Though patent law appears to be a meritocracy, that narrative is true only in the context of a distinctly Euro-American understanding of human progress. Those on Chakrabarty's side—and eventually the Supreme Court—embrace a narrow frame for "making" that excludes traditional knowledge that cannot be patented.

Other amicus briefs in favor of Chakrabarty mirror this rhetoric and sentiment, recalling the language of colonial discovery in the context of science. Genentech, for instance, goes so far as to argue that patent law is "neutral,"[42] functionally denying any race- or coloniality-based claims that might be made against Chakrabarty. The "question before the Court," Genentech contends, "is neither one of ethics, for [p]hilosophy, nor politics. It is one of statutory interpretation, of grammar leavened with reason."[43] The appeal to statutory interpretation and grammar erases the racial implications of *Chakrabarty*, casting it instead as a mere question of law and economics. The internal logic of the patent system to which the amicus brief appeals is a racial one, which separates indigeneity from civilization.

While Chakrabarty ultimately won this case, he did so by demonstrating in one instance that he could contribute to human progress, measured by a particular raced and colonial yardstick. His victory left in place the nature/culture binary through which the Supreme Court measured traditional knowledge. In this respect, the Court's decision to side with Chakrabarty is less important than the manner in which it chose to do so. Leaving space for a pluriversality of knowledge instead of excluding particular forms of knowledge would have allowed precarious peoples to protect their making as traditional knowledge instead of as having been transformed into a marketable commodity. Only making space for multiple forms of knowledge production can effectively decolonize intellectual property law. The danger of *Chakrabarty* is that it incorporates people-of-color experts into a schema of inventorship that is associated with a restrictive notion of human progress, which values science and law above nature and traditional knowledge, without any material confrontation with the racial scripts or structural inequalities that underlie those concepts. Economic language offers a veneer of race neutrality that suggests a false separation from racialization and (neo)coloniality while also obscuring racial capitalism.

When read through this frame, the Supreme Court's binary distinction between nature and science constructed through its appeals to manufacturing and composing—notions that also inform the Agreement on Trade-Related Aspects of Intellectual Property Rights (TRIPS)—are racially and (neo)colonially noteworthy.[44] Historically speaking, the former binary favors the inventions of whites, who not only have had greater access to education, wealth, and social power than their people of color counterparts but also have structured the very colonial classification systems upon which science is culturally constructed. As Geoffrey Bowker and Susan Leigh Star explain, "Whose voice will determine the outcome is sometimes an exercise of pure power: [w]e, the holders of western medicine and scions of colonial regimes, will decide what a disease is and simply obviate systems such as acupuncture or Ayurvedic medicine."[45] In this sense, "made by man" is not race neutral but rather privileges epistemological frameworks of expertise and whiteness that consistently devalue the traditional knowledge of people of color and overvalue items produced at the hands of often already propertied white men in the Global North.

As Sandra Harding explains, conceptions of expertise historically structured colonial societies and offered modes of claiming dominance over indigenous peoples.[46] Indigenous scholars including Aroha Te Pareake Mead, Winona LaDuke, and Linda Tuhiwai Smith critique the racial hierarchies implicit in expertise and their tendency to exploit traditional knowledge for its commodity value while refusing to treat it as patentable. Indeed, the Supreme Court's invocation of the statutory term "manufacture" endorses a vision of expertise in which biological innovation happens not in everyday life but in a laboratory, in ways shaped by the flow of racial capitalism. The language of manufacture further evokes the patriotism and pride of the Fordist assembly line. The term compels us to imagine the innovative spirit with which Henry Ford approached automaking and the remaking of industry in science, via employed racialized labor for economic advantage. Similarly, the term "composition of matter" reads nature through a scientific lens, transforming a bacterium into a set of component parts. Composing is the skilled practice of a scientist, distinguishable from discovery in nature.

Further, the Supreme Court's reading of patenting human life as part of the broad grant of constitutional authority to protect ingenuity invokes violent and nostalgic notions of discovery and the frontier. The majority writes in *Chakrabarty*, "Mr. Justice Douglas reminded that the inventions most benefiting mankind are those that 'push back the frontiers of chemistry, physics, and the like.'"[47] Though the case involves the work of an Indian microbiologist, it nonetheless invokes metaphors of the frontier that have consistently been used to subordinate people of color. Historically speaking, the frontier myth, as Richard Slotkin explains, is deeply embedded in

Manifest Destiny and Indian Removal.[48] It is intertwined with public feelings of patriotic pride, which function to invoke a nostalgic and sanitized version of the violent and expansionist history of the frontier as a means of mobilizing power in the present. Wendy Brown writes of the racial and colonial deferral that such nationalism requires:

> Identification with power, which is what I am suggesting "my country is always right" patriotism entails, calls for loyalty to power rather than principle; it glories not in the goodness of America but in its power; it needs other nations and peoples to defer to this power and suffers a narcissistic wound when they do not. This is a dangerous political condition, not only because of the volatility and aggression in this kind of patriotism, but because it breeds anti-intellectualism, contempt for thoughtfulness and collective introspection.[49]

Brown's words draw attention to the inherent danger in appealing to state power and highlight the manner in which that danger can bleed into other areas of everyday life. This is certainly true in the context of patents on life. As Leah Ceccarelli demonstrates, the rhetoric of the frontier is not limited to juridical contexts. Rather, "scientists are imagined to be blazing ever forward, or crossing boundaries, or climbing ever upward."[50] The myth of the frontier and the epistemic whiteness of expertise are updated for patent law, as they are used to justify the colonization of human life in ways that, as biopiracy critics have demonstrated, result in the extraction and commodification of the traditional knowledge of people of color.

The triumph of *Chakrabarty* calls upon those racial scripts of white supremacy through which Europeans justified colonization and genocide of indigenous peoples. Such language was evident not only in *Chakrabarty* but also in public cultural engagements with the case. The *New York Times*, for instance, noted in 1980 that *Chakrabarty* "opens the way for patent protection for the rapidly burgeoning field of genetic engineering."[51] Genentech proclaimed: "The Court has assured this country's technology future."[52] The language of opening and technological futures has an expansionist tone, one that suggests the need to explore and conquer, particularly in the service of economic prosperity and human progress. Notably, the case did open such paths. *Ex Parte Hibberd* (1985) (hereinafter *Hibberd*) extended patent protection to seeds, plants, and plant tissue cultures, facilitating the ownership of genetically modified crops by corporate entities.

Moore followed shortly after, in 1990, enabling the commercialization of human tissue without the permission of the patient. Discourses of scientific discovery, purification, and refinement were instrumental in the expansion of the metaphorical "frontier of science,"[53] which unavoidably revived nostalgic sentiments about the settler colonialism of centuries past.

Chakrabarty set up a binary in which Indigenous peoples who functioned outside of the circuits of knowledge production legible to the scientific-industrial complex were merely noble savages living in nature, not inventors capable of "discovery." In the context of patents, expertise was rhetorically shaped through notions of discovery, invoking not only frontier myths but also tropes of "ingenuity" as evidence of scientific innovation and the larger mythology of the American Dream. Here too the episteme of whiteness is apparent in the larger mythologies of "discovery," in which whites are cast as agents of creatorship, while people of color are those whose knowledge is discovered. Stuart Hall writes that the trope of discovery is fundamentally white, noting that "racism was so *ubiquitous*, and at the same time so *unconscious*—that it was impossible to get any critical purchase on it—the very idea of *adventure* became synonymous with the demonstration of the moral, social and physical mastery of the colonisers over the colonised."[54] Adventure and discovery went hand in hand, with the outcome of adventure being the discovery of new places and objects, including humans, flora, and fauna.

Returning to the Doctrine of Discovery set forth in *Johnson v. McIntosh* (1823) serves as a reminder of the manner in which discovery was coded as uniquely white as well as a means of protecting property rights for whites, from a settler colonialist perspective. In addition to devaluing traditional knowledge,[55] "expertise barriers" in Parthasarathy's words, "make it difficult for those without knowledge that is recognized as relevant and legitimate to engage as equals."[56] The relevant distinction here is not that some science must unfold in laboratories or that traditional knowledge is sometimes unusable in its current form. Rather, it is that discourses of expertise, discovery, and manufacture serve gatekeeping roles, transforming legislators and judges into arbiters of invention and, therefore, property rights. As countless scholars have demonstrated, the rules that these actors develop rarely protect traditional knowledge.

Moore, a patent case that cites the holding in *Chakrabarty*, also strengthened the relationship between expertise and whiteness by allowing doctors to commercialize cell lines without patient permission and failing to address the implications of such a practice for people of color. John Moore, who was treated for hairy-cell leukemia at UCLA Medical Center in 1976, alleged that his doctors had engaged in conversion by commercializing "certain blood products and blood components"[57] without his consent. The Supreme Court of California, in finding no conversion, privileged the doctors' "commercial and scientific efforts"[58] over Moore's right to ownership of his body. The court declared that "[p]rogress in medicine often depends upon physicians, such as those practicing at the university hospital where Moore received treatment, who conduct research while caring for their patients."[59] It went on to explain that Moore could not possibly own the cell line that his doctors developed because it was, by virtue of their scientific expertise, both factually and legally distinguishable from his body:

> Federal law permits the patenting of organisms that represent the product of "human ingenuity," but not naturally occurring organisms. Human cell lines are patentable because "[l]ong-term adaptation and growth of human tissues and cells in culture is difficult . . . and the probability of success is low. It is this inventive effort that patent law rewards, not the discovery of naturally occurring raw materials.[60]

Moore not only marked a new era in the ownership of human bodies, a historically and racially violent practice, but also gave a nod of approval to the use of Black tobacco farmer Henrietta Lacks's posthumously named HeLa cells without her permission or consent.

The implications of such a pronouncement are not simply about the outcome of the case; they are racially epistemic. On a broad level, *Moore* endorses the notion that experts, an already racialized group, have a more valid claim to bodies than the individuals who live in those bodies. The case fundamentally commits to creating a world in which propertizing bodies is thinkable. Such an outcome, historically and contemporarily speaking, produces hierarchies of personhood and citizenship and disenfranchises people of color like Lacks. Though John Moore is white, those deemed to be property are generally not white, partly because they are categorized as such through the persistent racial scripts assert that they lack fundamental traits of humanness. *Moore* enables the calculation that some are less than human; indeed, any and all may become objects emptied of their humanness should they lack expertise. However, such a judgment is always already raced and tied to understandings of who may and who may not be a full citizen.

Moore rhetorically entrenched the damaging binary of expert/non-expert and marked definition of that binary as the domain of whiteness in a number of ways. Like *Chakrabarty*, the decision reinforced the nature/science binary by making a legal distinction between products of nature and products of human ingenuity. Also as in *Chakrabarty*, in *Moore* "human ingenuity" operates as a racialized term, from which people of color have historically been excluded by racial scripts and racial feelings that deem them non-humans, incapable of higher forms of thought and knowledge production.

Moreover, while the Court is factually correct that doctors are important agents of innovation in medical science, *Moore* elides the manner in which medical expertise has been historically dominated by white men who do violence to people of color. The Court's decision to place the economic and research interests of the doctors above the bodily autonomy of their patients necessarily transforms human tissue into a commodity in a system of racial capitalism. The discussion of doctors caring for their patients is also a sanitized one, which erases the history of doctors exploiting vulnerable patients, particularly women of color such as Lacks, who never had the opportunity to contest the use of her bodily tissues.

Once again, the importance of the decision, then, is less about Moore himself and his identity and more about the racial implications of the economic practice of legally allowing corporations to propertize and own bodies. Here, racial capitalism explicitly endorses the ownership of those marked as less than human and less than citizens in a manner that facilitates the invocation of racial scripts. Especially when read in conjunction with *Chakrabarty*, *Moore* signifies a clear commitment to the crass objectification and extraction of economic value from people of color. The political economy of patent law is intertwined with the assessment that some people, predominantly people of color, are less than whites.

Marlon Rachquel Moore refers to the practice of commodifying people of color in this way as "bioslavery,"[61] historicizing its connections to physical slavery. Returning to the two-body problem that Stephen Best identifies reveals that *Moore* marks the refusal to acknowledge that people of color inhabit their own bodies, instead disambiguating, even erasing them, from their physical form through the language of expertise. The rhetorics of the case thus invest in the ideal intellectual property citizen—i.e., that expert who can take the bodies of those who are less than and produce economic value.[62] Laura Foster explains that such a calculus is a biopolitical one, which "privatizes some women's bodies and their knowledge over others, while promising innovations that may only be accessible to certain groups."[63] Similar calculuses were evident even before *Moore*.

In 1951, Henrietta Lacks came to Johns Hopkins Medical Center for a biopsy of a cervical tumor that ultimately took her life. Decades later, her family discovered that HeLa cells, which were the first human cells successfully immortalized in a laboratory, had not only been instrumental in developing a polio vaccine but were also widely used in scientific research across the United States.[64] While Lacks's family eventually came to an agreement in which they were compensated for scientific use of HeLa cells,[65] the story nonetheless underscores the manner in which people of color become objects for exploitation in the name of medical science. Numerous examples, from the syphilis studies conducted on African Americans in the 1930s to the forced sterilization performed on Native American women in the 1960s and 1970s, reveal the tendency of medical expertise to focus on whites as the agents of change and people of color as the subjects upon which experiments are performed.[66]

Moore offered a post facto judicial alibi for the treatment that Lacks received, while rendering invisible the history of race and gender exploitation that laid the groundwork for the outcome in the case. Notably, recirculated racial scripts about the inability of people of color to make informed decisions, feel pain, or experience loss provided moral justification for experimentation without consent. These racial scripts were amplified with respect to Black people, who, as Dorothy Roberts points out, continue to be denied access to the same medical care and pain management that their white counterparts receive.[67] It is only through the devaluation of people of color that their bodies can be deemed property and they can be marked as less than citizen and less than human. Patent law's embrace of binaries of nature/culture and scientized understandings of expertise provides important precedential language through which that process of dehumanization unfolds.

In addition, *Chakrabarty*, *Hibberd*, and *Moore* were stepping-stones to the broad acceptance of practices of bioprospecting. The term "bioprospecting" originated with Walter V. Reid et al., who published the handbook *Biodiversity Prospecting: Using Genetic Resources for Sustainable Development,*[68] in 1993. The practice has been defined numerous times since then as "corporate drug development based on medicinal plants, traditional knowledge, and microbes from the 'biodiversity rich' regions of the globe—most of which reside in so-called developing nations."[69]

Notably, the "prospecting" portion of the term, which is "borrowed from the practice of prospecting for gold or oil,"[70] is consistent with Western representations of intellectual property as oil or other precious commodities that must be extracted and refined. As with the theft of raw materials from colonies, bioprospecting is a taking of biological resources from the developing world to benefit the developed world, often at the cost of the economic well-being and access to knowledge (A2K) of the former. Vandana Shiva observes that "[b]ioprospecting creates impoverishment . . . by claiming monopolies on resources and knowledge that previously enabled communities to meet their health and nutrition needs and by forcing those communities to pay for what was originally theirs."[71]

Disputes over patent applications for neem oil, turmeric, cowpeas, basmati rice, and hoodia exemplify the breadth of the products and forms of traditional knowledge that Western science has attempted to own and commodify.[72] In the context of bioprospecting, a process analogous to the objectification and commodification of bodies unfolds in the context of knowledge resources. Bioprospecting facilitates the treatment of people of color knowledge as a resource in the production of scientific knowledge.

Bioprospecting also normalizes the relationship between expertise and whiteness by locating the Global North, specifically multinational corporations, as the source of discovery, refinement, and purification and the Global South as the source of raw materials in a (neo)colonial system of exchange. People of color were not the primary beneficiaries of the intellectual property rights regime, particularly the international one that developed after TRIPS entered into force in 1995.[73] Instead, traditional knowledge was merely a resource from which the developed world, particularly predominantly white companies with considerable economic and political power, could claim ownership through aggressively propertized notions of expertise.

As Ikechi Mgbeoji explains, "The patent concept is not an instrument of interstate conviviality or camaraderie; rather, it is an instrument for the pursuit of perceived national economic self-interest, even when this leads to the appropriation of indigenous peoples['] knowledge."[74] The patent is a legal rhetorical construct that is also "an artifact of a society that values technological innovation."[75] The European patent tradition that informs both U.S. and international law demonstrates that patents are also an artifact of a society that values whiteness and white supremacy, particularly as indices of expertise in inventorship.

As Laura Foster observes in the context of South Africa and the commodification of the indigenous appetite suppressant hoodia, colonial legacies of ordering and naming in the creation of experts, nature, and discovery frequently disenfranchised people of color as they "severed our knowledge of plants from their precolonial histories."[76] In this sense, patents were not and are not innocent tools of colorblind science but prefigured structural mechanisms for protecting whiteness as property and racial capitalism as economic system through the invocation of people of color as unintelligent and provincial. Indeed, "the Western biases of the patent concept itself"[77] aid in reallocating property rights from the Global South to the Global North and ensuring the continuity of whiteness as property, often through feelings of nationalist pride around inventorship.

Even those people of color whose expertise is recognized as worth patenting are not immune from the narratives of race liberal creatorship. Melamed notes that the embrace of anti-racism frequently means that people of color "become subject to (and within) destructive normalizing and rationalizing systems.[78] This is true in the context of intellectual property law, particularly patent law. People of color may innovate and create, yet they are frequently exempted from American and global imaginaries of expertise. As America's recurring H1B visa discussions demonstrate, the "attraction of brains"[79] or "brain drain"[80] does not mean that people of color are understood to have intrinsic worth beyond their capacity to produce.

Rather, the flow of immigrants of color to the United States is "another example of the silent extraction of resources from the Global South"[81] in a manner that objectifies and commodifies the literal and figurative brain but does not eliminate the forever foreigner racial scripts that prevent people of color from being accepted as American citizens. People of color are also imagined to exist outside of the narratives of (white) expertise upon which patent law depends because they are read through beliefs that treat them as exceptions to the rule and unimaginative copiers, not as true experts with the capacity for innovation and creativity.[82] Persistent racial scripts about the inhumanity of nonwhites ensured that expertise continued to be a powerful tool of white supremacy and racial capitalism, both of which were used exploit intellectual properties created by people of color without genuinely embracing them as citizens of the American nation.

COPYRIGHT THUGGERY AND THE SAMPLING WARS

In a manner that both resembled and departed from the articulation of expertise in the context of patent law, copyright law in the race liberal era reinforced whiteness as (intellectual) property through the doctrinal language of "originality" and "newness," which implicated the standard of true imagination, and the structural violence of racial capitalism. America's refusal to embrace people of color as full citizens after the civil rights movement was driven not only by persistent racist scripts about their unfitness to be members of the body politic but also by the intentional provocations of public figures in national discourse.

Jack Valenti was a particularly important figure in both keeping alive the racial scripts applied to people of color and fueling racist and xenophobic feelings of pride, anger, anxiety, and fear in American publics. While the full depth and breadth of Valenti's racist and (neo)colonialist rhetorics are beyond the scope of this project, I want to mark him as a key source of domestic and international anti-Black and anti-Asian discourses in American trade and intellectual property disputes over supercomputers, VCRs, films, and music in order to trace racial scripts in copyright law, especially in relation to American citizenship.

In 1982, Valenti testified before the House of Representatives Subcommittee on Courts, Civil Liberties, and the Administration of Justice about the importance of the film industry for the United States. "I am merely coming to start off," he said, "by talking about the American film and television industry, not as an economic enterprise, but as a great *national asset* to this country."[83] Valenti then wove a tale about the significance of the American film and television industry as a trade asset across the world, crafting a proud and protective narrative of both.[84] While Valenti's audience was Congress, his ideas were taken up more broadly by film and music industry executives, who spent the next decades fortifying Hollywood and the music industry against real and imagined threats. The globalization of American entertainment, Valenti continued, "happened because of the *quality* and *caliber* and the *imagination* and the way people construct fragile imaginings that we call the American film."[85] In his testimony, he characterized the United States as exceptional in its intellectual property production.

Valenti's narrative of intellectual properties, particularly film and television, as central to national identity fueled a narrative in which threats against copyrighted materials were read as threats against America itself. Over the course of his career, Valenti mythologized the nationalist and economic value of the high-quality American imagination, locating it as a site for production of national identity. Yet he did not merely announce the importance of the film industry; he also cultivated anxiety, anger, and fear about potential threats to it. He spoke on behalf of the Clint Eastwoods of the world as well as "hundreds of thousands of men and women who without public knowledge or recognition, who are not besieged by fans, but who are artisans, craftsmen, carpenters, bricklayers, all kinds of people, who work in this industry."[86]

In his narrative, intellectual property is a "national asset," a product that must be stewarded and protected in a persistent and vigilant manner. Production of intellectual property outside of the structure that Valenti imagines enthymematically threatens the American nation and the American economy. Those who lack the characteristics of Americanness, in reality or perceptually, are cast as questionable citizens and threats to nation and economy. Moreover, the threats that Valenti described mobilized public feelings in favor of intellectual property maximalism, as a tool for protecting American jobs. Valenti racialized these national security threats in later years, in the contexts of the VCR Wars, the Sampling Wars, Asian piracy, and the War on Terror. While this chapter focuses on the Sampling Wars, each of these examples could serve to illustrate the racialization of infringement.

Three cases—*Grand Upright Music, Ltd. v. Warner Brothers Records, Inc.* (1991) (hereinafter *Grand Upright Music*), *Campbell v. Acuff-Rose Music* (1994) (hereinafter *Acuff-Rose*), and *Suntrust Bank v. Houghton Mifflin Co.* (2001)(hereinafter *Suntrust Bank*)—illustrate how Valenti's rhetorics about intellectual properties, patriotism, and nationalism evolved into anti-Black rhetorics about true imagination and attendant racial scripts. I coin the term "copyright thuggery" to describe a "strategic rhetoric of whiteness"[87] through which powerful, white industry and political actors weaponized familiar racial scripts of Black men as dangerous, deviant criminals who threatened the nation and its well-being, particularly through moral panics about urban crime and obscenity. The anti-Black, anti-Asian, and anti-Arab language that policymakers and industry executives, such as Valenti, alternately used to frame infringement as "theft" in individual moments of public address became instrumental in the production of structural copyright racism. Valenti's pro-industry language reverberated throughout the music industry and legal cases, often by way of networked power and appeals to raced narratives of bad citizenship.

Copyright thuggery manifested in legal cases in which primarily Black artists were forced to demonstrate that their art was not obscene and did not steal from others. Through the embrace of restrictive laws against sampling and relegation of the works of people of color to the category of parody, the protections that courts afforded to non-whites increasingly became *exceptional* instead of *ordinary* moments of creativity that merited special protection instead of a categorical recognition of citizenship, personhood, and the capacity to create. The functional ghettoization of creators of color through copyright doctrine reinforced notions that they could not create with the same degree of innovativeness as their white counterparts and rendered invisible a larger system of agency capture via "mafia capitalism,"[88] in Kaushik Sunder Rajan's words, which actors like Jack Valenti, Jay Berman, and Joe Biden have worked to maintain from the 1960s until today.

The emphasis in the Sampling Wars on remix as an economic wrong and a criminal act perpetrated by Black people was a red herring that erased the structural inequalities—including urban decay, failing education systems, redlining, and so on—that produced the very need for such music in the first place and incentivized obsolete and racially white conceptions of authorship. Moreover, it ignored that copyright is a rhetorical formation that draws upon racial epistemes and structural power to protect whiteness as intellectual property, not operate in a race neutral manner in a race neutral market economy.

In 1984, concerned mothers Tipper Gore and Susan Baker unleashed a Pandora's box of "anti-Black" and "anti-poor" rhetoric and sentiment after their Parents Music Resource Center (PMRC) took steps to police the purportedly unsafe world of popular music. The organization named the "Filthy 15," a group of songs that, in its estimation, needed to be marked for objectionable content. While the songs were originally ones that were focused on violence, sexuality, and language, the PMRC evolved into an organization that policed the boundaries of race, obscenity, and creativity.[89]

After a number of public hearings, the Recording Industry Association of America (RIAA) released a series of self-policing labels, modeled on the MPAA's self-imposed rating system, to make consumers aware of violent and sexually explicit content. By 1987, Ice T's *Rhyme Pays* became the first hip hop album to have the "Parental Advisory" sticker affixed to it.[90] In the years that followed, hip hop and gangsta rap were brought under intense public scrutiny for their obscene, sexualized, and violent musical content. Then, in 1990, N.W.A. was arrested in Detroit after an incident during their performance of "Fuck Tha Police." When asked about the content of N.W.A.'s music, Ice Cube commented: "We didn't invent no words. We ain't teaching nobody nothing new when it comes to that. They can't blame us if their kids use profanity. They can't blame us for no crime rate in no city, because there's always been violence and there's always been crime."[91] When asked about the concert, he said, "Ain't nobody caused no riot and said, 'Yo, N.W.A. made me do it.' At our concerts, a little thing happened in Detroit, which was the police's fault."[92] According to Ice Cube, undercover police started the riot, in a show of police power.[93]

Ice Cube's quote, much like hip hop and rap more generally, points to racial epistemes and structures of oppression as sites for the production of the language of domination and also resistance. The same year, the members of 2 Live Crew faced misdemeanor obscenity charges for releasing the album *Nasty as They Wanna Be*. In the opening argument of that case, defense attorney Bruce Rogow said: "This is not violin music. This is not piano music. But this is serious art, even though it may be different.[94] A familiar struggle over the demonization and appropriation of Black art had begun, this time in the context of hip hop and rap, with copyright and obscenity operating as tools of entrenching racial inequality.

In addition to being a historical outgrowth of Valenti's moral outrage–based film politics, the PMRC's response to hip hop and rap brought fear and anxiety of Blackness and crime into the music context. The Parental Advisory labels quickly became a means of marking Black artists as threatening and deviant. Former vice president Dan Quayle and former president William Jefferson Clinton added fuel to the fire by criticizing the "irresponsible corporate act" that led to Interscope Records and TNT Records publishing the album *2Pacalypse Now* and comparing Sista Souljah to David Duke.[95]

Such critiques set up an important binary: Black urban youths who participated in hip hop and rap subcultures were cast as threats whose presence marked zones of decay and "social death,"[96] while white suburban youths who participated in technology and Internet subcultures were cast as innovators whose presence marked zones of flourishing and "reproductive futurism."[97] This dichotomy was fundamentally about white fantasies of the moral innocence, purity, and potential of their children, who were largely insulated from accusations of criminality in the intellectual property infringement arena through racial double standards and vulnerable to imagined corruption at the hands of Black hip hop and rap artists.

In a broader political and cultural context, President Ronald Reagan's conservatism, which operated through the demonization and punishment of Black men who lived in urban spaces,[98] provided a lens through which sampling could be read as a distinctly *criminal* threat to the nation. More specifically, copyright criminality became a conceptual possibility through the overlay of racial scripts of *Black* criminality, amplified by Reaganism and Clintonism—which advanced anti-Black welfare reform, mandatory minimum sentencing, and discourses of superpredators—onto emerging understandings of technological innovation and musical sampling. Napster's creators and Napster's users were criminalized through understandings of Black people, not white people, as inherently dangerous, threatening, and immoral. Such a world allowed (white) hackers to position themselves as intrepid explorers and suburban naïfs.[99]

When read and experienced alongside the fear-of-crime rhetoric that flourished in the 1970s and 1980s in the nation's major cities, comments such as Quayle's and Clinton's blurred the boundaries of Blackness, crime, obscenity, and artistic production. Criminality and creativity were imagined as fueling each other, not because of anti-Black structural violence but because of the inherent immorality of Black people. Rhetorics around hip hop and rap revived racial scripts about Black people as dangerous criminals with an innate desire to steal, because they had no work ethic or sense of imagination. That blurring, in turn, spilled over into copyright law, where judges presented Black artists as per se criminals instead of resourceful individuals who produced creative music. White tinkering with technology and the Internet, however, came to be imagined as a vital economic engine for the nation, into the present.[100]

The lyrical and musical complexities of appropriation art, including but not limited to hip hop and rap, were largely lost on courts, if not in theory certainly in practice. Even when Black artists prevailed in defending their appropriative practices as creative fair use, it was in ways that were steeped in white supremacy and racial double standards. An early copyright-infringement case involving sampling, *Grand Upright Music*, showcased the tendency of courts to presume criminality and bad intent on the part of Black artists, in a way that they rarely did when considering white infringers.

In deciding that Biz Markie had engaged in copyright infringement when he sampled Gilbert O'Sullivan's "Alone Again (Naturally)" on the album *I Need a Haircut*, Judge Frank Duffy began his opinion with a now infamous appeal to the Seventh Commandment. "Thou shalt not steal," he wrote, "has been an admonition followed since the dawn of civilization."[101] He went on to rhetorically link Blackness, sampling, and theft, noting that the defendants violated "not only the Seventh Commandment, but also the copyright laws of this country."[102] Most significantly, Duffy assessed that Biz Markie's infringement was knowing and willful and offered neither compassion nor understanding for the creativity of the album. The remarkably ungenerous opinion continued: "Their only aim was to sell thousands upon thousands of records. This callous disregard for the law and for the rights of others requires not only the preliminary injunction sought by the plaintiff but also sterner measures."[103]

The "sterner measures" were unprecedented recommendations of criminal prosecution in addition to customary civil penalties. Duffy's tone mirrored that of the earlier PMRC years both in terms of moralizing admonition and in the call for harsh and racialized punishment in this, the first-ever case to rule on the legality of sampling in the context of music. Unlike previous cases, which had primarily involved interracial disputes and settled mostly on co-writing credits for those artists who successfully proved infringement, *Grand Upright Music* involved an intraracial conflict and the explicit threat of criminal punishment. Even compared to future cases, the language that Duffy used was exceptionally harsh and particularly racialized.[104]

Instead of identifying and making conceptual space for Biz Markie's original redeployment of O'Sullivan's song,[105] something that he could have done through a broad reading of fair use or a relatively narrow exercise of judicial activism, Duffy embraced a strict liability approach to copyright infringement, which presumed the bad faith and bad artistry of the defendants. O'Sullivan is the "thoroughly credible and believable witness,"[106] while Biz Markie was the malicious thief who derived unjust benefit from the creativity of others even when they denied him licenses. Invoking the racial scripts of Black men as unimaginative, disingenuous, malicious, and dishonest criminals in a simple copyright case both harks back to the true imagination cases of earlier eras—i.e., making Phillis Wheatley prove she wrote her own poems and finding a Mexican Charlie Chaplin imitator to be a deceitful fraud—and takes a punitive and affectively charged approach to regulating sampling. Low-stakes sampling is transformed into high-stakes theft, with Black copyright thuggery as a presumed norm. Moreover, Duffy's language invokes ambient racial feelings about Black criminality, particularly through his references to bad intent.

This presumption of Black criminality as the norm is at odds with the hardworking honesty of the American Dream. Sampling becomes the mark of failed American citizenship, a feeble attempt to derive profit from exploiting the work of others. The court's decision in *Grand Upright Music* perpetuates ideologies of Black theft that "cloaked issues relating to property and theft in racial language, effectively racializing property crimes."[107] The court erased any non-economic motive that Biz Markie may have had, highlighting instead the desire to sell "thousands upon thousands of records."[108] Despite the fact that this is doubtless the motive of many, if not most, authors and artists, Biz Markie's choice to sample the work of O'Sullivan negated the creativeness of his own work and transformed him into a thief with no justifiable motives. As Siva Vaidhyanathan contends in the documentary *Copyright Criminals*, Judge Duffy was uninterested in making space to recognize Black art as creative.[109]

By treating Black appropriation, particularly in music and literature, as prurient instead of creative from the outset, courts overdetermined racial scripts and racial feelings about Black criminality, effectually deeming hip hop and rap musicians bad creators and bad citizens. Such a reading flattens out the complexities of the "thug imaginary,"[110] which uses fantasies and realities of criminality to imagine opportunity and cultural cachet for the nation's Black urban poor. At its root, thug life romanticizes the successful hustle, a creative and lucrative enterprise intended to help struggling Black people and families in increasingly segregated and dilapidated cities make ends meet, in a radically new and technologically and musically innovative musical form.

This is not to excuse the role of hip hop and rap in contributing to toxic masculinity, particularly in terms of violence and sexism. Rather, it is to acknowledge the creativity and social commentary of the genre, as well as the appropriateness of, if not finding sampling to be fair use, certainly not demonizing its practitioners. White conservatives and white liberals intentionally and unintentionally misread hip hop and rap not as complex negotiations with the structural oppression of the post–civil rights era but as shorthand for racial scripts about Black laziness, theft, and lack of creativity. In doing so, they amplified the racial feelings around Black criminality while minimizing those of Black creativity. Particularly when read alongside early social and political commentary about Napster-prompted infringement as harmless play, the racialization of sampling is clear. Innocent white suburban teenagers downloaded music from the Internet, while devious Black teenagers engaged in theft in order to create dangerous new forms of music. Though the latter discourse evolved over time, largely for economic reasons, it remained less punitive with respect to white infringers than it did with respect to Black ones.

While 2 Live Crew's victory in *Acuff-Rose* and Alice Randall's victory in *Suntrust Bank* seem to be affirmations of Black creatorship and Black creativity, they are better read as the race liberal exceptions that prove the racially regressive rules of Black criminality and unimaginativeness. In finding that 2 Live Crew had engaged in transformative fair use of the song "Oh, Pretty Woman," by Roy Orbison and William Dees, the Supreme Court crafted a rule of parody that functionally ghettoized Black creatorship instead of marking it as original in its own right. Put differently, the rules of copyright infringement remained prefigured in a manner that privileged particularly white and Euro-American norms of "originality," with little space for fair use, at the expense of people of color.

Parody merely operated and operates as a limited and discretionary solution to the problem of lawful infringement, intertwined with culturally specific notions of legal doctrinal terms such as "transformativeness." Predominantly white judges served as gatekeepers of originality and, historically and contemporarily speaking, do not tend to read Black artists' work generously. 2 Live Crew, then, was marked as exceptional not because the group's work was the best or most creative of those who sampled but because it fit within the contained judicial space of parody. The very obscenity that led to the group's criminal indictment became the justification for finding a reason to find the song "Pretty Woman" to be fair use. The continual insistence on "newness" suggests an individualistic and limited Euro-American frame for judging knowledge production that privileges a culturally and racially specific model of Romantic authorship.

Transformativeness, a doctrinal standard that asks whether an infringing work engaged in "new expression, meaning, or message,"[111] is one factor in whether a defendant's use of copyrighted material falls under the fair use exception to the Copyright Act. But though *Acuff-Rose* discussed one example of a parody, it did not provide a clear blueprint for all future disputes over fair use.[112] Quite to the contrary, the Supreme Court held that the question of fair use—and by extension the evaluation of transformativeness—is "not to be simplified with bright-line rules, for the statute, like the doctrine it recognizes, calls for case-by-case analysis."[113]

As a result, since *Acuff-Rose*, lower courts have treated transformativeness as a central organizing concept of the four-factor fair use test, but they have not categorically embraced all appropriative uses as fair use or completely overturned *Grand Upright Music*.[114] Though not dispositive of whether fair use exists, a finding of transformativeness provides strong evidence of the defense, in part because it suggests that the infringer has produced a new creative work with "social benefit."[115]

Defining "new expression, meaning, or message" and "social benefit" has been a racialized process that offers only post facto releases from liability and has led to multiple contradictory holdings. The racialized outcome in *Acuff-Rose* coupled with the inconsistency of the standard of transformativeness is ultimately a mechanism that, even though it appears to protect 2 Live Crew, reinforces the power of predominantly white judges to be gatekeepers of creativity. *Acuff-Rose* protected 2 Live's Crew's music, but it did so by affirming the lower court's notion that "Pretty Woman" "'was clearly intended to ridicule the white-bread original' and 'reminds us that sexual congress with nameless streetwalkers is not necessarily the stuff of romance and is not necessarily without its consequences.'"[116]

Here, 2 Live Crew became an exemplar of the momentary originality and creativity of the Black hip hop artist, and parody operates as a tool for leaving existing racial scripts and racial feelings about Blackness, unimaginativeness, and criminality in place. 2 Live Crew's "Pretty Woman" was protectable because of the group's play with obscenity (i.e., the sexuality and crassness of the streetwalker) and criminality (i.e., the originary associations and specific performance of the thug imaginary on the album), not in spite of it. The Court framed the exceptionalism of the production of the social benefit of musical parody in a manner that suggests that the same does not exist in other instances.

In this way, parody in the fair use context cannot operate, as Robert Hariman contends, as an unfettered "strategic refunctioning of preformed linguistic or artistic material."[117] Rather, parody is subject to the disciplinary whims of lawmakers and judges. The majority in *Acuff-Rose* writes: "Parody's humor . . . necessarily springs from recognizable allusion to its object through distorted imitation. . . . When parody takes aim at a particular original work, the parody must be able to 'conjure up' at least enough of that original to make the object of its critical wit recognizable."[118]

In his concurrence, Justice Anthony Kennedy goes on to further limit the bounds of parody by appealing to the implicitly racialized narratives of free riding and economic exploitation. "We should not,"[119] he writes, "make it easy for musicians to exploit existing works and then later claim that their rendition was a valuable commentary on the original."[120] *Acuff-Rose* thus draws explicit and narrow boundaries around creativity that refuse to embrace a notion of fair use that would allow for sampling as per se original or transformative. As the last line proclaims, rap and hip hop still "exploit." The only option is to create a high bar for fair use. In his reading, Kennedy at least partially embraces a racist understanding of property as underwritten by racial scripts and racial feelings about Black intelligence and norms of theft.

As structured in copyright law, the parodic is necessarily infringing. It is only through a successful fair use defense that it can be judged "good parody." The closure of space for Black appropriative art is one of legal rhetorical and argument structure. The creation of an exception for certain parodies cannot resolve the problem of the parodic writ large. Not only does such a framing of the parodic refuse the notion that Black sampling practices could be sufficiently original to merit protection on their own accord, but it also forces artists to declare their works to be parodic even when they are not parodies.

The overinclusivity/underinclusivity problem of parody results in a moving target that allows white artists to derive profit from their works even as they refuse to protect the radically innovative creative works of artists of color. Henry Louis Gates writes about this issue at length, naming "signifyin'" or "playing the dozens" as culturally specific ways that Black people appropriate language to communicate in coded ways, particularly in the face of racial oppression.[121] Gates's framing, which is much broader than that of the *Acuff-Rose* majority, recognizes that nearly all hip hop and rap music engages in signifyin'. The Supreme Court's decision to craft *Acuff-Rose* narrowly reinscribes race liberal creatorship, allowing space for Black creativity only within narrow bounds determined on a case-by-case basis by predominantly white and largely culturally anti-Black judges.

That 2 Live Crew won, then, is of limited utility for Black creators. Their success is allowable only because, for a brief moment, Black artistry comported with the overarching structures of white creatorship. Once again, the double bind of true imagination created a no-win situation for artists of color, specifically those Black artists who were interested in creating hip hop and rap music. In the period after *Grand Upright Music*, licensing became a gatekeeping structure to keep sampling at bay. However, the economics of the practice, as Kembrew McLeod and Peter DiCola demonstrate, made the production of music nearly impossible, because it was so expensive to get permission to use samples.[122] Licensing and parodic exceptionalism, then, were not merely economic mechanisms for regulating music; they were also examples of racial capitalism through which white industry executives maintained power and control.

Perhaps no case showcases the complexities of parody's overinclusions and underinclusions better than *Suntrust Bank*, which involved a lawsuit between Margaret Mitchell's estate and Alice Randall over an "unauthorized" retelling of *Gone With the Wind* from the point of view of the plantation Tara's slaves. Unlike "Pretty Woman," which one might credibly read as a parodic critique of "Oh, Pretty Woman," Randall's *The Wind Done Gone* is, despite the Eleventh Circuit's protestations, a difficult fit with common understandings of the parodic as comedic rewriting of existing creative material. The novel appears to get shoehorned into the category of parody as a means of post facto creating an argument for its fair use.

The case also revealed the underlying tendencies and desire of judges—here the district court, whose discussion of the problems with "tainting"[123] Scarlett O'Hara's racial history and ruining the "reputation of their copyright"[124] was later reversed—to rely on a narrow and white understanding of memory with nostalgic attachment to the Antebellum South. The judicial choice to read *The Wind Done Gone* as parody of the nostalgic *Gone With the Wind* incentivizes the creation of appropriative parodies but disincentivizes the creation of radically innovative forms that might not be parodic. Fair use's compartmentalization of particular literary forms and unspoken racial desires creates a narrowly bounded space for non-white creatorship and validates the citizenship of some individuals by invalidating the racial memories and racial traumas of others.

Placing *The Wind Done Gone* in the category of parody, despite the Eleventh Circuit's acknowledgment that sometimes there is "strong public interest in the publication of the secondary work,"[125] is a problematic act that, like *Acuff-Rose*, fails to make easily legible a space for diverse genres of creative fair use and offers only a narrow remedial measure for pushing back against white supremacist (intellectual) property norms.

Suntrust Bank's overinclusiveness discourages the creation of appropriative art that does not fit into the category of parody because if it is mere satire or social commentary, it is likely infringing. Its underinclusiveness fails to reward creative works that appropriate as other than parodies. Though broad and detailed in its characterization of *The Wind Done Gone* as parody, the Eleventh Circuit retains an underlying conservativism and race liberalism in its understanding of fair use and actively refuses the racial restorative justice that is the antidote to perpetrator perspective. The Eleventh Court's restrictive definition of fair use once again leaves in place the racial underpinnings of creativity and, perhaps more importantly, the racial capitalism that protects white originality as inviolable property and Black signifyin' as potentially transformative parody, in the right circumstances. *Suntrust Bank* became an actual and sublimated negotiation over the protection—to echo Claudia Rankine and Beth Loffreda from the Introduction's epigraph—of a white literary imaginary. While *Gone With the Wind* was always a book about the romanticization of the Antebellum South, *Suntrust Bank* turned it into a public negotiation of that romanticization of public memory in the context of copyright in order to protect whiteness.

The district court's description of a "parasitical" work of authorship, in reference to a Black woman, described through the anti-miscegenist reference to protecting Scarlett O'Hara from the "taint" of Randall's novel, echoes notions of the Black welfare mother articulated in the Moynihan Report and repeated throughout the Reagan years. *Gone With the Wind*, and particularly O'Hara's whiteness, must be kept from intermingling with Black blood in the tale that Randall tells of O'Hara's biraciality and in the very act of writing a counterhistory that opposes Mitchell's narrative. The moral opprobrium against free riding that Judge Duffy invoked in *Grand Upright Music* is evident as well, in the Court's need to police the desire to "capitalize on and thus benefit from . . . notoriety."[126]

Even the Eleventh Circuit, which refuses this narrative of miscegenation, does so in the narrowest of ways, suggesting *not* that the lower court's racist language is unacceptable but that such opinions ought not be attached to copyright. Racial anxiety and fear of miscegenation are not reprehensible; they are merely presented in the wrong forum and too overtly. The Pyrrhic victory in *Suntrust Bank*, though it creates space for parodic art, reinforces the racial scripts and racial feelings that underlie race liberal creatorship. The racial desire to protect whiteness as (intellectual) property remains ideologically and structurally in place despite Randall's victory.

Read together, *Grand Upright Music, Acuff-Rose,* and *Suntrust Bank* showcase the relationship between definitions of fair use, parody, citizenship, and racial capitalism. Edward Schiappa theorizes definitional rhetoric as "discourse that defines."[127] Such definitional rhetoric constructs and endorses a particular view of reality, one with cultural and political baggage. In the appropriation cases examined here, legal definitions of parody masquerade as race neutral language of fair use while concealing an ideological investment in racial capitalism, underlying racial anxieties about Black people, and judgments about those who make parodic works.

Portraying all infringement and copying as piracy not only invokes the rhetorical baggage of the colloquial term "piracy" but also obscures the racial capitalism through which intellectual property works. The definitional landscape of fair use leaves little room for exceptions, making the parodic a rare occurrence, not a norm. Read in the larger history of the period, this definitional choice mirrors the creation of civil rights law, which operates in the interests of political stability and cultural consistency instead of racial reparation.

The cases in question here are best read as moments of racial conflict in which Black musicians demonstrated their creative capacities, claimed full citizenship, and contested the mafia capitalism that political and economic actors, including Valenti, Johnson, Reagan, and Clinton, systematically used to normalize white exploitation and white ownership of Black people and Black culture. Hip hop and rap, through the construction of a deeply radical and deeply political thug imaginary, pushed back against the oligarchic racial capitalism that led to the uncompensated theft of Black music and the production of segregated cities and, increasingly, prisons filled with urban working poor. Sunder Rajan writes that mafia capitalism describes "despots that operate personal fiefdoms under formally liberally democratic conditions . . . one in which vested corporate interests don't feel the need to operate with a veneer of institutional propriety. It signifies a return to the robber-baron capitalism of late nineteenth century America."[128]

This definition is particularly apt in the context of copyright law, where a remarkably small number of individuals, primarily white men with race liberal politics and long connections to one another, disproportionately shaped seemingly democratic and race neutral decisions about the direction of legal change. Court cases that drew from the broader rhetorical culture around fear of crime and obscenity were significant because they rendered whiteness and structural violence against people of color invisible by employing normalized racial scripts and racial feelings. Copyright mafia capitalists and the powerful public figures who sided with them managed impulses to racial equality by selectively repeating and amplifying the parts of the thug imaginary that resonated with racial scripts and racial feelings about Blackness and obscenity, criminality, violence, deviance, and sexuality, and minimizing the ones that emphasized Black dignity, self-determination, responsibility, creativity and innovation, and hustle. They transformed Black criminality into decontextualized fact

The landmark copyright and race cases of the time, because they adopted and reinforced these repetitions and amplifications, became important spaces for the hegemonic struggle over the identity of Black hip hop and rap artists. The cases constructed Black creators as intentionally immoral and unscrupulous infringers, copyright thugs who operated outside of the prescribed boundaries of American citizenship, and not deliberately innovative and savvy creators who epitomized its ideals. They used consistent rhetorical strategies revolving around intent to do harm, creative exceptionalism, and racial compartmentalization to portray Black hip hop and rap artists as guilty-until-proven-innocent "copyright criminals"[129] with a "mark of criminality,"[130] instead of representing them as bona fide copyright creators.

Reading hip hop and rap exclusively as hypermasculine, oversexualized, violent, and anti-feminist forms of expression misses their radical class politics, remakings of Black masculinity, and emancipatory storytelling. They are, as scholars such as Tricia Rose have argued, in fact complex art forms that confronted and confront anti-Black and anti-poverty rhetorics through their real and fantasy performances of masculinity, braggadocio, aggression, and violence. Hip hop and rap offered new and transformative racial scripts and racial feelings for Black persons, primarily men, who lived in grim conditions in heavily policed urban spaces.

Davarian L. Baldwin writes about another, less recognized radical aspect of hip hop culture, namely its criticism and reimagining of the mafia. He observes that the mafia-style rhetorics and recording practices of Roc-A-Fella, Death Row Records, and other artists "cannot be divorced from the actual rise during Prohibition of the Irish-American Kennedy family or the Italian-American Gambino family."[131] Their lifestyles also showcased, in often ostentatious and aspirational ways, the "Horatio Alger narratives [which] have served as models for this country's 'formal' economy."[132]

Ice Cube's comments underscore this same point, as they highlight not only the perpetuity of violence, particularly racialized violence in America, but also the manner in which it is racially, economically, and affectively structured through legalized mafioso activities, such as police incitement of riots at hip hop and rap concerts. The clash between the "mafia state," which made and enforced copyright policy, and the hip hop and rap "mafia," which appropriated and redefined the terms of the mafia contract, came to a head in obscenity and copyright cases. In this sense, hip hop and rap invocations of mafia language, including its associations with a particular kind of hypermasculinity, were deeply political, resistive, and creative.

The counterhegemonic impulse that hip hop and rap embodied was threatening to the underlying mafia capitalism of copyright law. *Grand Upright Music*, *Acuff-Rose*, and *Suntrust Bank* are in one sense about the economic logics of analogue music and its operations. They are about protecting structures and institutions in which the entertainment industry, an industry forged by the networked connections of powerful individuals, is invested. But they are also about whiteness as the default, which is maintained through even sporadic cases that compartmentalize and contain the work of artists of color. In order to be protected from the mafia, Sunder Rajan notes, individuals must pay the mafia.[133] That is, in a manner of speaking, a broad retelling of the history of race and sampling: hip hop artists paid and continue to pay industry licensing fees to meet industry rules about licensing. But they also paid and pay a racial tax on creativity. The signifyin' art that Gates describes critiques structural power, including the insularity of copyright's mafia capitalist structure. Yet it is taxed, so to speak, for that critique of whiteness and racial capitalism, in ways that recenter and reinforce whiteness supremacy itself while mimicking racial progressivism.

TRADEMARKING FEARS OF RACIAL MIXING

The nation's racial anxieties were evident not only in copyright and patent contexts but also in the trademark context, where laws intended to protect the economic value of trademarks seized upon familiar rhetorics and fears about the erosion of the links between whiteness and property. The growth of multinational corporations and global neoliberalism fostered an era of the brand in which trademarks took on greater meaning and value for publics and corporations and required greater legal and economic protection. Companies like Coca-Cola and Mattel led the charge, pioneering lawsuits against fans and pushing the boundaries of legal doctrinal theories of intellectual property protection, such as tarnishment and blurring.[134]

Dilution law, the subset of trademark law concerned with preventing the use of famous trademarks on non-competing products, legally termed blurring, and in contexts that might harm their reputations, legally termed tarnishment, added a new dimension to trademark protection. Unlike traditional trademark doctrine, which is intended to protect consumers from "confusingly similar" products in the marketplace, claims of dilution by blurring and tarnishment aim to protect the identity of the trademark itself—provided that it is deemed "famous"—by treating it as a valuable piece of property with a reputation to be maintained.[135] While dilution law has not been widely litigated, the area of trademark litigation is symbolically important to the discussion of race, citizenship, personhood, and intellectual property in two ways. First, it reflects the structural relationship between doctrinal authorship and whiteness in the context of intellectual property law—i.e., how articulations of legal doctrine get taken up in racially unanticipated ways and, accordingly, define the boundaries of (intellectual) property protection. Second, it repackages national anxieties about whiteness, racial mixing, and national identity pollution in the language of corporate protection, in a manner that exceeds the consumer gaze.[136]

Whereas early standards of consumer confusion used a white male consumer gaze to turn people of color into objects to be consumed, trademark dilution disciplined consumer gazes that were not white, heterosexual, and/or male. In essence, dilution law mobilized the language of mixing and morality as a means of delegitimizing practices of looking at that were not consistent with the white, heterosexual male consumer gaze. As such, it seized upon racial scripts of people of color as immoral deviants—in this instance, as individuals who sought to destroy the value of trademarks and impugn the good names of corporations.

First laid out in a piece by Frank Schechter in the *Harvard Law Review* in 1927, trademark dilution was meant to address "the progressive ingenuity of commercial depravity."[137] "Depravity," particularly in 1927, signified moral deficiency, which many believed was biologically based, racialized, and incorrigible. Schechter went on to argue that trademark infringement is intended not only to protect against consumer confusion but also to insulate the reputation of the trademark owner.[138] Trademarks mediate the flow of goodwill between the producer and the public in a manner that relies on the integrity of the trademark owner's identity. Accordingly, Schechter proposed a standard of trademark dilution, which he described as "the gradual whittling away or dispersion of the identity and hold upon the public mind of the mark or name by its use upon non-competing goods."[139]

Over the years, courts periodically granted relief on the basis of dilution legislation.[140] However, dilution was a relatively unsuccessful means of protecting trademarks until 2007 when, in response to the landmark case *Moseley v. V Secret Catalogue, Inc.* (2003) (hereinafter *Moseley*), Congress passed the Trademark Dilution Revision Act (TDRA). *Moseley* involved a lawsuit by V Secret Catalogue against the owners of the adult novelty store Victor's Secret. Ultimately, because no actual economic harm occurred, V Secret Catalogue was unable to prove its dilution claim.[141] The TDRA legislatively overturned the Supreme Court's decision in *Moseley* by clarifying that actual dilution is not required for proving the existence of blurring and tarnishment. It ushered in a new era of dilution law.

Moseley is emblematic of the categories of cultural content against which trademark dilution protects. Historically, blurring and tarnishment are causes of action used to police representations of sexuality, violence, and drug use.[142] Richard Schur theorizes another dimension of the cultural significance of dilution by adding that this area of law mediates race, albeit unintentionally. He observes: "Despite its relatively recent vintage, dilution nonetheless retains a foundation of nineteenth-century conceptions of racial identity."[143] His argument rests, in part, on persistent white racial anxieties around racial dilution of power, as evidenced by such cases as *Plessy v. Ferguson* (1896) and *Gratz v. Bollinger* (2001). Schur goes on to note that "[ironically], both Plessy and Gratz sought to protect their individuality by contesting the social meaning of their ascribed, or adopted, racial identity."[144]

For Schur, trademark law works *through* the negotiation of identities, particularly racial ones. Schechter's discussion of the need to avoid "the gradual whittling away or dispersion of the identity" is eerily similar to the language of miscegenation and racial purity used in the 1800s and 1900s. A piece in the *Congressional Globe*, for instance, describes the parade of horribles brought about by racial mixing: "But [the Negroes'] aim is to embody the miscegenation of the races in the [S]outhern States as part of their system. They have noted the permanent national degeneracy and weakness produced in other countries by this blighting curse,"[145] through which they replace whites as "absolute masters of the people."[146] In addition to disciplining those who associate famous trademarks with sex, violence, and drug use, dilution law intersects with important histories of race and racialization, such as those related to drug panics.

Though there appears to be no explicit historical connection between the racial origins of dilution and the practices of anti-miscegenation, tracing the implicit rhetorics of fear of loss of white racial power in dilution law is a useful exercise. Trademark dilution law mediates white anxieties about racial intermixing and political economy, specifically those around legal authorship and control of the consumer gaze. Despite the uneven implementation of dilution law and the intense anti-Semitism of the era, Schechter became a doctrinal author with considerable influence over trademark law. Consistently invoking Schechter's theories in the service of globalizing trademark law ironically functions to protect legal doctrinal authorship as racially white and Euro-American, his Jewishness notwithstanding.

Furthermore, Schechter's rhetorical appeals, which reemerge in cases that discipline various forms of cultural production and cultural deviance, speak to white anxieties about eroding economic power, even if not intentionally. Dilution law, in the forms of both blurring and tarnishment, operates to manage and protect the trademark relationship between whiteness and property, in part by refusing to diversify the consumer gaze vis-à-vis Black and Brown authors. Cyclically reimagining Schechter's theories created a mechanism for reasserting a white and male consumer gaze in the era of racial liberalism.

Ironically, the Nazi anti-Semitism of the 1930s and 1940s was instrumental in creating a rhetorical culture in which Schechter's theory could be used to fortify the connections between whiteness and authorship. For Nazi eugenicists, degeneracy and deviance, which were born of racial dilution, were incompatible with works of genius. Adolf Hitler's *Entartete Kunst* (Degenerate Art exhibition) drew upon Max Nordau's 1895 book, *Degeneration*, to make pseudoscientific connections among modern art, mental pathology, racial inferiority, and deficient perceptions of the world.[147] While the exhibit focused exclusively on turns in European art, its more important purpose was to normalize the "traditional," including Aryanness and whiteness, over the "avant garde," including theoretical and artistic innovation.[148]

Entartete Kunst opened in Munich in 1937 as part of a series of exhibitions organized by Minister of Popular Enlightenment and Propaganda Joseph Goebbels "for the purpose of clarifying for the German public by defamation and derision exactly what type of modern art was unacceptable to the Reich, and thus 'un-German.'"[149] It included 650 works of art by Cubists, Expressionists, Surrealists, Symbolists, and other modern artists including Ernst Barlach, Max Beckmann, Marc Chagall, Otto Dix, Lyonel Feininger, Wassily Kandinsky, Paul Klee, Oskar Kokoschka, and Emil Nolde.[150] Each of the exhibition's galleries highlighted a different form of degeneracy: German citizens were reminded that mocking Jesus Christ, practicing Judaism, glorifying "inferior" races, protesting war, supporting Bolshevism, and criticizing industrialization were contrary to the Nazi project.[151] Over three million visitors—more than most art exhibits in history had garnered—viewed *Entartete Kunst*.[152] Perhaps most importantly, the exhibit contributed significantly to the acceptance of cultural and rhetorical norms against deviance and dilution, in Europe and the United States.

The horrors of the Third Reich demonstrate how concepts of degeneracy were deployed far beyond the scope of art. Specifically, the concept of "degeneracy" was employed to demarcate the lines between humanness and non-humanness that underpinned eugenic crusades. Once *Entartet* was conceptually identified with biological inferiority, psychological defect, and fear of miscegenation, groups including Jews, gypsies, homosexuals, and the disabled, among others, became targets for complete dehumanization and murder.

Indeed, even before *Entartete Kunst*, "the fusion of political and aesthetic themes, and the use of the term *Entartet* to designate supposed inferior racial, sexual, and moral types had been in the air for several years."[153] By the 1930s the avant garde had become inextricably intertwined with degeneracy. Modern art, racial impurity, sexual deviance, and leftist politics, all understood to be fundamentally anti-German, were blamed for the downfall of the Weimar Republic and lumped together under the label of "degenerate."[154] As theories of eugenics spread to the United States, the anti-miscegenation sentiments of the Jim Crow era gained new life. The rhetorical culture of the United States, even without Nazi eugenics connotations, had a new set of conceptual resources through which to perceive threats of dilution. This is not to say that dilution law was marked by an explicit investment in eugenics or that it grew in proportion to anti-Semitism. Rather, it is to point out that shifts in rhetorical cultures toward whiteness as property were the anxious and angry definitional response against which conceptions of Romantic authorship and trademark dilution were articulated, particularly as a tool for managing "threats" to trademarks produced by "deviant" authors and artists. The networked connections among dilution, blurring, tarnishment, and miscegenation have shaped the racial logics of trademark law and conceptions of authorship in ways that are written into case law.

The ideology of the law of dilution is culturally constituted through rhetorical associations between the manipulation of trademarks and historical concepts of miscegenation. Etymologically speaking, "to dilute" is "to make thinner or weaker."[155] In his *Dictionary of English Etymology*, under the entry for "scarlet," Hensleigh Wedgwood notes that "the mixture of a colour with white is considered as a dilution or weakening of the colour."[156] "Blur" originates from the word "blear," meaning "to blot, stain, obscure, or blemish."[157] "Tarnish" (originally meaning "to cover, darken"[158]) comes from the German word meaning "to diminish the luster or purity of."[159] Read in tandem with the term "*Entartet*," or "degenerate," these three words take on new meaning: like degeneracy, the terms "dilution," "blurring," and "tarnishment" constitute a fundamental weakening through lost purity. Indeed, dilution, blurring, and tarnishment, all of which have negative connotations, are processes through which degeneration occurs.

The outcome of constant dilution, then, in the form of blurring and tarnishment, is ultimately degeneracy, or the complete inability to associate the original object with its present incarnation. To speak of dilution, blurring, or tarnishment, even used in a radically different context from the Nazi deployment of the term "degenerate," evokes genocidal histories. The failure of dilution law to gain widespread acceptance notably does not negate these connections. Instead, it suggests that dilution is a tool for managing identity, against period crises. Given its reputational components, dilution law served as a tool for managing cultural anxieties and the white masculine authority of the consumer gaze.

The consumer gaze, as theorized in the previous chapters, was shaped by white masculine formulations of political economy. Trademarks and trademark infringement were formed around the racial episteme of white men looking at white women and people of color. Dilution law called upon familiar rhetorics of miscegenation in the context of consumer goods. By doing so, it suggested a set of racial scripts and racial feeling about the impurities and threats associated with non-whiteness, in both the body politic and streams of commerce. The ebbs and flows of dilution law are certainly legal and economic insofar as they rest on the decisions of lawmakers, lawyers, and judges in specific disputes about blurring and tarnishment. However, they are also returns to racial rhetorics that reflect white anxieties about the loss of consumer and capitalist influence. In the race liberal era, cases such as *Moseley* and legislation such as the TDRA, keep alive vocabulary around the value of whiteness and the dubious value of non-whiteness.

Dilution cases also marked certain identities as threatening and deviant, particular via the embrace of famous trademarks as reputational personas. More specifically, dilution law operated as a frame through which deviation from white heterosexual masculinity is treated as morally and economically dangerous to increasingly anthropomorphic brands. Race liberal dilution cases, intentionally and unintentionally, cultivated moral panics, much in the same way that copyright cases did around race.

In the originary dilution case, mouthwash company Odol made a claim for dilution, "geggen die gutten Sitten," against a steel company. Dilution, which the court described as "contrary to good morals,"[160] protected Odol, which would "lose selling power"[161] without intervention. The moral framing of dilution—in the context of both blurring and tarnishment—produces an affective, ethical, and economic justification for its implementation.

Contemporary cases reflect that moralizing, in ways that construct brands as needing protection from those who are racially, sexually, and culturally impure and who thus threaten the social fabric of the nation. As in the context of consumer confusion, dilution law imagines and protects a white, male, middle-class consumer, one who has the right to interface with trademarks that are not blurred or tarnished by other products in the marketplace. Here, the specter of the consumer gaze implicitly reemerges. Whiteness is reinforced by that which is deemed immoral, lewd, and deviant. As Richard Dyer puts it, "[W]hiteness as race resides in invisible properties and whiteness as power is maintained by being unseen. To be seen as white is to have one's corporeality registered, yet true whiteness resides in the non-corporeal."[162]

Dilution litigation, which prompted brand purification by keeping trademarks bounded and safe from pollution, suggested an underlying desire for social purification of racial and sexual deviants. Mary Douglas writes that "[e]asy purification enables people to defy with impunity the hard realities of their social system."[163] Such a desire, of course, was consistent with the purity-obsessed politics of individuals like Valenti, Nixon, Reagan, and Bush and that of organizations like the MPAA, RIAA, and PMRC. Valenti's policies used moral purity as a weapon against people of color, cultivating a perpetual threat that justified increasingly harsh punishments. Reagan followed Nixon's racist anti-drug policy, in order to manage the "morally polluting men and women whose low character hastens the decline of *Pax Americana*."[164] For Reagan, (white) Americans were moral and pure. Their hard work and sense of individual responsibility distinguished them from lazy and dangerous racial Others, primarily Black people and Latinxs, and marked them as deserving of the spoils of the nation.[165]

Cultural and political obsessions with purity are not merely coincidentally related to dilution law. Instead, as the history of the racial scripts and racial feelings around intellectual properties demonstrates, obsessions with crime, danger, and morality were deeply racialized and affective commitments, which moved between bodies and spaces. Purity operated as a vehicle for reinforcing racism in and out of intellectual property contexts. Trademark law functioned to create communities of belonging based on lines of race and sex.

Imagined conceptions of wholesome Americanness and intellectual property citizenship served the dual purpose of increasing corporate profits and cultivating nostalgia for the 1950s nuclear family. Holding those who placed trademarks in contexts involving "deviant" drug and sex practices liable for dilution, though economically motivated, was also implicitly raced in its use of trademark law to capitalize on the nation's anxieties. In short, protecting brands became an alibi for identity policing. Moreover, through dilution rhetorics, those who engaged in acts that blurred and tarnished trademarks were constructed as threats to American national identity, and they themselves became second-class citizens.

Take, for instance, *Coca-Cola Co. v. Gemini* Rising (1972) (hereinafter *Gemini Rising*), in which the court found that "Enjoy Cocaine" posters would harm Coca-Cola's reputation by associating the company with drugs. Writing that "plaintiff's good will and business reputation are likely to suffer in the eyes of those who, believing it responsible for defendant's poster, will refuse to deal with a company which would seek commercial advantage by treating such a dangerous drug in such a jocular fashion," the court took a conservative stance in a pro-drug era.[166] Coca-Cola's refusal to be associated with cocaine not only erases and ignores its own history, into the early 1900s, of producing beverages containing the drug but also erases the racial histories that make visible the ways in which people of color were forcibly involved in the production and use of the substance. As Michael Cohen explains in his history of cocaine:

> At the root of the drug-prohibition movement in the United States is race, the driving force behind the first laws criminalizing drug use, which first appeared as early as the 1870s. In an era in which African Americans, Asian and Mexican immigrants, as well as most European immigrants—Jews, Slavs, and Catholic Irish and Italians—were considered racial others, white racial fears amplified the sense of public menace posed by drugs and drug users.[167]

Jim Crow and anti-cocaine sentiments coalesced in the late 1800s and early 1900s, stoking fears of "Negro cocaine fiends."[168] Popular news sources contended that Black people became criminals when under the influence of cocaine. That statement belied the reality that the substance was widely available to people of all races and included in many consumer products. Given this racialized history at drug production and treatment of criminality, Coca-Cola's trademark claim of equity functions as a means of sanitizing history and the company's brand. The company consistently refuses to acknowledge its own role in the production and subsequent erasure of racial hierarchies.

By the time the case was filed in the 1970s, the War on Drugs was gaining strength and pushback against civil rights victories was growing. In *Gemini Rising*, trademark dilution became a rhetorical mechanism for enforcing a racialized morality that rendered invisible the past oppression of people of color, gave moral force to the War on Drugs targeting them and their humanity, and strengthened racial capitalism via multinational corporations. This same racialized morality reinforced existing narratives about intellectual property citizenship, particularly around the criminality of people of color, as in the Sampling Wars. The return to racial scripts and racial feelings about the criminality of Mexicans underwrote dilution law's disdain for drug use. Through the management of discourses of drug use in *Gemini Rising*, intellectual property law echoed the protection of whiteness as (intellectual) property through familiar national racial scripts and racial feelings.

Moseley, decided three decades later, demonstrates the return to rhetorics of morality as stand-ins for protecting whiteness. By employing a doctrine barely mentioned for decades, the case, in which Victoria's Secret sued the retail shop Victor's Little Secret, owned by Victor and Cathy Moseley, revitalized dilution law.[169] Victoria's Secret filed suit for trademark infringement and dilution by blurring and tarnishment, citing a complaining male army colonel who assessed that the Moseleys sold "unwholesome, tawdry merchandise," a practice that allegedly undermined the wholesome reputation of the lingerie company.[170]

The military official's moral sensibilities—here his disdain for adult novelties—prompted the trademark suit. Dilution law offered a means of protecting the value of the trademark while simultaneously endorsing a morality that was fundamentally white and male. Managing sexuality in such a way, Jasbir Puar argues, "constitutes a systemic, intrinsic, and pivotal module of power relations."[171] In this instance, enforcing the morality of the complaining army colonel upholds racialized practices of regulating sexuality, specifically by treating the sale of sex toys as material evidence of tarnishment.

While the Supreme Court reversed two lower court decisions finding dilution because "[t]he officer was offended by the ad, but it did not change his conception of Victoria's Secret,"[172] Congress legislatively overturned *Moseley* in 2006, with the passage of the bipartisan TDRA. The statute made "likelihood of dilution" actionable and broadened the economic and moral reach of trademark law.[173] Ultimately, the district court found a likelihood of dilution and the Supreme Court declined to grant cert to hear the case a second time.

Moseley and *Gemini Rising*, cases from the 1970s and 2000s, respectively, are emblematic of the issues that arose and continue to arise in dilution cases. Moreover, they are representative of the biopolitical evolution in trademark law after the civil rights movement. Dilution law, which implicitly anthropomorphizes trademarks, treating them as having discrete identities that can be blurred and tarnished, attempts to contain those individuals and actions that would threaten trademark reputations. Instead of formally excluding people of color from owning trademarks and then circulating racist images, the race liberal regime of trademark law imposed moral ideals in ways that implicitly and explicitly denigrated people of color in favor of maintaining a white male consumer gaze. In essence, *Moseley* and *Gemini Rising* are examples of how dilution law attempted to prevent people of color—and other precarious persons—from talking back to their objectification in the trademark arena.

Dilution law did not effectively quell resistance to the disciplinary discourses about race that arose in the context of intellectual property law. Nonetheless, it is productive to map the ebbs and flows of dilution law alongside those of white resentment and white nationalism in order to render visible the relationships between whiteness and (intellectual) properties. Dilution discourse contributed to understandings of the categories of good citizens/bad citizens, often drawing upon the same fear of crime and moral panic that animated racialized discourses in copyright law.

Other moves toward trademark maximalism—for instance the passage of the Trademark Counterfeiting Act of 1984—operated to set up and parallel dilution law by criminalizing trademark infringement and reinforcing racialized constructions of counterfeiters. Together with the racialized rhetorics of the Sampling Wars—and even evolving linkages between whiteness and expertise—intellectual property law in this era replicated its racial investments through the language of morality and criminality. The collision of numerous social wars reflected and constructed an increasingly militarized and racialized way of thinking about racial capitalism and consumer goods while maintaining an appearance of race neutrality.

In short, intellectual property law, a site for the simultaneous projection and creation of anxieties about race, national identity, economic prosperity, personhood, and morality, continued to invoke racial scripts and racial feelings that denigrated creatorship by people of color and elevated creatorship by whites in the race liberal era. In the postracial era, intellectual properties continued to operate as deeply racialized spaces, increasingly through the revival of rhetorics of individual self-determination.

CHAPTER THREE

THE POSTRACIAL INTELLECTUAL PROPERTY CITIZEN

What's more, we're going to aggressively protect our intellectual property. Our single greatest asset is the innovation and the ingenuity and creativity of the American people. It is essential to our prosperity and it will only become more so in this century. But it's only a competitive advantage if our companies know that someone else can't just steal that idea and duplicate it with cheaper inputs and labor. There's nothing wrong with other people using our technologies, we welcome it—we just want to make sure that it's licensed, and that American businesses are getting paid appropriately.
—PRESIDENT BARACK OBAMA, Remarks by the
President at the Export-Import Bank's Annual Conference

BEGINNING IN APPROXIMATELY 2008, the inaccurate but seductive notion that the nation had moved beyond race as a category of discrimination took on new life in the United States. As the country transitioned from President George W. Bush to President Barack Hussein Obama, discourses of hope and national unity dominated public cultural spaces, with Obama himself adopting the language of postracial egalitarianism.[1] The language of postraciality, which often drew upon narratives of hard work, economic exceptionalism, and competitiveness, created a veneer of equality in policy discussions while leaving in place the structural constraints that prevented people of color from being able to attain equality. As Obama moved through his presidency, a militantly conservative and oppositional Congress, persistent police brutality, growing global protests about economic uncertainty, and brewing white nationalism showcased the naïveté of the nation's postracial zeitgeist.

Against this backdrop, Obama pursued intellectual property policies that were consistent with those of his Republican counterparts, investing in copyright, patent, and trademark maximalism while simultaneously preaching about the race neutral links between creatorship and the American Dream. Legislation such as the Leahy-Smith America Invents Act anchored a platform of economic nationalism and individual achievement. In the postracial era, the narrative of race liberal creatorship evolved into a similar but different one of postracial creatorship.

Reading intellectual property citizenship through the lens of postraciality reveals how the latter functions as language of obfuscation, by investing in the postracial creator as a mechanism for erasing structural inequalities at home and blaming them on hyperracial infringers abroad. Postracial creatorship, as a rhetorical formation, had two central features. First, it articulated a postracial intellectual property citizen domestically, through the familiar ideologies and rhetorics of the American Dream. Second, it implicitly constructed a racialized intellectual property anti-citizen internationally, by projecting economic anxieties onto people of color in the developing world who were cast as perpetual pirates and counterfeiters. As such, postracial creatorship continued to reinforce narratives of meritocratic achievement, in race neutral language, while projecting racial scripts and racial feelings internationally, onto racially othered infringers labeled as threats to the well-being of the nation.

From the beginning of his presidency, Obama wove narratives of the self-made American with the desire and capacity to innovate that he used to justify his proposed economic and entrepreneurship policies. He stressed the importance of creatorship to economic growth in messages that echoed those of Republicans. From his position in the executive branch, he crafted an economic and cultural fantasy of a postracial American Dream achieved through creatorship, which was purportedly accessible to all because of the nation's strong and race neutral intellectual property policies. He also continued the practice of invoking threat rhetoric in creatorship/infringement contexts, noting that he would "aggressively" protect the nation's intellectual properties against those who tried to capitalize on them.

Nonetheless, despite talk of moves toward postraciality in the area of intellectual property law, public cultural representations of creatorship remained grounded in histories of white masculinity that called on familiar racial scripts and racial feelings, not the egalitarian fantasy of copyrights, patents, and trademarks that Obama espoused. Ideological and structural barriers continued to keep people of color from producing knowledge or benefiting from the knowledge they did produce at the same rate as whites. In short, postracial intellectual property policy and discourse was anything but race neutral. It remained beholden to the nation's racialized under-standings of creatorship/infringement and attendant anxieties about threats to the nation. Attachments to racial categorizations of good intellectual property citizens/bad intellectual property citizens remained implicitly but firmly in place domestically and internationally.

This chapter traces the emergence of the postracial creator, who offered a means of reconciling opposing cultural imperatives of colorblindness and white supremacy. The figure embodied the innovative spirit of the American Dream for the twenty-first century and represented ideals of racial equality, even while entrenching nostalgic histories of white, male creatorship. Curi-ously, the postracial creator functioned through the contradictory *refusal* of racial scripts about the incompetence of people of color and the *embrace* of racial scripts about the competence of white men. The figure also operated as a space of constant negotiation in public culture, requiring, in Hasian's words, consideration of "what the speaker and the audience *co-produce* in forensic discourse."[2]

The postracial creator reflected and constructed the racial and economic culture of the times, through rhetorics of colorblindness, neoliberalism, and the American Dream. However, it also worked in binary opposition to the figure of the hyperracial infringer, an international pirate-counterfeiter who was simultaneously invoked to emphasize American nationalism and exceptionalism. The hyperracial intellectual property anti-citizen became a site for displacing racial scripts and racial feelings about the incapacities and incompetencies of creators of color, in ways that seemingly no longer applied at home. Domestically, Obama and Biden, among others, used the imagined ideals of postracial intellectual property citizenship to justify their intellectual property and economic policies. Internationally, they invoked the familiar threat of the hyperracial intellectual property anti-citizen to justify imposing maximalist intellectual property policies on a hostile and infringing Global South. Colorblindness/color-consciousness worked in mutually constitutive ways, disabling discourses of anti-racism domestically and internationally via economic fantasy.

Obama's emphasis on individual responsibility and ingenuity, the core principles of postracial ideology, was consistent with emerging colorblind economic rhetorics in intellectual property law. The trademark dispute in *Matal v. Tam* (2017) (hereinafter *Tam*), which divided Asian American and Native American anti-racist activists, is emblematic of the colorblind economic rhetorics that rendered structural inequalities invisible domestically in the United States. In *Tam*, though Simon Tam earned the right to trademark the band name the Slants, his victory marked a libertarian ethic that reinforced a white, male, consumer gaze. Committing to deregulatory market-based solutions to racism without addressing the underlying racial investments of the capitalism created a Pyrrhic victory in which people of color could trademark freely but came no closer to producing the mythical "level playing field" required for equal opportunity.

Similarly, in the area of patent law, human progress continued to be articulated in the colorblind but structurally unequal language of scientific discovery and expertise. Yet the controversy in India in *Novartis AG v. Union of India and Others* (2013) (hereinafter *Novartis*) demonstrated that human progress as conceived of in American and European patent law functioned as a means of reinforcing racial and (neo)colonial hierarchies, in a manner inconsistent with postracial discourse. Specifically by using strict and narrow interpretations of coercively negotiated intellectual property agreements the United States justified marking India as "insolent democracy" that willfully subverted international patent norms around pharmaceuticals.

A similar (neo)colonial turn of events occurred in the area of copyright law, in *Golan v. Holder* (2012) (hereinafter *Golan*). *Golan*, despite its purported investment in adhering to international intellectual property law and finally protecting foreign authors, did so through (neo)colonial management of the public domain through norms of true imagination for the economic benefit of US content owners, not the embrace of A2K. Together, these rhetorics relegated people of color to second-class creator and citizen status, largely by playing on familiar racial scripts, racial feelings, and economic language. While they were promised the spoils of the American Dream, people of color globally were systematically disadvantaged by the economic choices that the United States pursued and its enforcement of intellectual property rights.

NARRATING POSTRACIAL CREATORS AND
HYPERRACIAL INFRINGERS

Post- culture, including postrace, was invested not only in the purported transcendence of identity categories but also in a renewed and exaggerated commitment to meritocracy, individual achievement, and self-help in an increasingly neoliberal world.[3] The post- was, fundamentally, a do-it-yourself myth of transcendence taken to its cultural and economic extremes.[4] As Ralina Joseph puts it, "[t]his narrative of individual post-racial, post-feminist success is one of *rising above* racism and sexism to the point where identity categories themselves no longer exist."[5] The individualism of postracial ideology worked in tandem with the individualism of the American Dream, creating an imaginary in which people of any race, color, or creed could purportedly pick themselves up by their bootstraps. The central problem with postracial ideology, however, was that the United States had not actually moved beyond racial categories or toward racial equality in any meaningful way. Catherine Squires writes, "How is it that in what's termed 'post-racial America,' people keep finding ways to talk about race?"[6] The arguments that Joseph and Squires make point to the ways that the postracial functioned to render the hyperracial invisible, in a rhetorical and structural strategy of concealment, particularly at the international level.

The production of a postracial creator required the production of its double, the hyperracial infringer. More specifically, postraciality's obfuscation of structural inequality operated through the overdetermination of race in outsider spaces. As Michael Ortiz contends, invocations of the postracial strengthened whiteness through their disavowals of race, in part because they allowed structural inequality to persist unnoticed. He writes that (racial) capitalism works by dividing and conquering, a strategy that produces a kind of hyper-racism in the guise of self-protection:

> [O]ne specific way hyper-racism is generated is by fueling white racial anxiety through accentuating and amplifying a false narrative of "otherness." It creates this sense of an "in" crowd and an "out" crowd, of the need to protect the values and attributes of the "in" crowd at all costs from "deviant outsiders."[7]

In the postracial era, racial overdetermination played out through domestic invocations of postracial creatorship, which were built around persistent

nostalgia for histories of white male making, alongside foreign policy invocations of hyperracial infringement, which blamed other countries for stealing
America's most valuable commodities. Hyperracial infringement constructed
Americans as good intellectual property citizens who are innocent and hardworking victims preyed upon by bad intellectual property anti-citizens who
pirated and counterfeited the nation's intellectual properties.

As B. Zorina Khan points out, there is truth to the idea of the "democratization of inventorship."[8] Nonetheless, political discourses and popular
culture chose to romanticize creatorship, crafting a feel-good narrative of
DIY-maker culture consistent with the postracial zeitgeist. The postracial
veneer on creatorship that facilitated erasure of domestic structural inequalities in authoring, inventing, and trademarking was evident in Obama's discussions of intellectual property. Across his intellectual property speeches,
his rhetorics emerged as postracial ones, which emphasized personal agency
as the path to the American Dream. His narrations of the postracial creator
as a hardworking, ingenious, and innovative figure, imagined colorblind
opportunity, an American Dream for the contemporary era. That American
Dream was intertwined with positive, yet intensely competitive and oppositional, public feelings that were also deeply racialized.

The Obama administration consistently contended that "ingenuity and
innovation serve as the foundations upon which we will continue to grow
our economies and bridge our cultural identities."[9] Referring to America
as "a Nation of inventors and creators making bold ideas real and blazing a
trail of technological advancement"[10] made creatorship a vital component
of citizenship—notably intellectual property citizenship—itself. The postracial creator, here invoked through the language of the undifferentiated
"Nation of inventors and creators," was a source of hope, pride, and progress. Intellectual property reflected and created collective national identity,
embodying America's most inspiring values, and ultimately producing the
"precious commodities"[11] that made the country run. Yet the above comments on World Intellectual Property Day elided the question of race, ro-
manticizing the United States as a unified nation of laborers, with equal
creatorial opportunity and equal economic access.

At the signing of the America Invents Act, a piece of legislation that awards
patent ownership to the first-to-file instead of the first-to-invent, Obama again
invoked a postracial imaginary of invention while calling upon histories of
whiteness, declaring: "One president who would have loved this school is the

person that it's named after—Thomas Jefferson. He was a pretty good inventor himself."[12] He went on to describe the inventor as central to American identity, through the histories of white men, before he discussed how young inventors could achieve the American Dream.[13] He opined to the audience, which included a number of high school students at Thomas Jefferson High School for Science and Technology: "Somewhere in this country—maybe in this room—is the next Thomas Edison or Steve Jobs, just waiting for a chance to turn their idea into a new, thriving business."[14]

While legal scholars disagree on whether the America Invents Act creates any meaningful change to the patent system or even benefits small inventors,[15] Obama suggests otherwise, stating that "[t]his change in our patent law is part of our agenda for making us competitive over the long term."[16] For him, it is the path to the smooth operation of (racial) capitalism and also the American Dream. The widely circulated visual image of the signing of the America Invents Act also evokes a postracial vision of invention. Obama sits in the center of a group of individuals of diverse identities, signing a piece of legislation that, according to him, makes it easier for the average American to invent. Women of color stand in the foreground, representing the potential for American youth to become inventors (Figure 3.1). While we might read this image as aspirational, it

FIGURE 3.1   President Obama signs the America Invents Act.

nonetheless contextually contributes to the erasure of the structural barriers that keep minorities from becoming successful inventors and perpetuates the fiction that any sufficiently educated person can achieve the American Dream through creatorship.[17]

Perhaps the clearest example of Obama's postracial creator narrative was his entrepreneurship platform, in which he linked the ideals of entre-preneurialism—particularly as a means of growing wealth via innovation, job creation, and ultimately U.S. competitiveness—with inventorship while ignoring their fundamental whiteness.[18] The latter was the clear path to the former in Obama's vision for the US economy. He used the same language to talk about intellectual property and entrepreneurship as he had used for invention, explaining, "Entrepreneurs embody the promise of America: the idea that if you have a good idea and are willing to work hard and see it through, you can succeed in this country. And in fulfilling this promise, entrepreneurs also play a critical role in expanding our economy and cre-ating jobs."[19] He went on to say, "America's always been a nation of doers. We build things. We take risks. And we believe that if you have a good idea and are willing to work hard enough, you can turn that idea into a success-ful business."[20] These examples demonstrate how creatorship could become rhetorically postracial, while simultaneously mobilizing US citizenship and US nationalism around the need to protect America from external threats to the American Dream, particularly hyperracial infringement.

Combining intellectual property rhetoric and economic rhetoric was not a new tactic in America, as Valenti's appeals to the everyman in the entertain-ment industry demonstrate. However, invoking the American Dream and the individual agency of the postracial era added a novel populist twist to Obama's rhetorics of intellectual property and economic policy. Whereas the VCR Wars and the Sampling Wars were largely about the success and failure of content owners, despite their appeals to the sentiments of the nation, Obama's intellectual property and economic policy called for Americans to come together around the common and colorblind goal of middle-class status. Intellectual property law was translated and made comprehensible to American publics through the language and mythologies of economic prosperity and entrepreneurship.

Intellectual property discourse functioned as method and object for perceptually carrying out the economic promises of the presidential agenda and the path for continued American global hegemony. Eco-nomics, as Deirdre McCloskey contends, has a veneer of false authority because it "claims to argue by logic alone."[21] Yet because the discipline is unavoidably culturally and logically constructed rhetoric, economics "participates in the false rhetoric against rhetoric."[22] In invoking colorblind economics, Obama engaged in rhetorics of concealment that obscured the racialization of his intellectual property policy. Economic language offered the alibi of logic, rationality, and race neutrality even though, as Angela Harris argues, "Macroeconomics as we know it today emerged in the twentieth century as a kind of Plan B in response to the dismantling of empires around the world, as part of a project to 'limit and reduce the operation of market competition, through increased management of finance, trade and migration, and above all through the prevention of a global market in labor.'"[23]

Postraciality, hyperraciality, and neoliberalism are intertwined in important ways, primarily because economics offers, as McCloskey and Harris contend, a veil of neutrality and objectivity from which to make claims about the world, here with respect to white supremacy. In the postracial era, discussions of economic prosperity offered alibis for continuing racial and (neo)colonial exploitation, generally by mobilizing fears and anxieties about people of color infringement in the developing world. For instance, at the MPAA's 2014 Creativity Conference, "Uncle Joe" Biden explained:

> More than any country in the world . . . America is hard-wired—hard-wired for innovation. It's what's enabled to give us the world—the world changing ideas, from the cotton gin to Microsoft. It's what made Hollywood. . . . It's the reason that I remain—and I mean this sincerely—I remain so optimistic about the future . . . [I]n the twenty-first century, the true wealth of a nation is found in the creative minds of its people. The notion of creativity and innovation as a tool for social and economic advancement is not just—though, just an American idea. It's [a] universal goal but not met very many other places.[24]

In addition to reiterating the story of the Romantic creator, Biden called upon two opposing but related sets of racial scripts and racial feelings in the speech, those of postracial creatorship *and* hyperracial infringement in order to weave a narrative about America designed to inspire pride and patriotism. The country is genetically predisposed for creatorship, he contends, because it culturally cultivates the skills required for innovation and ingenuity. For Biden, not all nations are capable of producing the unorthodox and outside the metaphorical box thinking that led, for instance, Steve Jobs to the slogan "think different."

Later in the speech, Biden pivoted away from America and by referring to the "face of piracy."[25] He cautioned his audience to be wary of those in "a far off country"[26] who engaged in mass theft. International law, he claimed, must keep up with their attempts to rob the American people—and occasionally the rare hardworking people in the developing world. The pirates that Biden speaks of are Indian and Chinese, sometimes even Russian.[27] They are the Orientalized enemies of Americans, who are uniquely culturally poised and accordingly entitled to be creators and achieve the American Dream.[28] In one short speech, Biden cultivates a range of racial feelings, including pride, patriotism, fear, anxiety, and resentment, about creatorship and infringement in the United States and globally.

Implicit in Biden's rhetoric here and in Obama's rhetoric in the previous examples is the construction of a category of intellectual property anti-citizens who actively work *against* the American Dream to which US citizens are entitled. While postracial creators are imagined as hardworking and innovative individuals deserving of the benefits of creatorship, hyperracial infringers are unfit for the rights and entitlements associated with citizenship. This view constructs citizenship as a rhetorical and ideological category organized around race that some individuals are entitled to occupy and other individuals are not entitled to occupy.

We must, as Rajeswari Sunder Rajan contends, "move beyond an earlier 'liberal and political science' understanding of the 'formal relationship' between the individual and the state"[29] and consider "'a more total relationship, inflected by identity, social positioning, cultural assumptions, institutional practices and a sense of belonging."[30] The hyperracial infringer, in this reading, becomes a hegemonic site for the negotiation of racial and economic authority and the right to define important concepts like true imagination and human progress. For the United States, the hyperracial infringer is the embodiment of the nation's fears and anxieties about loss of global leadership and economic decline. For the Global South, the hyperracial infringer is the embodiment of new postcolonial economic futures, ones in which former colonial subjects attain the rights to define knowledge production and its attendant economics in emancipatory ways. Attached to both visions of hyperracial infringement, of course, are narratives of stability/precarity that invoke familiar racial scripts and racial feelings.

TRADEMARK LIBERTARIANISM AS ENTRENCHING THE MALE CONSUMER GAZE

When Simon Tam set out to trademark his band's name, the Slants, he did not intend to alter the course of trademark history in the United States. However, that was what he did, in a case that resulted in the Supreme Court declaring that Section 2(a) of the Lanham Act is unconstitutional under the free speech clause of the First Amendment. In pursuing his lawsuit, Tam also created intraracial conflict by frustrating battles undertaken by Native Americans to cancel the racist Redskins® trademark (or "Washington football team's trademark"). The most generous reading of *Tam* is that it was a victory for the Slants, who were the victims of a federal government that refused to allow people of color to identify as intellectual property citizens, often by employing racial double standards. However, even though there is truth to that reading, the rhetoric of self-determination around *Tam* tends to ignore and dismiss the manner in which the case represents a move toward racial libertarianism, a philosophy with a laissez-faire, market-based attitude toward race. This move is consistent with post- discourses of self-actualization and self-branding that harm people of color by refusing to acknowledge that racism is ongoing and pervasive.

In *Tam*, the Supreme Court absolves the federal government of responsibility for managing racist trademarks by way of free speech. It also functionally endorses a hands-off system in which markets—systems largely governed by a predominantly white and male consumer gaze—must regulate brand racism. In a post-*Tam* world, the invisible hand and radical activism remain the primary available strategies for pushing back against disparaging trademarks. *Tam*, though it produces incremental gains in trademark recognition for Asian Americans, does little to represent them, or other people of color as full citizens and full creators. Rather, it incentivizes the repetition of racial scripts despite offering free speech and economics as solutions to racism. Read through the lens of historical trademark racism and the objectification of people of color, *Tam* reinforces the white masculinity of the consumer gaze by not only condoning the production of racist trademarks but also rendering invisible the structural whiteness of free speech and market economies. Deregulation flattens the category of intellectual property citizenship while leaving no legal doctrinal mechanism for managing racist trademarks.[31]

Tam involved an all-Asian rock band, the Slants, who petitioned for the right to register a trademark in their name, which the USPTO had found to be a "derogatory or offensive term."[32] The Supreme Court affirmed the Federal Circuit's decision, that the Slants, represented by Tam, had the right to trademark their name because Section 2(a) violates the First Amendment.[33] According to the unanimous Supreme Court opinion, Section 2(a), which permitted the USPTO to refuse to register a trademark that "[c]onsists of or comprises immoral, deceptive, or scandalous matter; or matter which may disparage or falsely suggest a connection with persons, living or dead, institutions, beliefs, or national symbols or bring them into contempt, or disrepute,"[34] "offends a bedrock First Amendment principle: speech may not be banned on the ground that it expresses ideas that offend."[35] More specifically, banning racist trademarks under Section 2(a), the Court unanimously agreed, is an overbroad act of viewpoint discrimination that is not justified even in the state interests of preventing the use of discriminatory speech or protecting the free flow of commerce.[36] The outcome of the case, which the Court subsequently determined invalidates all of Section 2(a), not simply its Disparagement Clause,[37] also gave the Washington R*******® stronger grounds to argue a right to trademark registration despite the invalidation of that trademark just a year earlier.[38] *Tam*, while a victory for the Slants, is a considerable loss for Native Americans fighting racist mascots, such as that of the Washington football team.

Racial libertarianism in the Disparagement Clause

In *Tam*, the Supreme Court opted to embrace a racial libertarian model of trademark regulation, by invalidating the federal government's ability to refuse to register racist trademarks. *Tam* reads not as an attempt to *empower* marginalized groups, as the courts and Tam would have us believe, but as a move to force individuals and markets to *self-regulate* racism in the context of trademark law.

This push for self-regulation, which intersects with but is distinct from racial liberalism, is what Joseph Lowndes defines as "a [William F.] Buckleyite racial libertarianism."[39] While the latter theorizes personhood and relationships to the state, often in ways that implicate marginalized persons, the former is the basis for the deregulation and individual self-responsibility of the post-racial era. Lowndes defines libertarianism in the context of the American Dream debate between William F. Buckley, Jr., and James

Baldwin. Drawing a fine line between the liberal and the libertarian, he writes, "Emergent liberal concerns over Black inequality provided a way for Buckley to make cultural and libertarian conservative arguments by placing Blackness at the center. But his racial target was often not African Americans themselves, but an interpretation of black social conditions and black behavior."[40] At the heart of his claim was "the libertarian argument that people were *individuals who made choices*—not merely products of economic circumstance."[41]

Read through the lens of Buckleyite racial libertarianism, *Tam* places its faith in the racial libertarian approach to (de)regulation of free speech by putting markets, individuals, and people of color in the driver's seat with respect to morally and economically devaluing racist trademarks and reclaiming injurious speech. The case sacrifices Native American protection from hate speech at the altar of Asian American freedom to reclaim speech, a bargain that necessarily pits people of color against one another in a divide-and-conquer strategy.

As Junot Diaz recently put it, "The amnesia that empire inflicts on us allows us to forget the connections we have with each other—how in the past we fought with and for each other."[42] In *Tam*, the Supreme Court engages in a racial bait and switch: Asian Americans gain the right to reclaim speech in an entrenched system of racial libertarianism that, through its ideologies of individual responsibility, makes addressing the structural dehumanization of marginalized groups in trademark law, including Native Americans, more difficult. The racial scripts around the Myth of the Vanishing Indian take on new meaning as the language of the First Amendment becomes a "racial technology" for erasing Native trauma.[43] These erasures are the result of the continued existence, though increasing invisibility, of a white and male consumer gaze. The persistent corporate and consumer investment in the Washington football team's trademark is emblematic of the still overwhelming role of white masculinity in articulating and imagining structural possibilities for brand identities.

The whiteness of both the First Amendment and the Disparagement Clause highlight the problems with relying on a deregulatory approach to managing racist trademarks. During the Antebellum Era and the post–civil rights era, the Disparagement Clause was used as a mechanism for protecting white masculinity, particularly through policing the morality of the nation in a manner reminiscent of dilution law. Early disparagement cases, decided in the period from 1890 to 1953,[44] referred to the morality of corporate behavior, generally in the context of slander or unfair competition and rarely in the context of trademarks.[45] This understanding of disparagement, as Tam argued in a legal brief for the Federal Circuit, likely informed the passage of Section 2(a) in 1939. Tam contends:

> The history of the disparagement clause confirms that it was not intended to protect racial and ethnic groups. The clause was added in 1939 to one of the bills that eventually became the Lanham Act in 1946 . . . It is very unlikely that members of Congress were concerned about trademarks that were disparaging to racial or ethnic groups in a period when much worse forms of discrimination were still common . . . The purpose of the disparagement clause was not to protect minority groups. Rather, the purpose was to bring American trademark law into conformity with American treaty obligations.[46]

In other words, judicial understandings of disparagement primarily treated the cause of action as a tortious one meant to protect property, which sometimes intersected with trademark infringement.

While the argument is a curious one for Tam to make, the notion that disparagement was meant to protect the value of the company is one that is supported by the historical construction of racial capitalism during the period. In 1939, the eve of World War II, brand integrity combined with the war economy to create the meteoric rise of trademarking that Lauren Berlant and Rosemary Coombe discuss. In the period from 1953 to 2008, the number of trademark disparagement cases skyrocketed,[47] with the nature of those cases changing as well. Consistent with the nation's turn to civil rights and formal equality after the civil rights movement, marginalized groups began to use the Disparagement Clause to invalidate discriminatory trademarks, not simply to protect juristic persons or corporate financial interests.

For instance, Marion Bromberg and Judith Horvitz argue that the trademark Only a Breast in the Mouth is Better than a Leg in the Hand was "disparaging to all people of a specific class, and in particular, women, in that it has false connotations and brings individuals, especially women, in contempt and disrepute; that the obvious double entendre of the mark indicates that it is lewd, lascivious, indecent, obscene, worthless, depraved, chauvinistic, degrading, and has no commercial value."[48] That using the Disparagement Clause to protect marginalized persons was a battle, not a

foregone conclusion, demonstrates how trademark law continues to operate to protect property rights through a white male consumer gaze, at least
structurally speaking, with equity and inclusion as afterthoughts.

The gains made by people of color in combating racist trademarks have
been offset by significant losses, including of the very cause of action upon
which their victories are based. Racial realists contend that the consistent
rollback of gains is emblematic of a system that is committed only to interest
convergence and not to long-term racial equality.[49] In essence, as I argued
in earlier chapters, maintaining whiteness as property while mollifying people of color, not true equity, is the central goal of the post–civil rights era.
Victories for people of color that hurt other groups of people of color are
emblematic of the precarity of civil rights gains that racial realists describe.

The two suits against Pro-Football, Inc. over the Washington football
team's trademark, particularly when read alongside *Tam*, demonstrate this
fundamental principle of CRT. They highlight the continued existence of
a powerful default white and male consumer gaze even in the face of the
fiction of postracial intellectual property citizens like Tam. The struggle to
cancel the Washington football team's trademark started decades ago. In
1992, Suzan Shown Harjo sued Pro-Football, Inc. for the use of the disparaging trademark. She ultimately lost the case on a claim of laches, an
equitable defense claiming that the suit was filed so long after the purported
cause of action as to be unfair to the other party.[50]

Though the TTAB stated that its opinion should not be read as taking a position on whether the Washington football team's trademark is a
disparaging term, it also held, affirming property over personhood, that
"during the period of delay, Pro-Football and NFL Properties invested in
the trademarks and had increasing revenues during this time frame."[51] This
ruling on the grounds of laches was an early one of many legal pronouncements about the much criticized football team trademark.

The ultimate outcome in *Pro Football, Inc. v. Harjo* (2005) (hereinafter
Harjo), though wrapped in the language of procedural obstacles, relies on
narratives of the unfairness of the lawsuit and the plaintiffs' failure to exercise due diligence around the litigation. The former argument erases the
law's historical investments in protecting white supremacy—particularly as
produced through a white male consumer gaze that objectifies indigenous
peoples as mascots—at the expense of people of color. The latter argument
recalls the racial scripts of the Prerequisite Cases, painting Native Americans

as incompetent and devious. In addition to grounding *Harjo* in the purportedly race neutral procedural workings of law, the TTAB implicitly invokes racial capitalism as a justification for erring on the side of the football team. Its decision paints Native American litigants as incompetent and greedy—a strategy that was also used to publicly manage the claims of Aunt Jemima actors to real-life profits from Quaker Oats—while rendering invisible the manner in which procedural rules like laches work in the service of protecting whiteness as property, here by safeguarding a team's investments in its racist trademark and erasing broader histories of structural inequality.

Still, the TTAB steadfastly maintains that its decision ought not be read as taking a position on whether the term "redskins" is disparaging to indigenous peoples. Nonetheless, it chooses to protect the value of Washington football team's trademark, which is built on the historical resonance of an image that diminishes the humanity of indigenous peoples, instead of deploying Section 2(a) in a racially remedial manner. The court's overall investment in a purportedly colorblind notion of "fairness," as described by the rule of laches and the value of the Washington football team's trademark, reveals its tunnel vision in deliberating on the two concepts. The outcome is a case that reinforces the racial liberalism that plagued the era from 1953 to 2008 and endorses the continuation of racial capitalism without legal recourse or remedy.

In 2014, Amanda Blackhorse filed suit against the Washington football team's trademark, also for disparagement. Blackhorse was ultimately victorious, and the TTAB invalidated the trademark under the Disparagement Clause.[52] However, *Tam*, which was decided soon after, complicated the outcome of *Blackhorse v. Pro Football, Inc.* (2014) (hereafter *Blackhorse*). Further, though the TTAB and courts have invalidated a number of racially disparaging and scandalous trademarks over the years, including Memphis Mafia, Khoran, Porno Jesus, Stop the Islamisation of America, and various iterations of the N-word, they have consistently done so in ways that are ad hoc because they have been made by individual examiners and judges with no clear rules. Ultimately, a section in a statute that was originally meant to protect the businesses of predominantly white men evolved into a tool of antidiscrimination, which the TTAB and courts inconsistently applied to protect marginalized groups and subsequently found to be unconstitutional.

The history of the battle to cancel the Washington football team's trademark demonstrates that courts, when faced with the prospect of invalidating a valuable trademark over claims of racism, are prone to finding tangible ways to protect (white) property interests. Doing so necessarily works against the notion of a postracial intellectual property citizen and in favor of a white, male consumer gaze. It was not until 2014, in *Blackhorse*, that the TTAB and the District Court for the Eastern District of Virginia found the Washington football team's trademark to be disparaging. However, *Tam*'s resolution signaled a turn to market regulation of racism. A cynical reading suggests that the Supreme Court embraced new ways to protect the property interests of white men when the previous ones were co-opted by people of color. A less cynical reading is that the Supreme Court unanimously made a decision that was consistent with the First Amendment libertarianism of the time.

Free speech and the (racist) free market

The obvious response to these critiques of *Tam* is that the case is clearly one of viewpoint discrimination, as even the most liberal members of the Supreme Court found, which involves neither a government subsidy nor government speech. Instead of engaging the free speech debate, which CRT scholars have compellingly done for decades, I contend that *Tam* was not destined to be a First Amendment case and, even if it had to be decided as such, the Federal Circuit and the Supreme Court could have taken different approaches to managing trademark's "words that wound."[53] *Tam* became a free speech case only after the Federal Circuit's sua sponte request for the parties to brief the question of whether the Disparagement Clause violates the First Amendment.[54] This move was a curious one and bears further examination because, for decades, courts have cited *In re McGinley* (1981) approvingly as precedent for not invalidating Section 2(a).

Framing the Slants question as *why now?* instead of *why this outcome?* provides a means of homing in on the racial politics of the case. The answer to the first question rests not with a close reading of First Amendment jurisprudence but with the evolution of liberalism, post- culture, and libertarianism and their intersections with the protection of whiteness as property. In choosing to treat *Tam* as a free speech case, the Federal Circuit intervened to create a narrow frame of analysis through which trademark law's racial histories, including its implications for the protectability of Native mascots, were sacrificed at the altar of the First Amendment. Such a move was made easier by the rise of post- culture and neoliberalism, which come together in praise of practices of individual responsibility, self-branding, and free speech. *Tam* ought to be read not merely as a free speech case, but as an extension of the racial libertarianism of post- culture, which flowed from the racial liberalism of the 1970s and 1980s. It emerged from and reinforces ideologies of individual responsibility and calls upon the "marketplace of ideas" to remedy the nation's structural inequalities.

In *In re McGinley*, the Federal Circuit wrote:

> With respect to appellant's First Amendment rights, it is clear that the PTO's refusal to register appellant's mark does not affect his right to use it. No conduct is proscribed, and no tangible form of expression is suppressed. Consequently, appellant's First Amendment rights would not be abridged by the refusal to register his mark.[55]

The Court cited a litany of sources from across the political spectrum that criticize *In re McGinley* as justification for the ruling.

But despite footnoting multiple law review articles that condemn Native mascots and noting the failure of courts to understand "the expressive power of trademarks,"[56] the circuit court did not discuss trademark law's relationship to hate speech or the commodification of cultural property, though these issues could have easily been brought into the conversation sua sponte, as competing interests to free speech. These omissions are deeply problematic ones, highlighting the continuing refusal of courts to acknowledge the violentness of racial scripts and racial feelings, the value of traditional knowledge, and the exploitative practices of racial capitalism in the trademark context.

The colorblindness of the Supreme Court's decision provides cover for a racially problematic decision. Indeed, federal courts, which have a history of refusing to protect people of color, particularly Indigenous peoples, under the First Amendment and Fifth Amendment replicate this harm in *Tam*. The silence sets up a divide-and-conquer strategy in which protecting the Slants and protecting the Washington football team's trademark are presented as mutually exclusive goals. This compounds the problem of Native American marginalization in the United States, in part by facilitating the circulation of images that validate racial scripts about the barbarism and dangerousness of Indigenous peoples that go back centuries. As Angela Riley observes, "For indigenous peoples, then, there is little protection against the appropriation of intangible cultural 'goods,' even if the appropriation is experienced by tribes as distortion, theft, offense, or misrepresentation."[57] This oversight on the Court's part illustrates the failures of trademark libertarianism and implicitly reinforces a white male consumer gaze.

Much like the Supreme Court, the Federal Circuit sets up a narrative in which Tam is the hero, the model minority fighting for the principles of free speech against a government that threatens his ability to be treated just like everyone else. "Mr. Tam conveys more about our society than many volumes of undisputedly protected speech,"[58] Judge Kimberly Moore writes. The court then segues into a discussion of viewpoint discrimination, concluding that though "[m]any of the marks rejected as disparaging convey hurtful speech that harms members of oft-stigmatized communities. But the First Amendment protects even hurtful speech."[59] Through this juxtaposition, *Tam* can be read as involving a figure fighting for the civil liberties of all Americans and as a model minority who does not attempt to create exceptions to the First Amendment to protect himself from hate speech.[60] "Mr. Tam and his band weigh in on cultural and political discussions about race and society that are within the heartland of speech protected by the First Amendment," Moore continues.[61] Tam seeks to "'own' the stereotype [that "slants"] represents."[62] The Federal Circuit emphasizes Tam's desire to reclaim the term, using his property rights as a vehicle to "take on these stereotypes that people have about us, like the slanted eyes, and own them."[63] "Own" takes on two meanings here, one that connotes the transformation of stereotypes into property, as in the context of trademark law, and one that connotes embrace, as in the context of reclaiming hateful speech.[64] Both of these readings of "own" suggest a shift of power that has not actually occurred. Tam can no more control the cultural deployments of stereotypes than any other marginalized groups can, and his claims to do so are dangerous ones.

The Federal Circuit and the Supreme Court mobilized Tam's purported transgressiveness as a rhetorical vehicle for diminishing racial harm to other people of color, including Native Americans. In applying a standard of strict scrutiny to the case, the Court engaged in a strategy of "rhetorical exclusion"[65] that is common in instances involving Native Americans. In essence, the Court marks Tam's trademark discrimination as more important than that of indigenous peoples, thus papering over a multi-decade battle over Native mascots.

Moreover, as Butler writes, "[t]hese definitions build upon and contribute to the assumption that the US federal government is democratic, legitimate, and inherently worthy of defense against any threats."[66] In *Tam*, rhetorical exclusion takes the form of framing and footnoting, as the Federal

Circuit and Supreme Court invoke the free speech question and then foot-note but never engage conversations about Native mascots. Indeed, both choose to diminish the harms of disparaging speech and refuse to consider the potential racial implications of trademark doctrine itself. For instance, Judge Moore speaks of the State's desire to prevent circulation of "the most vile racial epithets and images"[67] and then invokes the example of Abraham Lincoln gin to demonstrate the Disparagement Clause's lack of viewpoint neutrality. Though the Circuit Court also engages arguably more-egre-gious examples of disparaging trademarks, such as Stop the Islamisation of America and Squaw Valley, it frames their discussion through that of free speech, not harm to individuals, as critical race theorists have suggested is necessary to get to the heart of the issue with words that wound.[68]

Though *Tam* advances the rights of people of color to reclaim disparag-ing trademarks, it does so by buying into a system that is historically rigged against them, mainly because of the persistence of racial scripts, racial feel-ings, and racial capitalism. *Tam* results in a flattened category of trademark citizens, all of whom allegedly have equal formal access to the economic tools to protect their trademarks. The tragedy of *Tam* is that the economic rhetoric of protecting trademarks is a rhetoric of concealment, which makes continuing beliefs about the non-citizenship and nonpersonhood of people of color more, not less, invisible and pernicious.

In light of the decision in *Golan*, discussed below, *Tam* reads as a First Amendment double standard that upholds the links between whiteness and property. The Supreme Court, on the one hand, rules that it is acceptable to remove material from the public domain, largely for the benefit of largely white corporate content holders, but that trademarks must remain content-neutral, for the benefit of a free market that benefits white interests in the guise of protecting people of color. This contradiction is emblematic of the manner in which postracial creatorship rhetorics operate through racial bait-and-switch tactics that structurally protect whiteness through sentimental and nostalgic notions of American creatorship and the American Dream.

INDIAN PATENT INSOLENCE AS
COUNTERING HUMAN PROGRESS

Similar bait-and-switch tactics are evident in postracial/hyperracial patent discourse. While, domestically, the United States appeared to invest in col-orblind creatorship, including in the realm of scientific and technological innovation, internationally, multinational pharmaceutical companies moved to enforce TRIPS in constraining, (neo)colonial ways that purportedly work under race neutral terms.

For instance, in *Association for Molecular Pathology v. Myriad Genetics, Inc.* (hereinafter *Myriad*), a case that is traditionally read as a blow to biotechnology, gene patents, and even capitalism, the Supreme Court refused to protect naturally occurring genomic DNA (gDNA) sequences, but protected lab-produced complementary DNA (cDNA) sequences used in breast cancer and ovarian cancer screening. That decision has complex but significant implications for race. When read in the trajectory of *Chakrabarty* and *Moore*, *Myriad* continues the scientific colonization of the public domain through its reiteration of race liberal definitions of nature/science and expertise—and their attendant racial scripts.[69] The case endorses a vision of inventorship as a process that unfolds in a laboratory, at the hands of expert scientists. As Laura Foster writes, "Patent ownership is contingent on maintaining binaries of nature and culture, thus items discovered in nature are not patentable, only man-made cultural inventions."[70]

The result of this nature/culture distinction, as demonstrated in chapter 2's discussion of race liberal creatorship, is often to obscure the racial subjectivity implicit in definitions of both nature and culture. For instance, the Supreme Court declared that patentable subject matter must be "markedly different"[71] from its natural form. Yet, like doctrinal definitions in copyright law, this phrase invokes culturally and racially specific notions of (white) expertise, which require manipulation of natural material. *Myriad* also stands for the proposition that some bodies, often bodies of color, ought to be the objects, not agents, of patents. By endorsing cDNA patents, *Myriad* aligns itself with gene sequencing and genetic testing, practices that often target and exploit already vulnerable populations.

While perceptually jarring, the Supreme Court's decision to protect only cDNA produced through reverse transcription affected only 25 percent of *Myriad*'s patents and is likely to have very little long-term effect on either the company or the overall growth of biotechnology.[72] With limited exception, the postracial intellectual property citizen, despite the alleged colorblindness of the category of creatorship, had access to the protective capacities of patent law only when working through preexisting and predominantly white rubrics of nature, science, and expertise. As Jonathan Kahn has argued, expertise barriers in patent law also create space for naturalizing genetic race, through the characterization of certain "deviant" gene sequences as associated with particular racial groups and not others.[73]

Myriad is, as the American Civil Liberties Union declared soon after the decision,[74] a perceptual win for those who are opposed to patents on genetic material insofar as it overturns the long-standing precedent established in *Chakrabarty* that gDNA is patentable. However, the victory is a hollow one for undoing racialized nature/science distinctions. The case further entrenches the doctrines of expertise in the context of patent law that allow traditional knowledge to be exploited.[75]

In another consistent racially problematic move, rhetorics of postracial creatorship stoked racial panics about people of color in the developing world stealing valuable intellectual properties and fueled economic unease at the implications of such acts.[76] Yet nations, with whom the United States has important economic, military, and diplomatic ties, were not categorically exiled from engagement. Instead, they were constructed as chronically suspect, in Homi Bhabha's terms the mimetic barbarians that were perpetually "almost, but not quite,"[77] yet not so much of a lost cause as to be completely abandoned. Indeed, abandonment would forsake the structure upon which modern (neo)colonialism and neoliberalism are built, specifically through their reliance on a colonial periphery for the definition and operation of the (neo)colonial core.

With sufficient praise and discipline from the United States, hyperracial infringers (usually allied democracies such as India), like well-behaved children, could mature into adults with the capacity, with caveats, to fully participate in global affairs.[78] Accompanying this desire to discipline hyperracial infringers is an underlying refusal to understand the structural conditions of development in the Global South.[79]

As Aihwa Ong argues, "Neoliberalism as a technology of governing relies on calculative choices and technique in the domains of citizenship and of governing . . . Neoliberal governmentality results from the infiltration of market-driven truths and calculations into the domain of politics."[80] In the context of intellectual property law, hyperracial infringers were represented as neoliberal rebels and intellectual property anti-citizens because of their inability and unwillingness to abide by distinctly Euro-American and (neo)colonial market logics of knowledge production. Characterized as having "illicit economies,"[81] the logics of production in the Global South are marked as not simply unfamiliar but also immoral, based on a refusal to engage knowledge and commodity production on neoliberal—read: America's—terms. Defining which economies are licit/illicit is a profoundly racial and (neo)colonial practice that maintains American (whiteness) as property.

When Edward Said originally spoke of Orientalism in the late 1970s, he described a discourse of Otherization in which the so-called Orient became an object of study, fascination, and exoticization for the Western subject.[82] Orientalism is a useful starting point for thinking through how the United States crafts intellectual property policy vis-à-vis India, particularly in the context of both nations' attitudes toward patent law. Identifying democracy as a distinguishing factor between the colonizer and the colonized, a rhetorical practice that the United States appeals to often in the context of India, is a well-worn tactic of neo-Orientalism, the strand of Orientalism that focuses on the cultural backwardness of Islamic nations as the root cause of violent conflict.

It has been, for decades, accepted racist and (neo)colonial wisdom in international relations that "the peoples of developing countries must now acknowledge that liberal democracy is the only plausible form of governance in the modern world."[83] The production of a "new barbarism"[84] thesis in which the "backward cultures"[85] of Middle Eastern and Asian nations, as opposed to political and economic factors, serves to explain the inevitability of Oriental violence and highlight the consistent demonization of any and all deviations from Western neoliberal democracy. Intellectual property Orientalism, which I explore here, is another notable turn in Orientalist discourse that requires detailed investigation, study, and critique.

Disputes over India's policies around pharmaceuticals showcase US approaches to constructing and managing hyperracial infringement and the racial scripts invoked in its construction. By critiquing India for its "patent insolence," a term I coin to describe representations of the country as obviously anti-democratic but also anti-global governance and anti-intellectual property, the United States draws upon racial scripts of Black and Brown people, particularly in colonial and slave contexts, as anti-citizens who refuse civilized society. The disciplinary politics of insolence are not independent from Orientalism but rather intersect with it. Orientalism and neo-Orientalism are "[p]ared to the bone," legible as "species of a larger discourse of power that divides the world into 'betters and lessers' and thus facilitates the domination (or 'orientalization' or 'colonization') of any group."[86] On the one hand, the United States frequently touts India as a shining example of democracy promotion gone right, a once colony that is now the world's largest democratic nation.[87] A White House report titled "Democracy and Progress in India" demonstrates the historical consistency of this narrative: "Sixty-five years ago this week, India's post-independence democratic constitution went into effect, paving the way for the country to become not only a democracy but the world's largest democracy."[88] Cooperation on regional security, climate change, and nuclear non-proliferation policy has made India one of the closest and most consistent U.S. allies, a fact that is routinely flagged in U.S. diplomatic and foreign policy rhetorics on both sides of the aisle.

On the other hand, the United States also routinely chastises the Asian nation as epitomizing opportunistic infringement and using such claims as a (neo)colonial and racialized wedge to promote intellectual property policy. Beginning in 1972, under the leadership of Indira Gandhi and in accordance with the Indian Patents Act of 1970, until 1995, when the nation joined the World Trade Organization (WTO), India did not offer product patent protection for pharmaceuticals.

Then, in a move that transformed the nation into the "pharmacy to the developing world,"[89] India began producing cheap, generic drugs and lobbying for exceptions to TRIPS that would allow the developing world to access those lifesaving pharmaceuticals. The United States pushed back at India's perceived intransigence in complying with international intellectual property law. That pushback, as with the practice that resulted in developing nations capitulating to international intellectual property regimes, often materialized in complaints filed with the WTO, economic threats, and coercive diplomacy. Instead of deescalating the conflict and reconciling their differences, the nations' different readings of TRIPS culminated in a very public legal dispute with Swiss pharmaceutical company Novartis in 2013.

The lawsuit, decades in the making, began when Novartis submitted a patent application for the cancer treatment Glivec, whose active ingredient, Imatinib Mesylate, had already received product and process patent protection in the United States, in 1992. In the ten-year period from 1995 to 2005, during which India was preparing for TRIPS compliance, it created a "mailbox" rule for patent applications that were, under its new patent law, eligible for patent protection.

Novartis's patent was not reviewed until 2005, at which time the Chennai (Madras) Patent Office found that Glivec was not patentable in India.

The Madras High Court and subsequently the Indian Supreme Court affirmed that decision.[90] The latter's ruling in *Novartis* provoked strong reactions across the world. Developed nations, led by the United States, and pharmaceutical companies decried the decision, while global health organizations, including the World Health Organization, and activists celebrated the landmark pro-A2K outcome in the case. The decision's refusal to extend patent protection to Glivec in India, because it did not make a meaningful improvement in efficacy to an existing drug, a hedge against a practice known in the industry as "evergreening,"[91] signaled the nation's continuing refusal to comply with international law.

The case soon became an important site for racialized criticism of India's intellectual property law, particularly vis-à-vis the rhetorical construction of the nation as an Orientalized insolent democracy that defied emerging global intellectual property norms. This narrative is a pervasive one in public cultural discussions of India. Thomas Blom Hansen, for instance, describes imaginings of India as centered around "democratic deformities"[92] that posit the nation "as somehow incomplete and immature: full of corruption, vulgar manipulators, campaigning film stars, colorful imagery presented to impressionable illiterates not capable of making qualified choices."[93] Kavita Philip notes a tendency to deploy this rhetoric in the context of infringement, chastising Asia for "infantile democracy."[94]

The Glivec dispute implicates both of these narratives, but it also points to a willful intransigence that the United States names in order to chastise India for flouting international patent agreements in a way that is knowing, lazy, and selfish. Neither democratic deformities nor infantile democracy, though useful and necessary terms, describes the subtext of insolence in U.S. patent critiques of India. "Patent insolence," as rhetorical trope, draws on a set of colonial discourses in the context of intellectual property law, resulting in India's being labeled as a dishonest broker, invested in power politics and thwarting progress on knowledge protection.

"Criminal insolence,"[95] a term that can be traced back to the Greek polis, connotes a particularly virulent strain of incivility that suggests the character flaw of hubris. For Aristotle, insolence was "classified among slights that excite anger."[96] He defined it as "a form of slighting that causes shame for the receiver and pleasure for the sender."[97] To engage in insolence was to fail at the art of rhetoric, specifically the self-styling expected of those Greek men who participated in democratic oration as part of their citizenship duties.

In describing fellow Athenian orator Meidias, Demosthenes identified his insolence in "the tone of his voice (loud-mouthed, bellowing, and haranguing), his gestures (snapping his fingers at justice), his stance and physical presence (breaking the doors of Demosthenes' household, standing by the judges to intimidate them, and blocking the aisles), and his eyes (staring down at the rowdy section of the Assembly to silence them."[98] Together, these characteristics suggest insolence as part of an "extradiscursive, presentational system that . . . points to a unified character."[99] Perhaps most importantly, the performance of insolence is an existentially antidemocratic act, which implicates the willingness and the capacity to engage with others with a particularly Athenian understanding of decorum. The mere accusation of insolence negates any possibility of being read any other way. Instead, it points to inherent unequalness, a worse-than quality, which arises from complete lack of restraint and lack of civility. In a rhetorical double bind, "[if] a bully is humble and supplicating when threatened, it just adds to the punishment his characteristic arrogance and insolence deserves, for it proves that his hubris is deliberate and malicious rather than being simply his natural manner."[100] The implications of insolence for contemporary readings of race and civility are accordingly significant.

Translated into racial and (neo)colonial contexts, insolence becomes a marker of insubordination and rebellion. It not only points to democratic incapacity, it showcases the inhumanity of the colonial subject. In the American South, insolence was a marker of resistance, which had to be managed and contained. Though it was an effective tool of protest in the face of slavery, it was also "'sufficient cause' at law for a white person's beating and maiming of a slave."[101] Insolence was a meaningful rhetoric, against which settler colonists positioned themselves. As Allison Shutt argues: "The colonial civilising project was bound up with manners,"[102] specifically, "the poor manners of the dominated, glossed most often as insolence."[103]

In the time of Demosthenes, insolence was at odds with the functioning of the polis. However, it also threatened the prestige and honor of settler colonists, particularly "critical issues of state-building, most notably the debate over how to dominate unruly Africans within the constraints of colonial civility."[104] Yet the boundaries of insolence were blurry ones: much like pornography in the U.S. Supreme Court, settler colonists "knew it when they saw it." Insolence was a subjective act, defined by the fragility of whiteness, particularly white masculinity, and arbitrarily and capriciously wielded.

Unlike "intransigent," "democratic deformities," or "infantile democracy," the term "insolence" provides a theoretical frame for understanding U.S.-Indo intellectual property negotiations as spaces for continuing hegemonic contestation over racial and (neo)colonial power. India's entrée into the WTO did not mark a new era in U.S.-Indo relations. Rather, it marked the continuation of the push and pull of colonial modes of interaction, with American cultural fragility serving as justification to berate and punish India for its insubordination. As in the logics of slave and colonial subject insolence, India's behavior with respect to intellectual property provides a justification for treating the nation as willfully refusing to comply with international norms and creating a subject/object positionality that erases the historical colonial and structural economic reasons for doing so. This is not to say that India was not also trying to gain the upper hand in pharmaceutical negotiations. India was certainly trying to outmaneuver the United States in a practical legal sense. However, the latter resorted to familiar racial and colonial tropes to discredit India's attempts to do so.

The language of Indian economic roguishness serves to render the nation different and Other, in a frame that also casts it not as invested in remaking neoliberal intellectual property regimes but as a "lesser" country that cannot achieve democracy perfection. This projection of American identity is reminiscent of the Cold War, in which democracy served as a counterpoint to communism, an ideology whose spread provoked fear and anxiety. The U.S. government plays the role of the parental figure, counseling India to "both take its rightful place in international rule-setting and to accept the responsibilities that come with it."[105] India cannot play by its own rules because the rules have already been set over a long history, in this case by primarily European and North American powers.

The language of insolence, specifically colonial intransigence, is evident in U.S. discourses with and about India on intellectual property issues. India has been on the Special 301 Priority Watch List, a trade tool that the United States Trade Representative (USTR) uses to shame countries that refuse to comply with TRIPS and other international trade agreements, since the 1980s. In recent years, as the document has become longer and more substantive, criticisms of India have focused not only on infringement but also on exploitation of the developing nation provisions in TRIPS. In 2005, the United States pledged its commitment to "effective and appropriate use of the TRIPS health solution to facilitate life-saving medicines by countries in need."[106] However, American actions revealed a desire to coerce developing nations into a narrow reading of provisions for access to pharmaceuticals contained in TRIPS after a deeply hypocritical history of strong-arming them into international intellectual property agreements with less than favorable, or even fair, terms.

The lawsuit in *Novartis* affirmed that the United States and India had wildly different readings of TRIPS. In 2013, after years of persistent opposition by Novartis, the Supreme Court of India determined that the drug Glivec was not patentable in India. In short, because the beta crystalline form of Imatinib Mesylate, even though it increased bioavailability, did not represent a notable improvement in therapeutic efficacy over the prior formulation of the medication, no "inventive step" was required to create the drug and it could not be patented. The Indian Supreme Court relied on the controversial Section 3(d) of the Indian Patents Act of 1970, which excludes the following from the definition of patentable inventions:

> The mere discovery of a new form of a known substance which does not result in the enhancement of the known efficacy of that substance or the mere discovery of any new property or new use for a known substance or of the mere use of a known process, machine or apparatus unless such known process results in a new product or employs at least one new reactant.[107]

The Court found that, despite expert evidence of the greater bioavailablility of the beta crystal form of Imatinib Mesylate over the free base form, "we are completely unable to see how Imatinib Mesylate can be said to be a new product, having come into being through an 'invention' that has a feature that involves technical advance over the existing knowledge and that would make the invention not obvious to a person skilled in the art."[108]

The Court further noted that Imatinib Mesylate was already a known substance as per the terms of Section 3(d), having been disclosed in a prior patent application. Citing the dangers of evergreening pharmaceuticals, the high cost of proprietary formulas of Glivec, and the intent of the statute, the Court found that both statutory interpretation and public policy required denying Novartis's patent.[109] In articulating its justification for defining invention in a more restrictive manner than the United States did, the Court pointed to Section 5, Article 27 of the TRIPS Agreement, which states: "Members may exclude from patentability inventions, the prevention within their territory of the commercial exploitation of which is necessary to protect ordre public or morality, including to protect human, animal or plant life or health."[110] India claimed to be acting in complete accordance with TRIPS, on behalf of those in the Global South who needed access to affordable pharmaceuticals.

The U.S. government and industry response to the outcome in *Novartis* was predictably negative. Both the divisiveness of Novartis and the type-casting of India as anti-democratic villain were evident in Novartis's post-litigation discursive strategy. Ranjit Shahani, managing director of Novartis India, lamented, "How can we be expected to come up with new cures if the developing world runs roughshod over our IP rights?"[111] Novartis's objections are as expected, given its position as a global corporation whose profits depend on selling patented medications as well as the perception that intellectual property rights can and will be enforced universally. However, the manner in which the company pitted and is pitting itself against India—indeed, against most of the developing world—is notable, especially as a rhetorical maneuver rooted in while civility.

While there are certainly critics who contend that India simply circumvented TRIPS in a bad faith, there are compelling arguments that the country, particularly given the "crowbar diplomacy"[112] that the United States used to secure international intellectual property agreements, simply outmaneuvered its Western allies. Accepting the latter argument, however, would require recognizing India as equal to the U.S., not a state engaged in incomplete mimicry. Even in the least generous reading of Section 3(d), however, does not justify the campaign of systematic racial derogation and dehumanization through which the U.S. has approached a fundamentally economic question. Yogesh Pai, among others, encourages international recognition of patent diversity. This is one alternative to narratives of patent insolence.[113]

As it stands, Novartis, in addition to making an important volley in the conversation about global access to patented pharmaceuticals, has become part of a larger rhetorical strategy of casting India as a noncompliant player in international intellectual property politics, a nation that aids and abets counterfeiting through its role as past and present pharmacy to the world. U.S. government rhetorics, namely the 2013 Special 301 Report, which responds to India's refusal to extend patent protection to Glivec, echo Novartis's complaints. The report condescendingly chastises India for its non-democratic practices, stating: "The criteria, rationale, and operation of such [patent evaluation] measures are often nontransparent or not fully disclosed to patients or to pharmaceutical and medical device companies seeking to market their products. USTR encourages trading partners to provide appropriate mechanisms for transparency, procedural and due process protections, and opportunities for public engagement in the context of their relevant health care systems."[114] Yet such claims are often disingenuous moving targets that fail to recognize the power politics of (neo)colonialism and reflect profound racial and economic resentment at losing at one's own game.[115]

Despite *Novartis*'s sound legal basis and profound hypocrisy on issues of transparency, due process, and health care, the United States continues to criticize the outcome of *Novartis* as antidemocratic and unfair. One recent article on Indo-U.S. relations stated, "There are compelling reasons the leaders of the world's largest democracies would find common cause"[116] while another stated, "The [Indian government's new intellectual property] policy emerges as the Indian government faces sustained pressure over patent protection."[117] Patent protection remains a wedge used to portray India as a failed international team player.

As the Special 301 Report demonstrates, in the context of intellectual property, India, despite its democratic governance, is treated as a nation that is inherently suspect for its failure to enforce patent law not in a manner consistent with law but in a manner consistent with U.S. practices. The Indian government's refusal to adopt U.S. intellectual property standards, which are distinguishable from those articulated under TRIPS, is treated as India's refusal to embrace the nation's democratic potential and its place among the world's superpowers. India's insolence is patent both in the sense that it is flagrant and obvious and in the context of the law of inventorship. Not only is the nation refusing to ally itself with the United States, it is also refusing the (neo)colonial manner in which America leads and the rest of the (uncivilized and barbaric) world follows. As such, American critiques of Indian patent policy reflect age-old anti-Black and anti-Brown racial scripts that originate in particularly white and European understandings of the polis, civility, and their workings. The issue here is less about the *validity* of India's argument in *Novartis* than the racial and (neo)colonial double standards around who is permitted to access the power to define in the context of patent law.

The Obama administration's simultaneous narratives of India as ally/ obstacle speak to the relative positionality of the two countries as well as their relative—and racialized—places in international relations. More than a familiar international relations strategy of power politics, these rhetorics rely on an underlying narrative of racialized progress, in which an imagined Western trajectory of steady development operates as invisible ideal. India, because it refuses to comply with American pharmaceutical patent aims, becomes a target of rhetorics of irresponsibility. The détente in previously rocky US-India relations cannot smooth over continuing epistemological differences in patent law.

Novartis, then, is not simply a contravention of international intellectual property norms; it is also a battle in a larger war over the postcolonial realities of A2K and the authority to decide whose versions of democracy and capitalism will prevail. As Mari Korepela points out, "Westerners 'imagine' India according to their own needs."[118] *Novartis* and its attendant commentary reflect a need to paint India as a colonial upstart that, though democratic, refuses to abide by American patent norms. In the American imagination, those are norms upon which the national identity of the United States as a country of inventors and innovators poised to achieve the American Dream is built. The narrative of inventorship distinguishes Americans from Other—here Asian—nations. Lawrence Liang explains that Asian infringement is consistently pitted against American standards of innovativeness; the only way the former can be found momentarily not suspicious is by complying with the latter. Asians lack true imagination. They are forever infringers in Jefferson's framing and spectral threats to American economic stability in Valenti's imaginings. Indeed, even if India complies with TRIPS, it will be through U.S.-led paternalism, attached to the narrative that India could not become a world power without American role modeling and pressure.[119]

The Obama administration and the USTR set up a race neutral argument for changing Indian laws that appeals to the purported rules of realpolitik and neoliberal democratic governance. In doing so, the USTR erases the internal and external relationalities and realities that militate for flexible inventorship norms. Precarious bodies, both in India and across the developing world, are rendered secondary to the aims of a distinctly American democracy and the market. India's refusal to embrace U.S. patent standards is coded as unfairness, stubbornness, shortsightedness, and impertinence, as evidenced by references to "IPR regime deficiencies"[120] and the systematic inequalities they produce.

These terms, however, are not neutral ones. They are steeped in the language of coloniality, as theorists like Franz Fanon and Albert Memmi demonstrate. More importantly, they echo racial scripts that not only mark Indians as lazy and opportunistic thieves but also position them as being outside of the regime of human progress. Despite the flexibility of TRIPS patent provisions for nations like India, the U.S. claims sole authority to interpret the relationships between the exercise of that flexibility and the practical workings of neoliberal democracy. This is not to say that India is exclusively a nation of integrity and moral virtue, as it is certainly embroiled in its own complicated nationalist politics.

However, Indian commitment to producing pharmaceuticals, even if overbroad, is a politically prudent and socially responsible approach to intellectual property that originates less from insolence and more from a desire to compete, as the United States did, on a racially and economically level playing field. Even if, as some critics claim, India is too stable and too strong to justify exercising developing nation exceptions to TRIPS, such as the one for compulsory licenses, that decision ought to rest not with former colonies but with the formerly colonized as remedy for histories of domination.

Appeals to Western democratic norms as more fair than those in the developing world reproduce discourses of progress and civilization that elevate the United States over other nations. Not only are such claims ethnocentric in ways that recall racial scripts about patents as a space for human progress, but they also erase the contextual development processes that nations such as India have devised in order to modernize in a postcolonial world. Narrativized within a distinctly American economic framing imagined to promote global progress and innovation, the trope of India as patently insolent centers the nation's difference through implicit reference to its postcoloniality. The discourses of a former colony transformed into a democratic superpower through the embrace of norms of political participation, transparency, and free markets suggest outsider status, not equality in a world of international affairs. In the context of WTO and TRIPS, India's externally imposed "rogue" persona highlights its intransigent refusal to be fully "civilized" in a system of racial capitalism.

Despite passing a new, TRIPS-compliant intellectual property policy in May 2016, India reaffirmed the right to continue to use the developing country loopholes in TRIPS, including Section 3(d) of the Indian Patents Act, compulsory licensing, and parallel importation in protecting the most impoverished nations in the developing world. The United States, however, continues to criticize India for its embrace of such a regulation, flagging the nation's unfair indigenous innovation policies. In the section detailing India's place on the Priority Watch List, the USTR lauds bilateral negotiations that strengthen Indian intellectual property protection and promote entrepreneurial innovation but goes on to note that "[t]he pharmaceutical industry in particular faces a host of challenges related to IPR."[121] U.S. objections focus on, among other issues, Section 3(d), the provision at issue in *Novartis*. India and its generic drug continue to be characterized in Special 301 Reports, statements from pharmaceutical companies, and news reports as arising from the active refusal to comply with accepted democratic norms, shameless exploitation of Western innovators, as well as unfair circumvention of the WTO and TRIPS systems.

Doing so, of course, privileges an economic narrative of postracial creatorship over that of postcolonial modernization, rendering invisible the structural inequalities from which India emerged and their continuing implications. As Partha Chatterjee puts it:

> [T]he problem is that democracy, perhaps in most of the present-day world, cannot be brought into being, or even fought for, in the image of Western democracy as it exists today . . . it is not as though . . . the normative model itself remains universally valid and should be regarded as a beacon for aspiring democrats around the world. Rather, the problem is that the experience of postcolonial democracy is showing every day that those norms themselves must be rethought."[122]

The (mis)representation of India as insolent democracy fuels the racialization of infringement as well as the portrayal of Indians as intellectual property anti-citizens who are also the purported ringleaders of an intellectual property non-compliant and unruly developing world.[122]

With this narrative of patent insolence comes a narrative of incomplete personhood, one that posits Indians as being incapable of full (white) humanity because they refuse the purportedly objective economic frameworks and they cannot take part in directing human progress. Frames of patent insolence, in the words of Shampa Biswas, raise "anxieties about instability and disorder"[123] that are justified through "a series of racialized constructions of Third World people."[124] Raka Shome contends that racial hierarchy originates with "the organizing and commanding gaze of white eyes surveying 'other worlds' that seem to be permanently characterized by chaos and disorder."[125]

These tropes are the ones that must be dismantled in order to move be-yond intellectual property Orientalism and into decolonial pharmaceutical governance. The consistent attempts by the United States to force India into compliance with an imagined set of neoliberal and democratic patent norms move us away from, rather than toward, such a goal. In this sense, the hyperracial infringer is, as Philip puts it, "a transactional nexus rather than an essence."[126] The figure is more than a "heroic proletarian."[127] Rather, it is a collectively imagined, racialized character in a larger story about cre-atorship, neoliberalism, and (neo)colonialism. Through *Novartis*, human progress is marked, again, as the domain of the (white) Global North, at the expense of the (Black and brown) Global South. The Indian govern-ment, as I show in chapter 4, resists that narrative.

ZOMBIES, COPYRIGHT COLONIALITY, AND TRUE IMAGINATION

A final example in the context of copyright law, *Golan*, constructs the pos-tracial creator by claiming to protect the "foreign creator" while actually endorsing the exceptionalism of American content owners. The commit-ment of the United States to "copyright restoration"[128] in the case—i.e., the recognition of copyright in previously unprotected foreign works—ini-tially reads as a move away from American exceptionalism and toward the enforcement of international law.

However, the rhetoric through which the move is made, as well as the effect of the decision, serves to entrench American economic prosperity and Euro-American creation schemas in a manner that privileges white and West-ern "foreignness." True imagination, a standard that is never explicitly in-voked in the case but is nonetheless encompassed by the Supreme Court's discussion of "creative process," operates as implied justification for protect-ing domestic content owners, and their profits, in international markets. Ac-cordingly, *Golan* is a case that effectually protects American content owners as exceptional in their creative capacities, even as it wraps its justifications in the language of protection of foreign authorship. As such, *Golan* is an im-plicit affirmation of creativity—and the choice of when to extend it—as the domain of whiteness, not of those people of color being newly protected.

Golan evaluated the constitutionality of a statute finally implementing a portion of the Berne Convention, Section 514 of the Uruguay Round Agreements Act (URAA), which the United States had long refused to enact. The functional effect of Section 514 is to grant copyright protection to some foreign creative works that were not previously protected by copyright law in the United States, thereby removing them from the public domain. As the majority in *Golan* explained, "As a consequence of the barriers to U.S. copyright protection prior to §514's enactment, foreign works 'restored' to protection by the measure had entered the public domain in this country."[129] A group of composers, musicians, and libraries that relied upon works in the public domain, which would receive copyright protection anew under Section 514, sued.[130] A majority of the Supreme Court, after *Golan* had amassed a lengthy procedural history,[131] affirmed the right of Congress to change the contents of the public domain at any time, even post facto, because the public has no property right or First Amendment rights in the public domain.[132]

One reading of *Golan* is that it was a victory for "foreign authors" who had long remained unprotected under U.S. implementation of international copyright law and a blow to the Romantic author because of its refusal to protect the litany of European works, particularly of composers, cited in the opinion. However, a competing and complementary reading of *Golan*, through the lens of interest convergence,[133] reveals its complex relationship to the vested interests of content owners, embeddedness within systems of racial capitalism, and inconsistency with real or imagined possibilities of colorblind creatorship. Such a reading, which this chapter advances, focuses on how the majority protects copyright protection for content owners in the guise of extending copyright equality to diverse foreign creators. American conceptions of property rights worked as a vehicle for extending U.S. economic interests in (neo)colonial ways, with historic parallels to the negotiation of *Stowe* and its attendant domestic nationalism and protectionism.

First, (neo)colonial exploitation wrapped in the language of development economics operated as a tool for asserting fairness, justice, and race neutrality, despite the simultaneous invocation of racial scripts about the exceptional qualities of Western creatorship and true imagination. The underlying and continuing (neo)coloniality of the Berne Convention was rendered invisible through *Golan*'s simultaneous centering/decentering of Romantic authorship, the public domain, and the First Amendment. Second, through its categorical discussion of foreign authorship and the public domain, *Golan* homogenized the world in a manner that erased the inequalities wrought by global intellectual property regimes and (neo)colonialism itself. Congressional management of the public domain, as *Eldred v. Ashcroft* (2003) demonstrates, often reduces A2K in the United States and abroad, through both longer copyright terms and the retroactive protection of copyrighted works.

Derrick Bell writes of interest convergence:

> The interests of Blacks in achieving racial equality will be accommodated only when it converges with the interests of whites . . . the Fourteenth Amendment . . . will not authorize a judicial remedy providing effective racial equality for Blacks where the remedy sought threatens the superior societal status of middle- and upper-class whites."[134]

He continues: "Racial justice—or its appearance—may, from time to time, be counted among the interests deemed important by the courts and by society's policymakers."[135] Interest convergence describes the process through which racial justice gains unfold, specifically when the perceived interests of whites intersect with the interests of people of color. In Bell's narrative, interest convergence is fleeting and reversible. White interests are not only constantly changing but also intertwined with the desire to retain (intellectual) property and power, not commit to radical equality. Bell's conception of interest convergence, though applied here only to the context of *Brown v. Board of Education* (1954), applies generally to questions of racial justice in the United States.

More specifically, Bell provides a useful frame for describing and explaining the outcome of particular political and judicial negotiations. A corollary to Bell's theory of interest convergence is that in some instances the appearance of racial equality may belie the reality of continued racial injustice. *Golan*, far from being the outcome of commitment to racial equality, is a moment of interest convergence in which American national interests in the tradition of European intellectual property norms coincide with those of *some* foreign authors while simultaneously working against larger struggles for A2K in the Global South. The motives of the case, however, are not altruistic. They are fundamentally self-interested.

The development economics of the level playing field

By seemingly universally protecting foreign works that were previously unprotected, *Golan* purportedly contributes to a mirage of postracial creatorship in which the playing field is level and any foreign author can receive U.S.

copyright protection. However, the case largely ignores and even endorses myriad structural barriers to equality—including the coloniality of the Berne Convention and technical requirements for foreign authors—which operate as obstacles to global copyright justice. This is unsurprising given that the majority highlights *Golan*'s importance in protecting the "creative process" of authors and content owners *stateside*, specifically:

> Full compliance with Berne, Congress had reason to believe, would expand the foreign markets available to US authors and invigorate protection against piracy of US works abroad . . . thereby benefiting copyright intensive industries stateside and inducing greater investment in the creative process . . . Congress determined that exemplary adherence to Berne would serve the objectives of the Copyright Clause. We have no warrant to reject the rational judgment Congress made.[136]

This passage in the majority opinion provides rhetorical cover for marking American creativity as more protectable and more valuable than that of other nations. The argument is a coded extension of the racialized standard of true imagination, which implicitly overvalues white creatorship and undervalues people of color creatorship. *Golan* does not create a level playing field. Rather, it disadvantages the developing world in favor of protecting American true imagination. This is not to suggest that all foreign authors are white, only that *Golan* fails to create parity for foreign developing nations as compared to foreign developed nations. Golan's mechanism for enforcement, an international treaty that advances a (neo)colonial and propertizing agenda, is also problematic.

Reading into the Berne Convention suggests that it does not protect the developing world but rather makes the United States colonially whole. Through *Golan*, America reasserts its position as a global hegemon, in a way that suggests nostalgic attachment to a (neo)colonial model of governance in which the developing world agrees to the disciplinary demands of the developed world. Wendy Brown contends that such power struggle is inevitable because liberalism itself is constrained by a problem of Nietzschean *ressentiment* in which: "A strong commitment to freedom vitiates the fulfillment of the equality promise."[137] In the face of India's historic refusals to abide by American and international intellectual property standards and broader pushback on copyright, patent, and trademark issues in the Global South, such nostalgia makes good economic as well as racial sense. *Golan* weaves a story about a benevolent (white) nation invested in moral uprightness that abides by treaties meant to protect foreign creators even when they recklessly refuse to abide by U.S. law.

The Berne Convention is an international copyright agreement that went into effect in 1886. Passed after Victor Hugo witnessed the rampant infringement of his work in the United States, it requires member states to extend copyright protection to creators whose works are copyrighted in other member states for at least the life of the author plus fifty years, without any registration formalities, unless the work is no longer protected in the home country.[138] The United States, which was a net importer of copyright until after World War II,[139] refused to accede to the Berne Convention until 1988, when its own content production interests coincided with strong intellectual property protections.[140]

Even after its accession, in a have-it-both-ways move, the United States declined to pass implementing legislation related to those parts of the agreement that were not compulsory.[141] The nation finally implemented Article 18 of the Berne Convention, which it had previously sidestepped, after the 1994 URAA in the form of Section 514. Article 18, which fully implements the treaty, applies to "works which at the moment of its coming into force, have not yet fallen into the public domain in the country of origin through the expiry of the term of protection."[142]

Lateef Mtima posits that intellectual property conflicts between the developed world and the developing world are manifestations of "IP imperialism," an orientation to intellectual property in which Western nations, particularly the United States, built intellectual property policies based on their own national self-interests, often at the expense of developing nations.[143] Such IP imperialism is evident in the context of the Berne Convention, which was created by largely colonial powers and often implemented through colonial mandate not democracy.

An early critic of the treaty's copyright regime, Ruth Okediji, writes: "Intellectual property law was not merely an incidental part of the colonial legal apparatus, but a central technique in the commercial superiority sought by European powers in their interactions with each other in regions beyond Europe."[144] As demonstrated in the previous chapter, even when implemented via manufactured consent, intellectual property law in the 1950s and 1960s was frequently a tool of (neo)colonial economic and information control in an increasingly postcolonial world. Such structural disparities were not remedied in later years.

Peter Drahos expounds upon this colonial history of the Berne Convention, observing:

> The Berne system was run to suit the interests of copyright exporters . . . By the time many countries shed their colonial status, they were confronted by a Berne system that was run by an Old World club of former colonial powers to suit their economic interests . . . When eleven Sub-Saharan states joined Berne they were "so totally dependent economically and culturally upon France (and Belgium) and so inexperienced in copyright matters that their adherence was, in effect, politically dictated by the 'mother country' during the aftermath of reaching independence."[145]

Read within this context, consistent with the prior case study, the "lax" intellectual property policies of developing nations, which began to emerge after independence and continue today, were often attempts to balance the legal regimes that had been crafted to extract knowledge from former colonies for the benefit of the Western world.

Reading *Golan* within the colonial history of the Berne Convention and international copyright law suggests that the outcome of the case was a moment of interest convergence that, while it granted some foreign creators additional copyright protections, undermined A2K in the developing world. The passage of Section 514 was not a magnanimous move in favor of developing nations; it was a concession that the United States made as part of the larger context of its TRIPS negotiations. In other words, Section 514 was a necessary move for the larger cause of intellectual property harmonization, a process that was costly for the Global South. *Golan* is not a radical statement against (neo)colonialism but rather an implicit endorsement of American conceptions of true imagination at the expense of the rest of the world.[146] Any benefit that Section 514 extends to foreign creators in the developing world that might not have previously been able to protect their creative works is largely offset by the URAA's larger structural and cultural inequalities.[147]

Despite the entry into force of the Universal Copyright Convention in 1952 and the addition of an appendix to the Berne Convention in 1971, both of which allow developing nations to avail themselves of certain limited exceptions in abiding by international copyright standards, international copyright law continues to force developing countries to adhere to strict copyright standards that frequently run counter to their cultural and economic needs with respect to A2K. Even now, nations such India continue to contest the tendency of international copyright law to privilege Western creatorship and frames of intellectual property protection over those of developing countries. The balance of copyright protection and A2K in academic literature was the issue at the heart of the controversial Delhi University copyright case. The impoverishment of the public domain and the difficulty in accessing copyrighted works led the Indian Supreme Court to rule in 2016 that photocopying academic materials for a course pack is fair use.[148] This ruling came at the end of years of conflict over the Berne Convention's (neo)coloniality.[149]

Golan and criticisms of it largely elide questions of inequality, focusing respectively on the benefits of Section 514 for foreign authors and the harms done to those who used the copyrights that fell out of the public domain, predominantly musicians and composers.[150] The case begins with an explicit framing of characters that introduces the reader to the case through identification with a particular set of individuals. Justice Ginsberg's majority opinion focuses on the foreign creator, who has been deprived of the "perfect US implementation of Berne."[151] She goes on to weave a tale in which the United States failed to show foreign nations the kind of reciprocal protection that Berne promised them, even categorically excluding them from protection until 1891.[152] The U.S. stance of "minimalist protection"[153] sets up the case's narrative conflict and, according to Ginsberg, created discord with Mexico, Turkey, Egypt, and Austria, among others.[154]

In this narrative, ratification of Section 514 is a heroic moment, in which the United States redeems itself after a long history of refusing to grant copyright protection to foreign authors. The outcome of the case "places foreign works on an equal footing with their US counterparts."[155] When the Court finally addresses critiques of the decision, in Part IB of the opinion, it is again with resort to the narrative of protecting foreign authors. Ginsberg writes: "In aligning the United States with other nations bound by the Berne Convention, and thereby according equitable treatment to once disfavored foreign authors, Congress can hardly be charged with a design to move stealthily toward a regime of perpetual copyrights."[156] The remainder of the opinion provides historical examples in which Congress has altered the scope of copyright protection, and then notes the potential for copyright extensions to enrich the public domain through *dissemination* of copyrighted materials instead of *creation* of copyrighted materials.[157] In articulating Berne's relationship to dissemination, Ginsberg confirms that the Court is not primarily invested in the protection of foreign creators.[158]

The Supreme Court's ultimate justification for the outcome in *Golan* is stateside benefit, not foreign protection. These lines reveal that the case is consistent with past (neo)colonial justifications for the extension of Berne, which are invested not in the local knowledge of the developing world but the smooth operation of transnational systems of racial capitalism. Indeed, the reasoning in *Golan* underscores that it is a case about particularly American management of the public domain, focused on both protecting US intellectual properties against infringement and reinforcing national understandings of piracy. Moreover, Ginsburg's First Amendment discussion advances an understanding of property rights that reinforces racial scripts and racial feelings about who produces valuable intellectual properties. With respect to the First Amendment, the majority reminds the reader: "Anyone has free access to the public domain, but no one, after the copyright term has expired, acquires ownership rights in the once protected works."[159]

The opinion then goes on to name the creators of the works in which Petitioners have allegedly lost property rights: Sergei Prokofiev, Leonard Bernstein, and Aaron Copland. Ginsberg cites examples from earlier cases as well: Charles Dickens, James Fenimore Cooper, and Nathaniel Hawthorne. Each is European or American.[160] In the opinion, contested musical and orphaned works at issue are whitewashed, reduced to individuals who fit within the narrative of Romantic authorship. The interest convergence of *Golan* is evident in its examples.

Reromancing the public domain

Golan, a case about the public domain, imagines the concept in a (neo)colonial and economically unequal manner. Neither the majority's nor the dissent's understanding of the public domain considers the disparities of A2K, which countless scholars and activists have discussed. Instead, they erase the inequalities that permeate always already racially and colonially structured understandings of the public domain in favor of a tale of U.S. heroism.[161] By holding that *no one* has a property right to material in the public domain, the majority functionally proclaims the right of the United States to govern the scope, domestically and internationally, of publicly accessible and ownable knowledge.[162] In claiming control over the public domain, the majority doubly colonizes knowledge through its language, invoking the names of white authors whose works it refuses to protect but nonetheless chooses to highlight in endorsing a larger system of U.S.-led international copyright.

Notably, Justice Ginsberg closes by again invoking the framing of protecting foreign creators, holding that "full participation" in the Berne Convention is necessary for "securing greater protection for US authors abroad, and remedying unequal treatment of foreign authors."[163] Unfortunately, the latter was never at the forefront of the majority's examples or analysis, even as it declared U.S. Congressional sovereign authority over the public domain. Instead, it unproblematically embraced the public domain, with its attendant racial and colonial baggage, and placed the U.S. decision to comply with the URAA at its center.

The dissent criticized the majority's refusal to protect those who rely on works that are not copyrighted or copyrightable. However, it did not do so by pointing to the disparities of the public domain. By virtue of citing copyright precedent, it reinforced the narrative of copyright as a reward for individual creativity, writing "encouragement of individual effort by personal gain is the best way to advance public welfare through the talents of authors and inventors."[164] True imagination remains a requirement of copyright protection, and the racial scripts that attach to it have not been deconstructed. As the dissent shows, this rationale echoes back to 1892, perhaps earlier.[165] Section 514, the dissent notes, primarily covers foreign works produced between 1923 and 1989, in places such as Japan, Latin America, Australia, South Korea, Turkey, and Egypt. But here, the dissent did not appeal to the need to protect these foreign nations, particularly the non-white ones, or the richness of their cultural productions.[166]

The dissent pivoted in the other direction, noting that the public domain is more important than the works of authorship from those nations. Accordingly, it participates in that which Madhavi Sunder and Anupam Chander call the "romance of the public domain"[167] by highlighting the need to preserve access to these works for consumers, ostensibly in the United States.[168] Orphaned works took center stage for the dissent, which noted that "Mexican folk music" and "Jewish folk music"[169] would no longer be accessible under

Section 514. While there is no doubt that public access to such works is important and valuable, the dissent couched their protection in terms of cultural cost and infringement issues, not as matters of the inherent value of people of color creatorship. Sunder, in her monograph, contends that the latter valuations are necessary, because intellectual property justice requires moving away from a law and economics frame to one of "human flourishing."[170]

Specifically, the dissent's discussion focuses on the "high administrative costs" of restored copyrights and the temptation for some "to 'steal' or 'pirate' works rather than do without."[171] According to the dissent, "piracy often begets piracy, breeding the destructive habit of taking copyrighted works without paying for them, even where payment is possible."[172] Such language fuels the moral panic of piracy: because it cannot make a claim about piracy of orphaned works, the dissent weaves a contagion narrative in which infringement fuels infringement. Yet it does so while sidestepping the complex racial dynamics of orphaned works.[173] Despite a weak critique of Section 514's overinvestment in granting a monopoly to existing creators and the occasional reference to works of authors of color—e.g., "Motown"[174]—the dissent embraces a concept that has repeatedly failed the Global South, without concern for racial justice. As organizations such as Creative Commons and the Electronic Frontier Foundation (EFF) voiced outrage and anxiety about the possible collapse of the public domain, using loaded terms like "zombie copyrights" and "free speech" to make their case, they also obscured the complicated politics and histories of copyright in the developing world, specifically through their rhetorical strategies of reromancing the public domain and racial feelings around the perceived "taking" of items in it.

While organizations such as the EFF consistently seek to broaden access to the public domain in an attempt to make it more equitable, they often do so through a colorblind framework. An EFF press release showcases even progressive copyright's investment in the public domain from a position of invisible whiteness:

> Works affected by this law include Sergei Prokofiev's Peter and the Wolf, music by Stravinski, paintings by Picasso and drawings by M.C. Escher, and writings by George Orwell and J.R.R. Tolkien—material that has been used and performed countless times. Now that the works are back under copyright protection, use of the works may require paying *hefty license fees.* The lead petitioner, Lawrence Golan,

is a music professor and conductor who challenged the law because it made performance of many works *prohibitively expensive* for many small orchestras. By taking the works out of the public domain, Congress had *impinged on his vested free speech* interest in using those works. On behalf of the American Library Association and other public interest groups, EFF filed an amicus brief in support, explaining that an unstable public domain creates *dangerous uncertainty* about copyright policy, posing a *significant threat* to libraries, digital repositories, and others that promote access to knowledge.[175]

The press release calls on the audience to be incensed, fearful, sad, and vigilant at the shrinking public domain, as "hefty" and "prohibitively expensive" license fees and "dangerous uncertainty" threaten access to knowledge.

While the EFF is right in articulating a need to protect the public domain, its framing of the case replicates the colorblindness of the concept. As in majority opinion, the EFF's examples of creative works—those by Sergei Prokofiev, Igor Stravinski, M.C. Escher, George Orwell, and J.R.R. Tolkien—are invoked for their threat to the Western, particularly American, public domain. The EFF then turns to free speech, a deeply racially complicated civil liberty, in order to underscore the outrage the public ought to feel at *Golan*. The face of that lost free speech is Lawrence Golan, the obviously talented music director who nonetheless presents as white. The EFF concludes: "Word to the Internet: this is why we must never again let copyright maximalists ram through legislation under cover of night. Word to Congress: we're staying vigilant, if you won't protect the public domain, we will."[176]

The EFF's call to protect the public domain is couched in familiar racial and economic threat rhetoric. "Dangerous uncertainty" and "significant threat" are race neutral terms on their face. Yet read within the narrative of white authorial protection that *Golan* advances, they are racialized. In fact, the term "zombie" itself, as numerous scholars have demonstrated, marks racial anxieties as well as the collapse of contemporary systems of neoliberal capitalism.[177] Protecting the public domain as per *Golan* means that Americans must vigilantly police the boundaries and contents of the U.S. and European public domains, so that others can have access to (white) canonical works of creatorship. The racial scripts and racial feelings associated with the move are crafted around (white) Romantic authorship, not people of color creatorship or a desire for racial justice.

The language of *Golan* echoes the intellectual property libertarianism of *Tam*. That is not to say that people of color cannot ever hold equal property rights, only that their rights are still subordinated to the links between whiteness and property, which not only afford less protection to non-white foreign creators than white ones but also recognize the former as more fully human than the latter. It is also not to say that the public domain is an irredeemable concept, only that the raced dynamics of A2K must be an explicit and central focus of intellectual property activists and courts. Without active management, creatorship and the public domain are organized through racial scripts and racial feelings with long and established histories.

Both sides of the conversation in *Golan* miss important questions of racial justice and development economics, fighting instead for principles that protect whiteness as property. They participate in the construction of people of color foreign authors as less than complete persons, whose work does not drive intellectual property policy or economics. The racial scripts around reromanticizing the public domain come from a white libertarian, market-based philosophy of ownership that is unmoored from the social justice concerns of the developing world and firmly rooted in Romantic creatorship.

CHAPTER FOUR

RESCRIPTING CREATORSHIP, RESCRIPTING CITIZENSHIP

Your thousand years are up;
Now you got to share the land;
Section One, the Fourteenth Amendment says:
No state shall deprive any person
Of life, liberty, or property
Without due process of law.
—PRINCE, "Dear Mr. Man"

WHILE THE MAJORITY OF THIS BOOK has focused on the ways that racial scripts about the incapacity of people of color to create have prevented racial equality in creatorship, resistance to such narratives is abundant and productive. The racialization of creatorship/infringement is neither an uncontested development nor one-way enterprise. Rather, as with the meanings of intellectual properties themselves, people of color push back against categories of race, citizenship, national identity, and personhood by performatively critiquing and remaking Euro-American ways of knowing, valuing, and owning. The practices of individuals, groups, and institutions change the way that public culture thinks about creatorship/infringement and, as per the title of this book, the very color of creatorship.

Debora Halbert writes, "The work of asserting alternatives to intellectual property is an interpretive battle. Intellectual property remains in the process of definition—there is a struggle to define the scope and meaning of the law."[1] Examining the particularities of the struggle is useful for both imagining new ways of relating to intellectual property law and mapping new strategies for activism. The question of how resistance to intellectual property's racial scripts works is an important one—and one upon which Lawrence Liang's concept of porous legalities sheds light.[2] Liang contends that (racial) capitalism produces residual humans—including migrants, squatters, and pirates—whose labor value is rendered obsolete. In doing so, it creates space for seepages, "the action of many currents of fluid material leaching on to a stable structure, entering and spreading through it by way of pores."[3]

Seepages, by way of performative acts of resistance, erode (racial) capitalism and "gradually disaggregate its solidity."[4] The romantic academic ideal of willful resistance from a conscious understanding of politics and culture is far less common than unintentional transgressions that produce anti-racist and anti-colonial effects. The latter acts, when extrapolated across urban spaces, "[create] new conditions in which structures become fragile and are rendered difficult to sustain."[5]

Liang uses the concept of seepages to theorize the porousness of law, which he argues are created through "a profound distrust of the usual normative myths of the rule of law, such as rights, equality, access to justice, etc."[6] The concept of porous legalities provides a frame for understanding how alternative intellectual property worldmaking can take root in quotidian performances.[7] Transgressive performances that create new "performative repertoires,"[8] in Isaac West's words, have the potential to exploit the gaps in the law in ways that produce new legalities.

If (racial) capitalism and law can be eroded through the iterative performances of individuals, groups, and institutions, so too can the categories of race, national identity, and citizenship through which capitalism and law operate. This chapter focuses on understanding how creators of color have contested racial scripts around creatorship/infringement, mobilizing them in ways that undermine the racial scripts and racial feelings that animate them. Often, as Liang suggests, these strategies involve remaking capitalism or using it against itself and reorganizing public feelings in racially radical configurations.

The three examples discussed here explore how individuals and institutions perform race and ownership so as to exploit the legal porosity in intellectual property law, race, citizenship, national identity, and personhood. The first example considers how Prince Rogers Nelson, when he changed his name to the Love Symbol, eroded the music industry's monopoly over the identities and (intellectual) property rights of artists of color. While Prince explicitly confronted histories of anti-Blackness in the United States in many ways, the symbolic significance of his name change and his fight to own the copyright to his songs continues to influence generations of artists across racial identities, notably by encouraging them to own their music.

The second example considers how, in response to yoga piracy, Indians and Indian Americans produced new vernacular that aided in decolonizing intellectual property law. The Indian government, which took up this new vernacular, built the Traditional Knowledge Digital Library (TKDL), a digital infrastructure that literally intervenes in the workings of intellectual property law by preventing the ownership of traditional knowledge through online databasing.

The final example considers how Marshawn Lynch's ownership of (intellectual) property rights in his body, specifically through the Beastmode® clothing line, erodes racial capitalism and the racial scripts around Black bestiality. Lynch functionally confronts traditional modes of claiming whiteness as property while making space for Blackness as property. Each of these cases demonstrates the existence of liminal spaces from which to remake racial scripts and racial feelings about creatorship/infringement through language and practice. Moreover, they do so from different levels of discursive engagement, including the individual, the institutional, the national, and the international.

Halbert writes: "What the language of intellectual property masks is the global political economy of highly concentrated copyright and patent ownership where corporations, not people, are the beneficiaries of the system . . . resistance to the expanding idea of property is developing as people began to reimagine cultural work outside the language of property and rights."[9] Prince, Indians and Indian Americans, the Indian government, and Lynch engage in projects that fit that description, by remaking the disciplinary functions of (intellectual) property through individual and institutional discourses and performances. Such resistive endeavors, whether intentional or not, represent productive moments of hegemonic contestation through which law's race-based suppositions can shift, particularly as they are taken up more broadly in public cultural spaces. They also serve as important lightning rods for rewriting racial scripts and moving racial feelings, in part by making them legible and intentional instead of invisible and libidinal.

These examples also set the stage for thinking about how lawyers and activists who are invested in anti-racist and anti-colonial struggles might orient themselves toward intellectual property law. Thinking about and remaking legislation, legal doctrine, and precedent are certainly important. But so too is performative resistance within the confines of existing practice. Being conscious of the racial histories of intellectual property law and committing to progressive racial ethics can drive considerable change in the direction of equity while law is being reimagined.

PURPLE PERFORMANCES OF TRUE IMAGINATION

Prince intervened, quite vocally, in the racially disciplinary politics of intellectual properties, rejecting the ghettoization of Black art and confronting the inequalities that underlie information ownership. One primary way in which he did so was by changing his name to the Love Symbol. While not without conceptual complications, that decision represented the culmination of a career that had pushed against the racial scripts around Blackness, true imagination, and human progress. Until the end of his life, when he famously commented at the Grammys, "Albums still matter, like books and Black lives, albums still matter," Prince created space for valuing Black creatorship and Black personhood.[10]

Prince's performative engagements with race and slavery, in particular, asserted that Black artists were not only capable of true imagination and human progress but also deserving of equality of citizenship and personhood. Prince sought to imagine and represent new visions of Black ownership and Black masculinity that would ensure that intellectual property law could not be used against Black artists and inventors in exploitative ways. The continuing impact of his strategies for Black self-determination and Black capitalism among artists of color demonstrates not only the movability of racial scripts and racial feelings but also the porosity of intellectual property law and the extent to which people of color can remake it.

When Prince Rogers Nelson died unexpectedly at his estate in Chanhassen, Minnesota, digital natives who were used to turning to YouTube, Spotify, or Pandora for their music were at a loss. The superstar, who had become increasingly protective of his intellectual property rights once he gained the copyright to his music and witnessed the payout structures of streaming services, had virtually eliminated his music and videos from the Internet. In the weeks after his death, fans who wanted to hear Prince's music had no choice but to tune in to the radio, particularly Minnesota Public Radio's *The Current*, pay for a subscription to Jay-Z's Tidal, buy a song or an album, or pour out into the streets for impromptu dance parties.[11]

During this time, he managed to break a litany of *Billboard* records, including becoming the first artist since 1963 to have five albums in the

Billboard Top 10.[12] In life, Prince, who received the "Raspberry Beret Lifetime Aggrievement Award for extraordinary abuses of the takedown process in the name of silencing speech" from the Electronic Frontier Foundation, was maligned for his maximalist intellectual property practices.[13] But in death, the wisdom and radicalness of Prince's (intellectual) property management strategies became clear, particularly with respect to Blackness, citizenship, personhood, and economic equity.

Prince was neither the first nor the only artist to raise objections about the politics of race and intellectual property or race and inequitable contractual arrangements. However, he was exceptional in the consistency and explicitness with which he advocated for his principles around creatorship and Blackness over the four decades of his career. Intellectual property and ownership, bodily and otherwise, were of the utmost concern to Prince. Touré, in the biography *I Would Die 4 U*, tells the story of Prince's rage at being faced with a racist, sexist audience throwing things at him and the band while they were opening for the Rolling Stones in 1981. Prince reportedly said, "This is absurd. Why should we put up with that? Those are people who've grown up with the Rolling Stones and just look at my image in a multiracial group and me in my high heels and thigh-hi stockings, bikini briefs, no shirt and a trench coat. This is enraging them and I'm not going to put up with it."[14]

Flash forward to one of his last concerts, the Rally 4 Peace in Baltimore, Maryland, after the horrific death of Freddie Carlos Gray while in police custody. Prince announced to the audience: "The piece I'm talking about is p-i-e-c-e. The next time I come through Baltimore, I want to stay in a hotel owned by one of *you*. I want to leave the airport in a car service created and owned by one of *you*."[15] The inequity of ownership—and the interrelationships among property rights, intellectual property, bodies, and Black life and Black death—were always central concerns of Prince's in his life and career. His early and late performances stood against the racial scripts and racial feelings, particularly about capacity for creatorship, citizenship, and personhood, that were at the root of anti-Blackness.

Prince began and ended his career as a racial visionary and a perfectionist who required the utmost creative control over his work. In the late 1970s, before the release of his first album, he and Owen Husney, his manager at the time, negotiated a contract with Warner Bros. that guaranteed the eighteen-year-old artist unprecedented authority over writing and producing his music.[16] Even in his early career, Prince confronted the constraints of creatorship that Black artists faced. In addition to securing complete creative control over his work, he refused to be included in the Warner Bros. R&B catalog like other Black artists of his generation. Instead, Husney writes,

> [t]he first thing Prince told me after we got signed [was] he did not want to be pigeonholed as an R&B artist. Very few people had broken down the barriers before him . . . If you were a Black artist in those days, you had to go to your Black base, which is Black radio stations, and you had to build it and then crossover.[17]

Such barriers to creatorship had their roots in slavery and segregation as well as in the devaluation of Black art and Black creativity, all of which Prince took up in the course of his career. His refusal to begin with his Black base, something that not even Michael Jackson had avoided, having recorded with Barry Gordy at Motown Records, was an act of claiming equality of creatorship and ownership. Prince pushed back against the notion that Black art was inferior or deviant as compared to white art, that it lacked true imagination, as Jefferson had attempted to claim so many years before.

With Warner Bros., which adopted a primarily non-interventionist management strategy, Prince's career exploded. In the 1980s, he turned out hits album after album, among them *Dirty Mind, Controversy, 1999*, and in 1984, the stratospherically popular *Purple Rain*. Despite public relations debacles such as his much-publicized refusal to participate in the historic recording of "We Are the World" for USA for Africa, which according to former bandmate Wendy Melvoin was because "he felt like the song for *We Are the World* was horrible. And he didn't want to be around 'all those muthaf——as,'"[18] Prince's career soared. He continued churning out hits, ending the decade in 1989 with his immensely popular eleventh studio album, the sound track for *Batman*. It seemed that he could do no wrong.

But then, in 1994, his relationship with Warner Bros. ran aground as the pop musician became (in)famously known for his very public dispute with his record label. In a now legendary but then bizarre story, Prince changed his name to the unpronounceable Love Symbol. The Artist Formerly Known as Prince (the Artist, for short), as he was then often known, spent years appearing with the word "SLAVE" written on his face. Though his behavior was an unmitigated public relations disaster that prompted wild media speculation about the reason for the name change, neither

Prince nor Warner Bros. relented. The latter released Prince's greatest hits in 1996 over his objections, while the former attempted to break with his record label.

It was not until 2000, after Prince's contract with Warner Bros. expired, that he changed his name back, an event that he celebrated with a three-disc album titled *Emancipation*.[19] In the 1990s, much of the world had been mystified by his name change. The seven years that he spent referring to himself as a glyph resulted in several commercially unsuccessful albums and threatened to diminish his fan base. However, they also point to the power of symbolic resistance in critiquing American conceptions of intellectual property and ownership, particularly where race and its links to creatorship and labor are at issue.

Prince's decision to change his name to the Love Symbol refused the copyright and contract politics that had, over hundreds of years, reflected and condoned treating Black people as less than, particularly with respect to intellectual labor. By putting himself into conversation with American histories of slavery and racial capitalism, Prince pointed to the manner in which Warner Bros.' ownership of his labor recalled labor conditions that Africans and African Americans had faced centuries before.[20] Though Prince himself was not anti-capitalist, his labor politics called for practices that respected the health and well-being of humans and community, in ways that broke with ideals of formal equality and colorblindness.[21] Moreover, they presaged and critiqued new forms of wage slavery intertwined with the rise of corporate dominance, which while still racialized, were distinct from the chattel slavery that African Americans faced. Kevin Bales describes how American chattel slavery was transformed such that "[n]o longer viewed as property, people today are merely seen as disposable inputs into production."[22]

Prince's act of changing his name to the Love Symbol, though not effective as a legal escape clause from his contract, created productive space for him to contest the racially inflected disciplinary practices of record companies and courts in a manner that, in Cynthia Fuchs's words, "revises the idea of binarism, gestures toward what we (whoever 'we' might be) haven't yet imagined, because we can't say it."[23] The embrace of the Love Symbol both references and refuses slave-naming practices that attempted to deprive Black subjects of their personhood and identities. The Love Symbol is a new identity, one that claims the value of Black creatorship and Black entrepreneurship. It is also an unspeakable critique of the present, a marker of the past, and a representation of possible futures all at once. Through Black creativity and Black entrepreneurialism narratives, Prince rhetorically and performatively establishes the (intellectual) property value of his music by criticizing those who would exploit his labor by reproducing that music without paying for it, producing unoriginal covers of his songs, and inviting contractual arrangements in which he would not own his own work. In doing so, Prince imagines a radically Black capitalism.

The name change was significant, in part, because of the importance of naming as an emancipatory practice generally and in African American history specifically. In one of the most memorable scenes in Alex Haley's hit miniseries *Roots*, Omoro Kinte holds his child up to the sky and bestows upon him a name. After Kunta Kinte is forcibly taken to America, he's brutally beaten until he repeats that his name is Toby. "When the master gives you something, you take it," the man whipping him says. These scenes exemplify not only the significance of naming in African and African American cultures but also the psychological depersonalization that was central to slavery in the United States.

Terrence Epperson argues that the process of imposing names, usually of English origin, on enslaved persons was both a disciplinary and a proprietary practice, one through which slave masters intervened in every part of the social lives of their slaves. He also notes that slavery, like other forms of domination, required a dual process of marking as different and incorporating as the same:

> [A] slave master's imposition of English names upon recently arrived Africans would seem to represent an incorporative aspect of domination, yet even here is a subtle marking of difference and inferiority. The lack of family names and the overwhelming use of familial diminutives simultaneously connoted attitudes of condescension, parental authority, and intimacy.[24]

Naming became a practice doubly intertwined with citizenship—and the denial thereof. First, refusing the right of enslaved persons to engage in traditional African ritual naming practices denied them the autonomy granted to citizens. Second, the imposition of slave names and concomitant propertization of enslaved persons marked them as nonpersons incapable of participating in the politics of the nation. Neither were African Americans granted the rights as autonomous subjects to keep their given names or allowed to keep others from depriving them of their rights as persons.

Naming is accordingly significant not only as a cultural practice but also as a political one. It is "a powerful strategy of rhetorical colonialism,"[25] one through which groups can be assimilated, disciplined, and excluded from political participation. In the context of slavery, the lack of control over naming operated as a disciplinary mechanism, one through which domination and erasure were effected. While naming may not be everything, given the scope of the violence that slavery imposed on African Americans, it is certainly something. Reading Prince through the example of *Roots* provides an opportunity to think about the significance of the power to name and the resistive potential of performing authority over naming. Along with the right to name come not only the ability to perform culture but also the right to control one's legibility in a cultural context.

As he tells the story, through his no longer consensual contractual obligations to Warner Bros., the moniker "Prince" became a corporate entity, a brand delinked from the person who signed the contracts that the record company offered. Prince's anger and frustration with Warner Bros.' authority over his record production was a related but distinct problem from that of the company's authority over his given name, the "Prince" part of "Prince Rogers Nelson." On its face, one might read Prince's name change as proof that the musician had no control over his name or naming rights. After all, his corporate "master" had commodified the identity that his parents had given him, taking away his rights to control his name and erasing him as Prince the person in favor of transforming him into Prince the brand.

However, such a reading would miss the incompleteness of Warner Bros.' control over Prince the brand and the counterinterpellative force of Prince's decision to change his name to the Love Symbol. When the master gives Prince something, he doesn't take it. Fuchs continues, arguing that "[a]s Prince appropriates the power of designation, he's hardly a figure of oppression . . . Instead, he circulates, performative, unstable, queered, dismantling the conventional links between possibilities for naming and structures of oppression."[26] Fuchs's analysis points to the radical resistiveness of the instability and ambiguity of the Love Symbol, a cultural text with play and nuance in the joints, and multiple historical and future referents. Here, Prince appears to both understand and intervene in the complex relation of desire and fantasy that Homi Bhabha, much like Eric

Lott, argues underpins and fuels racial and colonial domination.[27] When read alongside and in relation to histories of slavery, civil rights, and Black creatorship, Prince's name change is even more nuanced and complicated than it initially appears. The renaming becomes a simultaneous act of unmaking and remaking Black creativity and Black personhood.

While slave names were forcibly and violently imposed on Black persons, the interpellative force of "Prince" the brand is bidirectional. Even as Warner Bros. owns the name, Prince's performance of that name constructs the company itself, which signed a young artist who consistently contested social constructions of race and gender and refused to be "owned." Though Warner Bros. denies Prince's authority to control his contract, it does so under a brand whose biggest artist is a transgressive, gender-bending, sexually provocative, Black creator, one who marks his identity with a simultaneously empty and overdetermined signifier. Prince's very persona highlights the practical impossibility of Warner Bros.' attempts to exercise creative control over him, even as it demanded that he produce records at its pace. When compared to the indelible structural imprint that Prince left on the music industry by refusing to be an R&B artist, Warner Bros.' claims to his labor are dubious at best. Prince not only exceeds the categories of true imagination and human progress but redefines them.

Prince's decision to change his name to the Love Symbol and write "SLAVE" on his face was anything but a subtle performative intervention and critique of Warner Bros.' attempt to own him, i.e., racial capitalism itself. In a 1995 press release, Prince commented on the labor position of having to produce particular types of records for Warner Bros. and do so on the company's timetable: "It seemed reminiscent of much that had been experienced by other African-Americans over [the] last couple of hundred years. They had turned me into a slave and I wanted no more of it."[28] He declared in 1996: "People think I'm a crazy fool for writing 'slave' on my face, but if I can't do what I want to do, what am I? When you stop a man from dreaming, he becomes a slave. That's where I was. I don't own Prince's music. If you don't own your masters, your master owns you."[29]

Prince's name change, in addition to being a mechanism for trying to get out of his contract with Warner Bros., served as commentary on his alienation from self. According to Prince, Prince Rogers Nelson the person had been deprived of his fundamental rights to liberty and property, instead being forced into the brutal servitude that LeVar Burton portrayed in

Roots. "Prince" is transformed from an artist—The Artist Formerly Known as Prince—into a laborer beholden to corporate masters without concern for creative autonomy. However, where Prince's story breaks with that of chattel slaves is that he chooses his renaming, embracing the Love Symbol as his new identity, his critique of Warner Bros.' exploitative labor practices, and his resistance to America's history of owning and naming slaves.

In *Excitable Speech*, Judith Butler argues:

> One is not simply fixed by the name that one is called . . . [T]he name holds out another possibility as well: by being called a name, one is also, paradoxically, given a certain possibility for social existence, initiated into a temporal life of language that exceeds the prior purposes that animate that call . . . injurious address may appear to fix or paralyze the one it hails, but it may also produce an unexpected and enabling response.[30]

Here, Butler is speaking of reclaiming hateful names, by performing their meaning in ways that resist their interpellative force and mitigate their injuriousness. Her argument points us to how Prince remade previously injurious speech, using it to push back against the violent practices of slave naming and create a new identity. Slave naming, an act intended to strip individuals of their subjectivity, still left considerable space for interpellative resistance. Kunta Kinte's repetition of his name is a performative refusal to accept the erasure of his identity.

The use of symbols such as the Love Symbol and the *X* in Malcolm X's name can be read as another form of interpellative resistance, which symbolically marks the practices of erasure that were inflicted upon slaves. Signifiers of aporia and overdetermination, the Love Symbol and the letter *X* simultaneously call forth memories of the trauma inflicted on Black persons and claim the agency to embrace new names. Read in this context, much like Malcolm Little's refusal of his slave name, Prince's refusal to be known as "Nell's son" and his rejection of his corporate brand name suggest that the Love Symbol is a sign of performative reclamation of Blackness.

Prince's use of the Love Symbol, however, is not without its theoretical complications. Warner Bros.' move to force Prince to adhere to the terms of his contract—i.e., produce four records per year—was hardly identical to the chattel slavery that African Americans faced in the United States. As a result, part of the backlash about his position was about the analogy that he was attempting to make. Nonetheless, Prince's claim that Warner Bros. placed him in an unequal bargaining position, the kind of situation that historically resulted in the contractual exploitation of Black musicians in the United States and the erasure of their artistic contributions, is an important one. As Kevin J. Greene puts it, "Time after time, foundational artists who developed ragtime, blues, and jazz found their copyrights divested and through inequitable contracts, their earnings pilfered."[31] While Prince is speaking to a different type of slavery than the chattel slavery upon which the nation was built, both resulted in tremendous anguish and loss for African American communities. Even as the comparison falls short, marking the denial of Black creatorship is both significant in its implications and transgressive in its meaning, particularly in the larger context of anti-Black education and contractual practices in the United States.

Due to the institutionalization of slavery and the advent of Jim Crow, African American illiteracy rates remained high into the 1920s. In 1870, 80 percent of the Black population was illiterate, as compared to 20 percent of the overall population. In 1900, 44 percent of the Black population was illiterate. Not until 1979 did rates of literacy of the Black population and the overall population become comparable.[32] Because they lacked the ability to read and write post-Emancipation, many African Americans signed documents with an X, a legally valid indication of their assent to the terms being placed in front of them.[33]

While this practice was not unique to African Americans, it disproportionately affected those people of color who were denied access to the right to read. The signatory X is a practical legal mark, which operates in a profoundly different manner than Malcolm's X or Prince's glyph. The latter mark absences, erasures, memories, possibilities, reclamations, reconstitutions, and impossibilities, while the former is an executory symbol enmeshed with practices of white supremacy. The diametric opposition of these marks is notable. Malcolm X and the Artist Formerly Known as Prince implicitly and explicitly comment on the signatory X, using their symbolic reinventions not as signifiers of their *illiteracy* but as markers of their *hyperliteracy*.

Prince's glyph exceeds the abstraction of Malcolm's *X*, as it marks a language of gender and sexuality that he has refined in public space over time. In the ultimate act of sublime inventional prowess, Prince's glyph was indecipherable to Warner Bros., whose literacy did not match that of their star artist. If anything, Warner Bros., which spent considerable time and money remarketing one of their top artists, in part by sending floppy disks with the glyph to media outlets and figuring out how to refer to the Artist, played the fool.[34] Specifically, Prince remade himself against their wishes, his recreation of his identity prevailed in the end. As Kimberly Benston observes, "The *unnaming* of the immediate past . . . was reinforced by the insertion of a mysterious initial, a symbol of the long, unacknowledged selfhood that had survived and transcended slavery . . . *naming*, a staging of self in relation to a specific context of revolutionary affirmation."[35]

Coupled with Prince's affect as a gender-bending, funk, popular artist whose musical performances exuded joy, the name change asked the audience to reconsider the racial scripts and racial feelings around creatorship. Prince offered palliative and critique of the racial and economic anxieties that plagued Reagan's America. The calls for social justice in his music, in songs such as "Ronnie Talk to Russia" and "Sign o' the Times," pointed to the need not only to rework the nation's racial scripts and racial feelings but also to build community and connection, often through religion and sexuality, instead of alienation and hate.

Prince's vindication with respect to his name came in 2000, at the expiration of his contract with Warner Bros. He began the celebration concert at Paisley Park, where he played songs from his three-disc album, *Emancipation*, with the booming voice of Dr. Martin Luther King Jr. preaching "Free at last, free at last, thank God Almighty we are free at last."[36] The symbolic significance of titling the album *Emancipation* and celebrating with Dr. King's victorious words is self-evident: Prince had finally reclaimed his contractual autonomy and his original identity. Still, the moment when Prince became a free agent was not the last in his personal emancipation or his work of emancipating creatorship.

In 2014, Prince, who decided to stop streaming his music with services like iTunes and Spotify, declared, "The Internet is completely over."[37] The precipitating event for Prince's decision to stop streaming his work was his renegotiation of his contract with Warner Bros., in which he gained ownership of his master records. Dissatisfied with the streaming models, dismayed by record company profiteering, and invested in controlling his own image, Prince chose to stream with Jay-Z's Tidal, which remained the only streaming site on which substantial portions of his catalog were available for a long period after his death.[38] Rarely one to make business decisions quietly, Prince famously declared: "I don't see why I should give my new music to iTunes or anyone else. They won't pay me in advance for it and then they get angry when they can't have it."[39]

On Twitter, he offered more insight into this thinking: "Essentially, streaming has offered labels the ability to pay themselves twice while reducing what is owed to artists."[40] Prince's militant protection of his copyright, which mirrored the language of those who zealously advocated for copyright maximalism, was a problematic but arguably necessary intervention into racial inequality. Critiques such as those that came from the EFF, while technically true, remained situated in a race neutral public domain, without engagement with the racial remaking of creatorship/infringement and (intellectual) property that Prince was undertaking. Emancipating his music, and creating space for other musicians to do the same, was one of his most ideologically and economically impactful achievements.

Once he was able to say, "I am my own master," Prince redoubled his efforts to combat intellectual property infringement. Take, for instance, a statement that he made several years ago in an interview with the *Guardian*: "We made money [online] before piracy was real crazy. Nobody's making money now except phone companies, Apple and Google. I'm supposed to go to the White House to talk about copyright protection. It's like the gold rush out there. Or a carjacking. There's no boundaries."[41] Though he never returned to the fan-targeted zealousness of earlier years, he remained staunchly anti-infringement.

Prince's statements, of course, are intertwined with larger rhetorics of hyperracial infringement. Though he directs his ire at corporations instead of demonizing particular groups, he nonetheless creates space for reading "piracy" as a floating signifier, that can be filled with new racial meaning. He also invites a narrative of racial uplift, one that focuses on the need for access to the American Dream. His call for property ownership in the Rally 4 Peace is emblematic of this focus, as is his lyric: "Your thousand years are up; now you got to share the land." Notably, however, the Rally 4 Peace was the antithesis of the postracial creatorship that President Obama espoused in his economic platforms.

Tied to Black Lives Matter and a long-standing investment in social justice, Prince crafts a narrative of Black entrepreneurship, that celebrates the work of Black creators, values Black lives, and calls for Black ownership. The narrative, which is taken up in shows like *Empire*, *The Get Down*, and even partially *Luke Cage*,[42] Black artists are equal citizens and full persons who have a right to access the American Dream. While each of those shows represents Black capitalism in a different way, they all engage with a larger, productive dialogue about the need for and the contours of such a practice.

Prince is unequivocal: Black creators have the right to demand ownership of their works as well as that which James Baldwin argues in his famous speech, "The American Dream and the American Negro," was never granted to them. Despite potential complications and contradictions in his strategy of advocating for maximalist intellectual property rights, there is considerable generative capacity in the world that Prince weaves. He makes space for understanding Black artists as autonomous knowledge producers and (intellectual) property owners. The model for musical ownership that he created, one embraced by musicians from Chaka Khan to Janelle Monae, resonates even today.[43]

YOGIC NARRATIVES OF HUMAN PROGRESS

As the example of Prince demonstrates, individual resistance can have considerable structural implications, particularly in terms of the organization of institutions. The Yoga Wars, the ongoing struggle between India and the developed world over the ownership, commodification, and practice of yoga, have for the last two decades been important sites for individual and institutional (neo)colonialism and decolonization of intellectual property rights. The use of the word "piracy" to describe other than the Global South's use of knowledge produced and protected in the Global North confronts the racial scripts that undergird contemporary understandings of (white) expertise and the "discovery" and "purification" of knowledge. Read vis-à-vis the examples provided here, flipping the script of piracy refuses to accept the notion that people of color can produce only the raw materials that are then transformed into "real" and protectable knowledge.[44]

One of the first printed uses of the term "yoga piracy," in a 2005 *Washington Times* article, set the terms of the conflict between India and the West over yoga. Vinod K. Gupta, head of an Indian task force on traditional knowledge and intellectual property, used "yoga piracy" to describe the predominantly Western propertization and monetization of yoga, both of which he criticized. "These [asanas] were developed in India long ago and no one can claim them as their own," he argued.[45] In this context, alternative narratives of intellectual property infringement emerged as discursive mechanisms for inverting the racial scripts of Asians as lazy thieves who lack the intellectual capacity or work ethic to produce knowledge. The struggle to claim yoga manifested in two primary ways: the use of decolonial vernacular by lay Indians and Indian Americans to remake the very language of intellectual property and the creation of a digital database by the Indian government to protect against intellectual property rights claims in knowledge that had already been "discovered" by people of color. These two resistive moves served to decolonize and dewesternize global patent law by making Euro-American biases visible and producing new institutional structures and knowledge categories that confront them.

Reframing ownership through decolonial vernacular

Vernacular rhetoric—"the rhetoric of the oppressed"[46]—offers a counterpoint to the rhetoric of those in power, including around discourses of race and citizenship. Significantly, even though it is the non-expert language of everyday life, vernacular rhetoric can trickle up to influence the language of those in power, changing the very words, concepts, and institutional structures that experts use to describe and manage areas of public concern.[47] For instance, vernacular discourses around yoga piracy helped Indian publics to inadvertently produce new approaches to categorizing and managing traditional knowledge, thus pushing against rhetorics of expertise that justified excluding people of color from circuits of knowledge production and knowledge ownership.[48]

In effect, rhetorics of piratical theft of yoga produced new, radical, and accessible vocabularies for discussing intellectual properties that, in turn, influenced government policymakers. The use of language in the context of yoga piracy operated as "decolonial vernacular," a practice through which quotidian uses of legal language contest (neo)colonial regimes of knowledge production.[49] One of the earliest and most famous rhetorical rescriptings of the infringement narrative came in Vandana Shiva's articulation of the term "biopiracy" in 1997. Shiva, who was responding to the rise of bioprospecting, sought to critique "the exploitation of biological resources and traditional knowledge without the consent of local people or authorities, and without adequate compensation."[50] She observes: "At the heart of Columbus' 'discovery' was the treatment of piracy as the natural right of colonizer . . . Patents are still the means to protect this piracy of the wealth of non-Western peoples as a right of Western powers."[51] The language of biopiracy, then, rewrites the racial scripts that Western discourses of infringement perpetuate, specifically pushing back against the relations of power that they implicate. Taking a cue from Shiva's successful struggles to invalidate patents for turmeric and neem oil in wound healing, those who contested yoga piracy named the problematic power relations through which yoga is consistently colonized and commodified.

The embrace of the concept of yoga piracy, as with biopiracy, was not an end point in the conversation about the protection of traditional knowledge. Rather, it was one outcome of a sustained engagement with questions related to the ownership of yogic knowledge, often in ways that functionally "remixed" the legal definitions in and around intellectual property and cultural property.[52] In a *Times of India* article titled "Kissa Copyright Ka," a series of individuals engage with the concept of commodification of traditional knowledge.[53] Supreme Court of India lawyer Ashok Jain said:

> Copyright is an ambiguous area. Anyone can claim copyright if he has developed or innovated a skill. For instance, Bikram Choudhury can be granted copyright on the 26 asanas developed by him. However, nobody can get a copyright on the "original" yoga asanas as written in ancient texts . . . Legally, Indians don't have a monopoly over ragas, curry or yogurt . . . we've only inherited them. The government of India should be filing for cultural patents . . . The cost of filing patents is nothing. We must take action now.[54]

Here Jain uses his legal knowledge and scientific know-how to complicate understandings of intellectual properties and cultural properties, reading copyright as an "ambiguous area" that can be stretched to protect cultural knowledge. He translates his argument into accessible vernacular, framing the claims made by artists in the rest of the article. Notably, he moves fluidly between discussing copyrights and patents, intellectual property, and cultural property. In a maneuver that illustrates the possibilities of vernacular rhetoric, he argues that asanas ought to be protected by copyright law, an area of law intended to protect creative works. He then argues that India should file for "cultural patents."

While interesting, these arguments, like Prince's name change, are not legally cognizable. Though at the time, a series of asanas might have been considered a chorographic work, administrative clarifications and legal rulings in both the United States and India have concluded otherwise. Moreover, because yoga is not an invention under the terms of the U.S. Patent Act, it cannot be the subject of a "yoga patent." Nonetheless, the term "cultural patent,"[55] which both the blog *SpicyIP* and my own research confirm is repeated in Indian popular discourse as a result of "doctrinal confusion"[56] about different types of intellectual property law, creates rhetorical space for imagining the mechanics of the protective public domain that Laura Foster theorizes.[57]

Combining international law's notions of cultural property—as, for instance, articulated by UNESCO—and patent law's notion of patentable inventions, the term "cultural property" is a productive malapropism, a confusion of related but different legal concepts in the context of intellectual property that helps to envision the legal intersections through which cultural property can be protected. The subsequent embrace of the term "yoga piracy" and the creation of the TKDL are arguably an outgrowth of such productive malapropisms, which gave rise to linguistic play as rhetorical resistance within intellectual property discourses.

Such forms of discursive reworking facilitate definitional evolutions that Halbert argues are necessary for resisting intellectual property maximalism.[58] They also confront rhetorical maneuvers that Endres contends use strategic definitions to render minoritarian groups invisible in legal contexts.[59] Misuse prompts redefinition, which implicitly critiques the (neo)colonial processes through which intellectual property law emerged. The eventual affirmation in both the United States and India of the non-copyrightability and non-patentability of yoga, as well as the embrace of the TKDL as prior art, demonstrates the efficacy of such definitional challenges. Legal misuse, then, is not simply dismissible; it is discursively reconstitutive, a productive rhetorical move that aids in eroding the power of racial capitalism and propertization.

"Kissa Copyright Ka" is rife with similar examples of decolonizing vernacular through misuse. Sudha Gopalakrishnan, director of the National Mission for Manuscripts, for instance, calls for World Heritage protection by UNESCO. Jiggs Kalra, identified as "gourmet guru," begins by citing the patenting of neem oil and turmeric and ends with this legally invalid claim: "I patent all my recipes after someone tried to steal them three years ago. But what if tomorrow, some foreigner files a patent for dhokla, tandoori chicken, mutton vindaloo?"[60] Sonal Mansingh, a dancer, analogously notes: "Even Bach and Beethoven never filed for patents. It's the Americans who are trying to patent everything as their intellectual property."[61] Ritu Kumar, a fashion designer, notes that she files for copyrights on her garments and that "[w]hile in Europe and the US, [her] distributors file for patents in their respective countries."[62]

Once again, the doctrinal confusion that Shamnad Basheer identifies juxtaposes legally sound and legally unsound arguments about intellectual property and cultural property law. The value of such a move is not that it makes a legally actionable claim for protecting yogic knowledge. Rather, as Gerard Hauser points out, vernacular rhetorics actively create publics and script the conceptual possibilities within which policy is made.[63]

The rhetorical significance of intellectual property's productive malapropisms is that they discursively invent and circulate the radical possibility of delinking decolonially in public culture. In Walter Mignolo's words, they help us "build knowledge and arguments that supercede the hegemony of Western knowledge."[64] Decolonizing vernacular around biopiracy gave rise to notions of cultural patents and yoga piracy, both of which were precursors to important structural interventions in intellectual property rights, such as the TKDL. This predecession is no coincidence: decolonizing vernacular in the Yoga Wars shifted the rhetorical culture around intellectual property and traditional knowledge in ways that facilitated new ways of thinking, including about the racial scripts around creatorship.

The term "yoga patent" is not a one-time misspeak. The concept pervades Indian and US newspaper articles on yoga piracy over the years. "India to Protest Grant of Yoga Patents by US," proclaimed the front page of a 2007 issue of the *Times of India*. "Patenting Yoga: The Issue Steams Up" reads the headline of an article in the *Delhi Times*. "Yoga Wars: India Blocks Patents on Poses!" announces *NPR*. "India Patents 1,300 Yoga Moves," declared *RIA Novosti*. Yoga patent language became internationally pervasive in the 2000s, intermingled with discussions of copyright, cultural property, and intangible cultural heritage. Though these claims are frustrating to intellectual property experts, they created a rhetorical culture in which the TKDL could easily emerge.

The TKDL, created in 2001 and spearheaded by Gupta, made information about multiple types of traditional knowledge available to the public as prior art, a designation that would block patent claims. The database also includes a catalog of asanas, which though now publicly available, do not effectively block any intellectual property claims.[65] Nonetheless, structurally speaking, conversations about yoga patents are both descriptive and proscriptive in the context of the TKDL. They describe the motives for creating a catalog of yoga poses and information that blocks patents on traditional knowledge. They also help make visible the overarching desires among Indian publics, notably to find a legally enforceable way to make yoga patents a reality and thereby protect traditional knowledge. Such productive malapropisms actively refuse the citizen scripts of the hyperracial infringer. The concept of yoga piracy implicitly declares the existence of a creator who exists outside the intellectual property imagined by modernity/coloniality, who made their work in a manner that demands legal and cultural protection. It also asserts the existence of a counternarrative of history, one that makes space for the "illicit" development models of the Global South and creates the possibility of a framework in which infringement is not a moral evil or threat to the developing world but rather the natural consequence of neoliberal racial capitalism.

The notion of yoga piracy does not negate the possibility of Indian intellectual property infringement or undo perceptions of India's noncompliance with TRIPS. It does, however, refute narratives of bad global citizenship in "discursive spaces for the disempowered"[66] and broader public spaces. Liang points out that one of the ways that US anti-piracy operates is through a redemptive narrative of citizenship in which Americans are posited as hardworking innovators, ideal citizens against which Asian infringers are compared.[67] Yet terms such as "yoga piracy" and "yoga patents" suggest not only that Indians make and circulate knowledge that is so valuable as to be worth stealing but also that they are entitled to protection for that information. Indians are not simply lawless intellectual property anti-citizens; they are makers of "pirate politics"[68] who are perhaps unwittingly part of, playing on Martin Fredriksson's phrase "the multitude of resistance."[69] Indian publics participate in the project of combating racialized understandings of infringers, particularly by creating conceptual space for so-called illicit economies and building rhetorical and cultural schema for Asians to be read as creators, citizens, and persons. The TKDL serves such a purpose by making Indian knowledge known to the world as prior art.[70]

Reframing the public domain through dewesternizing restructuring

The language of piracy was effective in the Yoga Wars because it created a shorthand for referring to the racially bankrupt (intellectual) property relations through which Westerners exploited yoga. It also created productive space for protecting yoga. As yoga legend B. K. S. Iyengar stated, "Yoga is an essential part of our heritage, and India has to protect it."[71] Conceptually, yoga piracy identifies Indian yogis as bona fide creators—not anti-innovative pirates—whose work can and should be protected from commodification that takes it out of the public sphere. The term "yoga piracy" critiques the underlying knowledge production regimes and racial scripts through which Western legal systems create ownership rights in traditional knowledge.

Instead of ceding control to intellectual property advocates to identify and racialize agents of infringement, the phrase rejects that framework, positing that Westerners are the thieves who are taking information from the developing world through contrived doctrines around expertise. This view not only claims space for Asian creativity but identifies infringement as a practice of asserting whiteness as (intellectual) property while taking traditional knowledge from racial and colonial Others.

The name also raises the important question of how the public domain is structured and what information in it is available for ownership. In terms of the framework that Foster uses to discuss the exploitation of traditional knowledge, the conceptual inversion of yoga piracy makes a significant distinction between the protective public domain, which accounts for the histories of traditional knowledge, and the open public domain, which is functionally the status quo.[72] As per her analysis, the public domain ought not be understood, as Boyle posits,[73] as the set of information that is unprotected by intellectual property.

Like Madhavi Sunder and Anupam Chander, Foster contends that "a protective public domain challenges articulations of indigenous peoples' knowledge as raw material and recognizes the inventiveness and dynamism of indigenous traditional knowledge."[74] Yoga piracy not only suggests the need for a protective public domain; it claims ownership rights in that protective public domain, labeling those who unjustly capitalize on yogic knowledge as thieves in their own right. The TKDL furthers practices of imagining and constructing the protective public domain.

The TKDL is an example of "dewesternizing restructuring,"[75] which centers Indian knowledge production and remakes global patent regimes, including their attendant categories of citizenship, while nonetheless giving in to a larger system of neoliberalism and its attendant violence. The TKDL, a project of the Indian government, catalogs information about yoga and traditional medicine that would otherwise be essentially inaccessible to most audiences. The digital database is managed by the

Council of Scientific and Industrial Research and the Department of AYUSH, short for Ayurveda, Yoga and Naturopathy, Unani, Siddha, and Homeopathy.[76]

According to the creator of the TKDL, Dr. V. B. Gupta, the digital database was intended to catalog traditional knowledge that demonstrates the existence of prior art barring issuance of a patent accessible to the public. The TKDL was also intended to prevent widespread ownership of yoga, because "someone claiming yoga as their own and charging franchise money is not acceptable."[77] Gupta's claim, while an interesting one, is not legally cognizable because yoga sequences are not copyrightable or patentable in the United States or India. Nonetheless, it is a means of rhetorically claiming space of creatorship and ownership, in a manner that refuses the framework of the public domain constructed by Western intellectual property law. In essence, Gupta claims India's attribution rights in yoga and proclaims that the practice is in the public domain and therefore cannot be privately owned.

In this respect, the TKDL is arguably emblematic not of practices of decolonization but those of dewesternization. Mignolo characterizes dewesternization as being a complement and contrast to decolonization, as a struggle "in the spheres of the control of authority and of the economy."[78] Whereas decolonization is primarily focused on the creation of new ways of thinking and "epistemic delinking,"[79] dewesternization is predominantly concerned with the authority of former colonies in international relations and political economy, as a means of sometimes leading to epistemic delinking. As such, dewesternization overlaps with decoloniality as a project but is not coextensive with it. As Mignolo puts it: "Dewesternization is not a geographic but a political concept and refers to all States (corporate states) which are consolidating their economies without following the dictates of the US, the EU, the IMF or the World Bank. Delinking here does not mean delinking from 'a type of economy' but from the instructions of the World Bank, the IMF and related institutions."[80] Dewesternization is an important move in terms of reclaiming authority in international politics and political economy, but it does not necessarily confront central problems of racial capitalism, national identity, citizenship, or personhood. Instead, it theorizes and creates economic structures that are parallel and intersecting with those of the West. Though potentially anti-colonial in effect, dewesternizing strategies can, by virtue of their interconnections with and investments in systems of global capitalism, mean business as usual in ways that reinscribe the problems of modernity/coloniality.

The TKDL uses a "novel classification system" called the Traditional Knowledge Resource Classification (TKRC) to create new categories for Indian knowledge, which are then integrated into the International Patent Classification (IPC).[81] The IPC, a standardized classification system for patented inventions, is one of the most widely used patent categorization systems in the world. Created in 1971 through the Strasbourg Agreement, the IPC "divides technology into eight sections with approximately 70,000 subdivisions. Classification is indispensable for the retrieval of patent documents in the search for 'prior art.' Such retrieval is needed by patent-issuing authorities, potential inventors, research and development units and others concerned with the application or development of technology."[82]

As originally conceived, the IPC focused on knowledge that was legible to Western patent authorities, not traditional knowledge. The TKRC changes this by creating 207 subgroups of traditional knowledge, much of it particularly Indian, under the categories of Ayurveda, Unani, Siddha, and yoga, which are integrated into the IPC and used to search for prior art.[83] In doing so, the TKRC intervenes in patent law, making space for traditional knowledge in a dewesternizing maneuver that renders traditional knowledge legible within Western inventive regimes. This upending of Western categories of knowledge restructures intellectual property law and also rejects (neo)colonial knowledge classification, which is rooted in colonial practice.

Further, it creates space for Indians to be read as creators and as equals in humanity and citizenship to their Western counterparts. As Chidi Oguamanam argues, moves to structurally and ideologically center traditional knowledge are important because they confront patent law's Euro-American biases, including those against traditional medicine, which serves 80 percent of the world. He writes, "The most critical factor is the colonial hierarchy of culture and power in which non-Western peoples and their knowledge systems are treated with disdain and derogation."[84] The TKRC represents one step in managing that hierarchy, by reconstructing the apparatuses of intellectual property law via Indian orders of knowing.

More specifically, the TKRC engages in "epistemic delinking,"[85] a process that involves disentangling institutions and ideologies from the constraints and boundaries of modernity and coloniality, including the racial scripts upon which they are built. The TKRC epistemically delinks patent law from the categories of invention that govern international legal practice and, accordingly, broadens the boundaries of citizenship and personhood. Dewesternizing restructuring, like Prince's pushback against the music industry, remakes the very systems of governance through which norms of creatorship are produced in patent law. While both decolonizing vernacular and dewesternizing restructuring have the effect of confronting the racial scripts of citizenship in the intellectual property context, they also remake the structures through which those racial scripts are produced.

Dewesternization, like decolonization, effects the epistemic delinking that Anibal Quijano and Mignolo contend is vital to creating a world emptied of colonialism, not simply a postcolonial world. The Indian government, through both the TKDL and the TKRC, asserts the authority to classify, a practice that has been largely carried out and governed via modern/colonial logics. Seizing such power is important not only to decolonization but to building new and multiversal futures. I turn to these issues in greater depth in the next chapter.

The process of building the TKDL and the TKRC, then, confronts the racial scripts of Asians as unimaginative, devious, and lazy by claiming knowledge that the West, particularly Americans, has already deemed valuable in a way that also seizes authority to build knowledge structures themselves. Confronting racial scripts in this way is a structural mechanism for rehistoricizing Asian creativity and Asian productivity as well as asserting full rights to citizenship and personhood through lenses other than those of modernity/coloniality.

The USPTO, the European Patent Office (EPO), and many others have embraced the TKDL and the related TKRC. The offices actively use the TKRC and the information cataloged in the TKDL to evaluate whether prior art barring the issuance of a patent exists.[86] While one reading of the incorporation of the TKRC into the IPC is that traditional knowledge is being integrated into Western models of intellectual property, an arguably more compelling view is that though individuals in the developing world remain skeptical of intellectual property law's ability to protect their interests, they are reconstructing its very foundations in a manner that actively resists its multiple colonizing tendencies.[87]

To this reading, Oguamanam argues, indigenous peoples have a complicated and disaffected relationship with intellectual property law.[88] Attempts to remake intellectual property law are always accompanied by trepidation about integration and appropriation. Moreover, modifications to the IPC such as the TKRC challenge core binaries of Western patent law and Western medicine and the attendant racial scripts upon which they are founded. Ogumanam writes:

> However, developments in the traditional medicine and genetic re-sources arena in the last five years suggest that developing countries have adopted a radically different strategy in their approach to intel-lectual property which may have positive implications for local knowl-edge. Unconsciously, they have sought to renegotiate the so-called local status of traditional medicine through foisting the latter on the formal patent system in what translates into a direct encounter be-tween the local and the cosmopolitan. In this way, they not only seek to empower traditional medicine but, by default, they confront the intellectual property system with the reality of cultural cosmopolitan-ism and the processual evolution of knowledge.[89]

The TKDL is one development that has "fueled epistemological encounter and dialogue,"[90] thus facilitating the evolution of racial scripts about tradi-tional knowledge, as well as the institutions through which it is negotiated and managed. This is a particularly notable intervention into inventive nar-ratives of human progress and the role of people of color with traditional knowledge in producing them.

BEAST MODE® AS INTERRUPTION
OF THE CONSUMER GAZE

Like Prince, Marshawn Lynch, using his clothing line, Beast Mode®, de-ployed his name and body in the service of remaking understandings of Black creatorship, Black citizenship, and Black personhood. He did so pri-marily in the context of trademark law. In 2013, Lynch, running back for the Oakland Raiders and former running back for the Seattle Seahawks, created the Beast Mode® retail line. Lynch named his company after himself. He earned the nickname Beast Mode, which describes his unique break-away style on the playing field, while still in high school.[91] One NFL blog commented, "What else does one think about when they imagine a hard running tailback other than a beast? Lynch is just that, a beast on the field, and he can turn it on when his team needs him to."[92]

Describing Lynch as a beast, while arguably flattering in the context of sports, also invokes overtly and inferentially racist stereotypes by calling on hundreds of years of representations of Black men as violent, hypersexual criminals with no capacity to moderate their bestial and brutish tendencies. In the context of Lynch's performances off the field as well as the NFL's racialized labor system, such representations take on even more racial significance. Jenn Jackson argues that the NFL mirrors the plantation system, in which "Black athletes occupy lowly stations providing fodder and one-dimensional performance art for viewers."[93] Black athletes are transformed into chattel, property that is expected to perform on the field in the most unbridled and animalistic of ways and then off the field in the most civilized and respectable of ways.

Lynch runs afoul of the implicit racial rules of the NFL by refusing the labor scripts imposed upon him during postgame press conferences. As Robin Boylorn explains, "I find Lynch's lack of engagement wickedly brilliant. Jenée Desmond-Harris frames Lynch's 'selective silence' as a way for him to resist the system and claim ownership of himself. His refusal to 'perform' for white entertainment outside the boundaries of his own comfort is his way of achieving/enacting his agency and refusing to be controlled. It is a way of demanding respect and exerting masculinity."[94] In the context of trademark law, Lynch's performances of Black masculinity are at least partially racially resistive ones, as they implicitly claim equal recognition and authority in creatorship, citizenship and personhood.

Lynch's nickname-turned-trademark simultaneously refuses white ownership of Black labor and claims property rights in the Black body. Because Lynch neither completely embraces nor completely refuses dominant conceptions of Black bestiality but instead crafts his own, his performance epitomizes disidentification, which José Esteban Muñoz describes as that "third mode of dealing with dominant ideology, one that neither opts to assimilate within such a structure nor strictly opposes it."[95]

In the context of a history of trademark law and the implicitly white male consumer gaze, Lynch's actions create space for Black production and Black consumption under capitalism. Lynch, in the manner he represents himself, is a self-actualized figure whose intended audience is Black people first and then all other individuals. He engages in a type of (de)propertizing disidentification, which pushes against the racial scripts that code Black men as bestial nonpersons who do not deserve to be granted full citizenship, let alone recognition as creators.

Lynch asserts the independent and unregulated right to make consumer goods in the face of the NFL's imaginings of the relationships among league, player, and audience. His trademark works both as a marker of the labor relations through which consumer culture was established—i.e., the exploitation of Black men as slaves—and as a means of eroding the authority of the Black brute narrative—i.e., complicating and recoding the stereotype. Though Lynch is not completely successful in remaking racial scripts and racial feelings about Black masculinity, his resistance is significant insofar as it realigns public cultural empathy with his recoded Black bestiality. It is also significant because it creates productive space for imagining and enacting Black capitalism, through celebrity rescripting of Black masculinity and subsequent redistribution of wealth throughout the community.[96]

One analogue to the raced and gendered figure of the mammy, the image of the Black brute, perpetuated, ideologically and visually, the subjugation of Black men. As Jefferson's articulation of racial scripts demonstrates, Black people were coded as animals, more capable than whites of doing labor of the body but not labor of the mind. From the time they arrived in America, Black men, in particular, were portrayed as unintelligent real or potential criminals who, by their very nature, threatened white women with their sexual aggressiveness.

In the postbellum period, they were increasingly portrayed as threatening not only to white femininity but also to racial purity. Charles Carroll's *The Negro a Beast* (1900) was instrumental in perpetuating the stereotype of Black man as beast. The book's biblical narrative posited that the Negro was not an offspring of Adam and therefore was not of the human family. Instead, Carroll contended that Black people were Cain's soulless offspring, mere "amalgamated flesh." The transformation of Thomas Dixon's *The Clansman* into D. W. Griffith's film *The Birth of a Nation* (1915) as well as the release of films like *Imitation of Life* (1959) and *Gone with the Wind* (1939) reflected similar views, particularly by stoking fears of Black men as uncontrollable beasts and brutes.

As Andrew Leiter argues, fear of Black masculinity, with all its associations, increased over time as "sexual policing revolved around the image of the African American male as a 'Black beast,' an enduring image of the segregation era characterizing Black males as sexually aggressive, only slightly removed from savagery."[97] Understandings of Black masculinity built upon and incorporated the beliefs of philosophers from Hegel to Hume and they have remained in the American consciousness for centuries. Black bestiality threatens whiteness, femininity, citizenship, and nation through its perceived uncontrollability, lack of self-regulation, physical prowess, and hypersexuality. While images of Black bestiality produced saleable commodities, that commodification worked through the simultaneous hatred and desire for Black masculinity. In other words, Black bestiality was the product of a consumer gaze that was interested in maintaining whiteness as property and white patriarchy but consuming exotic Otherness.

In contemporary contexts, stereotypes of Black bestiality and brutishness persist, in overt and inferential ways. In 2008, *Vogue* was accused of perpetuating racial stereotypes with a cover of LeBron James and Gisele. James, pictured screaming and dribbling a basketball with his arm around a famous supermodel in a strapless seafoam-green dress, evoked historic images of King Kong with a helpless Ann Darrow in his arms (Figure 4.1). While Gisele is smiling broadly in the Annie Lebovitz photo, echoes of Black bestiality and brutishness are undeniable. This image is one contemporary example of a familiar and troubling trope that refuses to die.

Whether in the Blaxsploitation films of the 1970s and 1980s, the drug wars of the 1980s and the 1990s, or the political representations of the 1990s and 2000s, the image of the Black beast and Black brute continued to circulate in the American imagination.[98] Suzanne Enck argues that in contemporary representations of sports, Black men are depicted as uniquely masculine and bestial, thus "legitimizing the racist notion that blacks are naturally superior physically."[99] Thomas Oates contends that the NFL draft eroticizes Black bodies in the service of white supremacy, thus updating hypersexualization of Black men through public homoerotic desire.[100] Calvin John Smiley and David Fakunle maintain that in the context of criminality, the Black man has transformed from "beast" or "brute" to "thug."[101] In no case was this more apparent than that of Seattle Seahawks cornerback Richard Sherman being called a thug on Twitter after a postgame interview with Erin Andrews.[102] Sherman's failure to "turn it off" after the game resulted in the invocation of the disciplinary language of thuggishness, code for unmanaged and undisciplined bestiality and brutishness.

Because of its centrality to American discourses of anti-Blackness, resisting the trope of the Black beast remains a central struggle for racial equality.[103] Read in the broad historical context of Black beast and Black brute and resistance to that imagery, Lynch's performances of selective silence are particularly notable. Though he does not and cannot undo the racial scripts of Black bestiality and Black brutishness completely, he disidentifies

FIGURES 4.1 and 4.2 Bestial images of LeBron James and Richard Sherman.

with them, performing them while redefining them. In this context, Beast Mode® operates simultaneously as an invocation and an interruption of the narrative of the Black beast, a means for Lynch to assert property rights and ownership in his own body.

Lynch has a long history of noncompliance and technical compliance with respect to the rules of the NFL. While his insistence on responding to questions at press conferences with answers like "Yeah," "Nope," "I'm grateful," and his infamous "I'm just here so I won't get fined" before declaring that time is up and walking off the field makes him a character in the football arena and a fan favorite, it also reinforces racial scripts and racial feelings of Black men as aggressive, willful, and stubborn in ways that refuse white ownership and control of Black men as property.

And in many ways, Lynch *does* gum up the smooth operation of the NFL's racial capitalism. The postgame interview is part of the sporting event's marketing. It is also a space in which Black men are expected to behave in accordance with the "rules of the game" in order to cultivate a strong fan base. But Lynch, instead of bringing the expected adrenaline and excitement to interviews, brings quiet frustration and refusal to engage, responses that are inconsistent with the NFL's imagining of postgame labor. Lynch sums up his position best by saying, "I ain't got nothing to say. I just want to play football." He is "bout that action, Boss," interested in "town business" back in his hometown of Oakland, California. More than anything, he is "thankful."[104] This is not to say that his performance of Black masculinity is without its problems, but simply to note that it makes important moves in confronting racial scripts and claiming property rights.

Lynch's words and performances, which helped him to cultivate a strong fan base, became the foundation for his brand, Beast Mode®. By also trademarking comments such as Bout that Action® for consumption by his fans, Lynch both refuses the NFL's attempts to control him and creates (intellectual) property value in his body. This dual process of propertizing/depropertizing disidentification is significant because it highlights how, even as Lynch embodies and invokes the trope of the Black beast, he unmakes and rescripts it. I have defined the terms propertization and depropertization previously, in the case of Lynch. Specifically:

> I invoke the term propertization to describe moves to conceive of a category of items, often intellectual properties, in real property

terms . . . I use depropertization to contrastingly refer to the process whereby Lynch, through his disidentifications, combats the policing of black bodies in the NFL and asserts his own agency. Through (de)propertizing disidentifications, Lynch defies the fugitive-slave-to-(intellectual)-property narrative that Stephen Best tells, redefining the black beast not as a laboring figure to be owned and exploited in a system of [racial capitalism] but rather as a commodity producer to be respected and emulated.[105]

Lynch's critique follows in the footsteps of that of Jean-Michel Basquiat, who in the 1980s pushed back against the racism of consumer culture, particularly with respect to intellectual property and the ownership of (Black) humans, through his Pop Art.[106] Unlike many other football players, Lynch accomplishes the same by calling explicit attention to his life growing up in the projects, as well as highlighting the need to support and revitalize his economically struggling hometown of Oakland.[107] Lynch simultaneously critiques and unmakes the white norms promulgated by NFL commentators and critics and remakes Blackness through his understandings and commodification of his own body, with integrity and investment in his community in California. Initially, Lynch's refusal of the narrative of white ownership of Black bodies and creation of property rights derived from his body contests the ideological connection that Best identifies between the rise of intellectual property rights and slavery, specifically Fugitive Slave Laws. It was through such laws that intangible parts of Black bodies, such as the *labor* of fugitive enslaved persons, became property independent of the bodies of Black men and women themselves. Mind and body were decoupled and propertized.

Beast Mode® not only complicates the NFL's management of postgame labor but also undermines the very premise that Black labor is ownable by whites, here through marketing the refusal to act in the way the NFL demands. By registering his words as trademarks, Lynch transforms his "labor actions"[108] into commodities, creating value in his resistance to the NFL and rewriting the script for Black masculinity. The Beast Mode® merchandise line makes Lynch's actions and body both desirable and valuable.

Beast Mode® signifies not simply the bestiality of Black men but also their ability to engage in strategic action in a world of white supremacy. Lynch's trademarks define his postgame behavior as refusals to condone the white supremacist system that created those expectations. As represented for the merchandise line, Beast Mode® depicts the letter *B*, stylized in such a way that it resembles mountains (Figure 4.3). Lynch visually represents Black bestiality as a sleek, Spartan image, a visual representation of his ability to persevere in the face of adversity. Beast Mode and Beast Mode® are sophisticated, attractive, controlled, and smart. Lynch thus effectively produces iconography for reimagining the stereotype of the Black brute, if only in part. As the popularity of Beast Mode® suggests, everyone should want to be the Beast Mode that Lynch embodies. Lynch is Black cool remade and reclaimed.[109] And while desiring Black men has been a problematic practice, desiring to be a Black man creates a narrative that centers Lynch's integrity.

Through his actions and marketing, Lynch creates an opportunity for subverting the consumer gaze that emerged coextensively with trademark law in the late 1800s to mid-1900s. As chapter 2 argues, the imagined "reasonable person" is the invisible American default, the white male upon whom the rights to liberty and property were bestowed and continue to be enforced. Lynch's Beast Mode® speaks back to the racially constitutive politics of consumer culture broadly and the whiteness of trademark doctrine specifically. Lynch's interventions offer embodied possibilities for understanding Black masculinity, citizenship, and personhood as mutable concepts with anti-racist potential even as they continue to evoke familiar racial scripts.

Though Lynch did not necessarily set out to confront the racism of the trademark system, by and through his disidentificatory embodiments of the Black brute, he asks us to inquire into the racial and national identity implications of commonly accepted and stereotypical visual images. Through the Beast Mode® trademark, he rearticulates the stereotype of the Black brute, claiming ownership and value in his systematically devalued and demonized body. His counterhegemonic performance of Beast Mode transforms the accepted meaning of the trope, recoding the figure's threatening sexuality, disobedience, incivility, and aggressiveness as inspirational Black masculinity. These actions together subvert the scopic regime that looks *at* Black men and instead looks *with* them through a lens that though not completely free of the white gaze, complicates it in productive and meaningful, if incomplete, ways.

Take, for instance, images that appeared on the Beast Mode® website. The front page shows only Black models wearing Beast Mode® apparel, with a representation of kids wearing Lynch's Fam 1st Family Foundation T-shirts at the bottom. The Women's, Men's, and Kids' pages are devoid of models, showcasing instead an array of clothing, from bodysuits to T-shirts. T-shirts are printed with phrases like "Justice for All," "I Am Beast Mode," and "Beast Me."

Unlike the spectacle of Black bodies in the context of the NFL draft, which Oates argues involves "erotic ruminations on bodily beauty (or its absence),"[110] the Beast Mode® website is minimalist in its representations of Black bodies, showcasing only a few models and Lynch, fully clothed in Beast Mode® apparel (Figure 4.4). Lynch sets the terms of engagement in this online space, not the white consumer gaze. Though white consumers still buy his products, he markets them in a manner that scopically subverts the spectacular and necrophilic pleasure associated with the consumption of images of Black men, living and dead.[111] That is not to say that there is no white consumption of Black bodies here. Phrases like "Beast Me" make the postracial suggestion that the wearer can "put on and take off at will."[112]

Yet this notion is counterbalanced by Lynch's agency in making the website as well as his redefinition of Beast Mode as a malleable performative space for countering anti-Blackness. The "About" section on the Beast Mode website also highlights this argument. There Lynch articulates the meaning of Beast Mode, which he does in ways that articulate a contemporary Black bestiality, though sometimes within the constraints of the concepts with which he is working. "There is only one BEASTMODE," the website declares, and it's "who you are, it's how you're built, it's part of your genetic makeup—it's a lifestyle." These descriptions, that Beast Mode is an identity, a biology, and a lifestyle, construct a category that is other than race; they refer to something that is other than a racial category. "Marshawn Lynch leaves almost everything on the field," the website continues.

While this may be read as proof that Beast Mode reinforces the bestial/civilized dichotomy that Black athletes are supposed to live by, an alternate reading in a larger racial context is that Lynch's website remakes the concept of the beast. The beast becomes deracialized through appeals to modes of functioning that do not comport with understandings of race, set side by side with an image that presents something other than a Black body. Lynch, when he is pictured, predominantly represents Black joy, dancing as he did on the field, or smiling widely. His affective recoding of Black bestiality

FIGURES 4.3 and 4.4 Marshawn Lynch's Beast Mode® logo and the Beast Mode® website's representations of Blackness.

provides a powerful counterpoint to racist codings of Blackness as danger and Black capitalism as a threat to the economic prosperity of the nation. Far from representing the threatening Black men imagined by public culture in the Antebellum period, Lynch offers a new set of visual images from which to feel related to Blackness and economics (Figures 4.3 and 4.4).

A Black feminist reading of Lynch also reveals an athlete from whom Black audiences, in particular, derive pleasure.[113] Black athletes, Enck contends, routinely "legitimiz[e] the racist notion that Blacks are naturally physically superior."[114] Yet physical superiority is only one aspect of Lynch's identity as Beast Mode. Unapologetic in his Blackness and committed to community, Lynch represents a new brand of Black athlete, one that breaks with the white consumer imaginary. As Herman Gray points out:

> The complex cluster of self-representations embodied in images of the Black heterosexual body as rapper, athlete, and movie star challenges racist depictions of Black masculinity as incompetent, oversexed, and uncivil—ultimately a threat to middle class notions of white womanhood, family, and the nation. But [they] are also . . . deeply dependent on traditional notions of heterosexuality, authenticity, and sexism."[115]

Lynch's Beast Mode® fits this mold. It is at once a contestation of the system of white supremacy that denies Black people their rights as citizens and makers of knowledge and a means of claiming the value of Black masculinity. Lynch's imagining of himself in the trademark context remains embedded in the traditional notions of Black masculinity that Gray describes. He is always-already an icon who is intense on the field, invested in "town business," heterosexually coded, laconic, and deeply true to himself. Nonetheless, he uses trademark law to confront the propertization and dehumanization of the Black body in powerful ways, as well as the legal (intellectual) property system that contributes to those practices. As one article contends, Beast Mode® is demonstrative of a new mode of Black subjectivity, "[a]ll of which is helping lead a new rising trend: athletes using technology to bypass traditional sponsorships in favor of everyone."[116] Yet that commodity value and integrity rest on a combination of OG authenticity and athletic prowess that is embedded within a traditional masculinity that does not undo patriarchy.

Nonetheless, Lynch's integrity is central to his success in using his trademark to claim space for Black citizenship. As the Prerequisite Cases demonstrate, people of color were historically characterized as lacking integrity, in the form of trustworthiness, moral uprightness, and commitment to nation. Lynch demonstrates each of these qualities through his performances and his investments in community, which are reflected in his trademarks. Beast Mode® highlights the personhood and autonomy of Black men by claiming property rights in words that Lynch spoke in the context of resisting the labor requirements imposed upon him by the NFL.

Both of these actions are significant when read in the context of anti-Blackness, citizenship, personhood, and (intellectual) property rights. The NFL's implicit requirements of threatening bestiality and passive obedience create a representational justification for investing in whiteness, not Blackness, as property. Yet Lynch not only claims property rights in racially recoded Black bestiality and his performative acts as a football player, he also demonstrates that he is entitled as a human to the bundle of rights associated with that category.

In "Whiteness as Property," Harris notes that one way that the legal system oppresses Black is that it "has refused to recognize group identity when asserted by racially oppressed groups as a basis for affirming or claiming rights."[117] While Harris is speaking of the erasure of racial identities in cases such as *Mashpee Tribe v. Town of Mashpee* (1978) in which the federal recognition of tribal existence was a prerequisite for granting rights, her argument applies in this context as well. The marginalization of Black masculinity rests in part on the refusal to acknowledge the histories and identities of Black people. Lynch's (de)propertizing representations refuse the very idea that whites should own or manage the labor of Black people or control their celebrity endorsements. They also assert the autonomy and value of Blackness in a manner that rejects the (white) consumer gaze. While Lynch's actions exist, as they must, within an oppressive world marked by racial capitalism and anti-Blackness, he disidentifies with the racial and economic regimes and constraints that prevent resistance, using trademarks to demonstrate that Blackness, citizenship, and personhood are synonymous and should be treated as such.

DECOLONIZING CREATORSHIP AND REMAKING PERSONHOOD

> There is, for example, a greater and more immediate need to understand the complex ways in which people were brought within the imperial system, because its impact is still being felt, despite the apparent independence gained by former colonial territories. The reach of imperialism into "our heads" challenges those who belong to colonized communities to understand how this occurred, partly because we perceive a need to decolonize our minds, to recover ourselves, to claim a space in which to develop a sense of authentic humanity.
> —LINDA TUHIWAI SMITH, *Decolonizing Methodologies*

THE FRAMES OF CREATORSHIP, citizenship, and nation have been organizing ones for my discussion of race and intellectual property. Copyright, patent, and trademark discourses have been intertwined with them for centuries, often through the reiteration of familiar racial scripts. Chapter 4 explored the notion of rewriting the existing racial scripts of intellectual property law and mobilizing new racial feelings as a potentially productive means of unmaking invisible white norms around creatorship and personhood. Each of the three examples discussed—Prince's seizure of creatorship as a space for Black creativity and personhood, India's pushback against Western commodification of cultural property, and Marshawn Lynch's deployment of Black bestiality as a means of contesting ownership of Black bodies—demonstrates the practical impacts of performative resistance to intellectual property law's conceptions of race and economic structures. Despite the possibilities that such moments of contestation offer, however, they are also fundamentally limited by cultural and material systems that perpetuate inequality. In particular, imagining that the whiteness of capitalism, liberalism, and citizenship can be undone through equal rights ignores the fundamental ideological investments of those systems and the failures of the civil rights movement. Even while recognizing the "epistemic violence"[1] involved in calling out inclusionary politics, Amy Brandzel notes that incrementalist approaches are fundamentally limited because

> these aspirations for inclusion re-create violence against vulnerable peoples. As a process, normative inclusion entrenches notions of proper versus improper, natural versus abnormal and normative versus abject. There is no such thing as a movement for inclusion and citizenship for some that does not further the vulnerability and disenfranchisement of others . . . longing for inclusion and citizenship reinforce violence against abjected others.[2]

Brandzel, who like Saidiya Hartman, Jasbir Puar, Roderick Ferguson, and David Eng, condemns citizenship, acknowledges the need for a "politics of presence,"[3] which engages in radical critique while nonetheless acknowledging the trauma of normative exclusion. In other words, she is cognizant of the imperative to both respectfully examine how inclusionary politics are integral to "navigating the visceral registers of pain, violence, and social death within the limiting structures of citizenship"[4] and fundamentally limited as singular avenues for pursuing emancipatory politics. In the practical space of law, racial and economic equity must come together with concrete agendas for policy reform.

This Conclusion addresses how to craft anti-racist and anti-colonial approaches to intellectual property law that radically confront racial scripts, racial feelings, and racial capitalism while not becoming hopelessly mired in deconstructionist impulses. Ravi Sunder Rajan contends that "[i]t is not the case that capitalized, corporatized, financialized, monopolistic capitalism cannot be benevolent,"[5] because even pharmocracy is informed by an underlying ethical value system. For him, undoing the structural discrimination that is built into the pharmaceutical industry requires engaging and remaking the very ethical system around which it is legally and economically structured. His work is emblematic of a larger desire in critical race studies and, I would contend, in Critical Race IP as well, to articulate concrete legal interventions into racist and (neo)colonialist systems. In that vein, the rest of this chapter turns to decolonial theory as a useful tool for thinking about undoing and rebuilding the racial base that underlies intellectual property law in the service of creating new and fundamentally racially and economically equitable copyright, patent, and trademark policies.

Even though this book has traced the historical links among race, intellectual property law, and citizenship, exclusively embracing rights-based understandings of national identity is *not* the path out of the colorblind racism conundrum that exists. As Brandzel notes and history proves, struggles for equal citizenship—as in Emancipation—generally have come at the cost of other marginalized groups. The divide-and-conquer politics of citizenship, which also marked the outcome in *Tam*, cannot undo the quagmire of race in intellectual property law. However, decolonial theory, particularly when coupled with understandings of the movement of racial scripts within intellectual property discourses, offers a racially and economically egalitarian approach to equity that is more effective than the equality-based civil rights remedies that marked the 1960s.[6]

Decolonial approaches to intellectual property law are helpful for combating the "hidden agenda of modernity"[7] that is deeply intertwined with racial and (neo)colonial oppression. They do not seek to reinvent the wheel, so to speak, of Critical Race Theory or Critical Race IP. Rather, they provide conceptual frames for imagining how to enfranchise people of color through divestment from intellectual property's racial histories and radically equal conceptions of creatorship and personhood. This concluding chapter situates intellectual property law within the divide of coloniality and modernity and explores how anti-racist and anti-colonialist activists working within intellectual property law might begin to think about naming and undoing the racial scripts, racial feelings, and racial capitalism that this book has foregrounded. It also focuses on "intellectual property fugitivity" as a grounding practice for remaking racially inequitable copyright, patent, and trademark policies and reorienting contemporary conversations about structures of knowledge production.

INTELLECTUAL PROPERTY IN THE COLONIALITY/MODERNITY DIVIDE

The previous chapters traced the development of racial scripts in and around intellectual property law in the United States. In doing so, they named but did not fully examine, as other scholars have done, the complex relationships between copyrights, patents, and trademarks and (neo)coloniality. That connection is not one that begins with the advent of biopiracy but rather stretches back before American independence to the colonial construction of knowledge itself. Colonial regimes were built, in part, on the devaluation of the intellectual capacity and knowledge production of colonial subjects. Practices of treating non-Europeans as less than human and incapable of producing knowledge were enacted in colonies across the world, including in Africa, Asia, and the Americas, through the binary articulation of rationality with Europeanness and intellectual incapacity with Otherness. Ramón Grosfoguel, for instance, writes that "[t]he hegemonic Eurocentric paradigms that have informed western philosophy and sciences in the 'modern/colonial capitalist/patriarchal world-system' for the last 500 years assume a universalistic, neutral objective point of view."[8]

Through the simultaneous denigration of non-European Others and the valorization of Western ideals of modernity and progress, Enlightenment thinkers represented colonial subjects as inferior non-humans to be civilized. Otherness connoted deviance, not difference. Given the fundamentally European character of American intellectual property law, those racially informed tenets have come to shape the contours of the nation's copyright, patent, and trademark policies, as demonstrated earlier in the book.

In language that presages Thomas Jefferson's racist proclamations about Phillis Wheatley, Georg Hegel contended that Africans were exempt from the universal norms of humanness. He wrote:

> The peculiarly African character is difficult to comprehend, for the very reason that in reference to it, we must quite give up the principle which naturally accompanies all our ideas—the category of Universality. In Negro life, the characteristic point is the fact that consciousness has not yet attained to the realization of any substantial objective existence—as for example, God or Law—in which the interest of man's volition is involved and in which he realizes his own being.[9]

Hegel concluded that Africans were therefore incapable of thinking at the level of Europeans and incapable of producing knowledge. Continental philosophers and American forefathers, including David Hume and Immanuel Kant, echoed the belief that all people of color were inferior to whites. Hume wrote, "I am apt to suspect the negroes to be naturally inferior to the whites. There scarcely was ever a civilized nation of that complexion . . . no ingenious manufactures amongst them, no arts, no sciences . . . [T]here are negroe slaves dispersed all over Europe, of whom none ever discovered any symptoms of ingenuity."[10] He dismissed counterexamples, arguing that a learned Black man, in Africa or other colonies, must be "like a parrot."[11] Not only did Hegel and Hume lay out Enlightenment justifications for slavery and colonialism, but echoes of their words are evident in American rejections of the creatorship of people of color and the non-universality of personhood and creativity.

Enlightenment conceptions of colonial subjects as barbarous, childlike, innocent, and without higher intellectual capacity came to be embedded not only in intellectual property law in the eighteenth and nineteenth centuries, but in the very logics of global copyright, patent, and trademark law as well. Ruth Okediji observes that, historically speaking, intellectual property law from the nineteenth century onward discriminated against the developing world, centrally building upon the idea that colonial subjects lacked the intellectual sophistication to produce knowledge. She contends:

> In essence, the extension of intellectual property rights was not directed at the inhabitants of the governed territories at all, but instead to facilitate commercial relations among colonial powers as trade between European powers occurred on and among the various territories on behalf of foreign sovereigns. Intellectual property law was not merely an incidental part of the colonial legal apparatus, but a central technique in the commercial superiority sought by European powers in their interactions with each other in regions beyond Europe.[12]

Similarly, Edward Said observes that "[o]n the one hand, there are Westerners, on the other there are Arab-Orientals; the former are (in no particular order) rational, peaceful, logical, capable of holding real values, without natural suspicion; the latter are none of these things."[13] Philosophers and political theorists in the pre-American era made similar claims as well, increasingly marking whiteness as a signifier of the capacity to engage in fully formed thought as well as qualify for the rights and entitlements of citizenship.[14] Colonial subjects, the objects of the production of European knowledge, could not be its creators. Instead, they were categorically excluded from the imaginary of the Romantic author, which crystallized in the eighteenth century.[15] In Rudyard Kipling's words, colonial subjects were "half devil and half child,"[16] suitable only to be taken up as part of the white man's colonizing burden. Because Europeans treated colonial subjects as other than citizen, colonized peoples had little ability to protect traditional knowledge. Intellectual property law was thus not simply an incidental means of protecting creators; it was an important element of colonial structural power and domination.[17]

While these arguments retread some of the ground I have covered earlier, they also raise a much larger problem in intellectual property law than that of even American racial scripts. They demonstrate that concepts such as true imagination, human progress, and the male consumer gaze are embedded within the ideologies of modernity and coloniality. The central organizing philosophies of intellectual property law—a body of legal regulation that protects the Enlightenment creator—have persisted for centuries. Martha Woodmansee observes that the figure of creator has been remarkably inelastic, not changing even as postmodern theorists have argued for its reconstruction.[18] The inflexible ideal of the creator is also an important nexus of the modernity/coloniality binary in intellectual property law, one that is, as earlier parts of the book have demonstrated, often tied to conceptions of national identity in the United States.

For Grosfoguel, (neo)colonialism is necessarily linked with a hierarchal understanding of knowledge production that is also fundamentally racialized. He writes: "This epistemic strategy has been crucial for Western global designs . . . European/Euro-American colonial expansion and domination was able to construct a hierarchy of super and inferior knowledge and, thus, of super and inferior people around the world. We went from . . . 'people without writing' to . . . 'people without history' to . . . 'people without development.'"[19]

Intellectual property law, without attentiveness to modernity itself, is a mechanism for maintaining, not undoing, the racial and epistemic hierarchy that Grosfuguel identifies. Traditional knowledge remains largely outside the scope of protection of intellectual property law because epistemic domination is deeply embedded within legal theory and doctrine. Adherence to Enlightenment conceptions of authorship and inventorship continues to decenter the knowledge of people of color while advancing purportedly universal Western development agendas. Larger-than-life global brands reinforce the epistemic domination that authorship/inventorship produce by signifying quality in raced ways and exploiting labor in a global, self-destructing system of racial capitalism.

Rewriting the racial scripts that undergird intellectual property law requires grappling with legal and economic structures but also fundamental orientations toward knowledge itself. In this sense, decolonial theory's emphasis on epistemology offers inroads into undoing intellectual property law's racial and (neo)colonial exclusions. The project of decolonization emerged from the Bandung Conference of 1955, which took on critiquing the epistemological foundations of modernity as a justification for (neo)coloniality as its central agenda.[20] As former colonial states gained their independence, they were corralled into international regimes of free trade and economic harmonization, which also created international intellectual property rights. TRIPS, in particular, operated as a predominantly Western project of international law, one in which "white men of letters and science . . . were the gatekeepers of Western and modern knowledge."[21] The conversations in Bandung laid the groundwork for future critiques of neoliberal colonialism, particularly as realized through international governance.

Reading intellectual property law through the lens of decolonization—as well as the related lenses of postcoloniality and dewesternization—allows for historical and structural engagement with (neo)colonialism, from its dismissal of particular forms of creatorship to its alignment with the Doctrine of Discovery. Decolonial theory offers a means of using modernity and coloniality as the fulcrums for theorizing intellectual property inequality and articulating resistive practices. Decolonial theory also offers insight into how and why racial capitalism developed, as part of colonial exploitation of physical labor, which was articulated in opposition to intellectual labor and how and why individuals might undo those linkages. Through the lens of decolonial theory, intellectual property law can be read as part of a larger system of advancing particularly Western development agendas under the aegis of protecting knowledge as a valuable commodity, in ways that definitionally marginalize people of color and their capacity to think original thoughts.

Alexander Weheliye's work implicitly underscores the need for such decolonization in undoing the violence of racism. He writes: "Apportioning personhood . . . [through citizenship] maintains the world of Man and its attendant racializing assemblages, which means in essence that the entry fee for legal recognition is the acceptance of categories based on white supremacy and colonialism, as well as normative genders and sexualities."[22] When read alongside the work of decolonial theorist Nelson Maldonado-Torres, who like Weheliye takes up the work of Sylvia Wynter in laying out his understandings of decoloniality, the links among race, intellectual property, citizenship, and personhood become clear. He writes:

> Taking Du Bois and Wynter's lead, I would like to suggest that from the perspectives of the repeatedly racialized groups of modernity, particularly indigenous people and people of African or Afro-mixed ex-slave descent, but also Jews and Muslims, a concept of Being premised on what is often referred to as the dialectics of modernity and the nation, and their supposed overcoming by the emergence of imperial sovereignty or Empire, miss the non-dialectical character of damnation. That is, in short, that what are changes for many, for those whom Frantz Fanon called the condemned of the earth seem rather to be perverse re-enactments of a logic that has for a long time militated against them.[23]

While legal scholars often aim to achieve intellectual property equality through policy reform, critical race studies scholars, and decolonial theorists direct us to the need to identify the *logics* that underlie racial inequality in copyrights, patents, and trademarks. Given that intellectual property law is intertwined with notions of citizenship, which are themselves rooted in the modernity/coloniality dichotomy because of their distinctly European genealogy and relationship to the emergence of the contemporary nation-state, such critiques provide a means of approaching the problem of racial inequality at the root, with ideological depth.

Decolonial theory offers a way of deracializing knowledge production as well as conceptions of citizenship, nation, and personhood, through the embrace of language and practices that are delinked from modernity. Epistemic worldmaking takes a variety of forms, often imperfect ones. But it begins to grapple with the larger racial assemblages and rhetorics of race that make creatorship into a category from which people of color are ideologically excluded, in whole or in part, merely on the basis of identity.

FROM RACIAL CREATORSHIP TO DECOLONIAL INTELLECTUAL PROPERTY

Because claims to citizenship are always already, by virtue of managing questions of belonging, couched in terms of proving that those who are Other are not Other, they often involve drawing distinctions that reinforce existing exclusions instead of embracing humanness as a space of profound difference. Citizenship requires norms that are "brutally enforced against non-normative bodies, practices, behaviors, and forms of affiliation through oppositional, divide-and-conquer logics that set up nonnormative subjects to compete against each other in order to gain the privileged access to citizenship."[24]

In the context of intellectual property, these divide-and-conquer logics are evident even in seemingly productive calls for inclusion. Prince's appeals to protect Black creatorship—as well as popular cultural texts such as *Empire* and *The Get Down* that echo them—do so at the expense of "pirates," even when those pirates exist in states of tremendous precarity. Indian and Indian American claims to have a cultural property interests in yoga feed virulent Hindu nationalism that justifies violence against Muslims.[25] Lynch's claims to own the labor of his Black body reinscribe the racial capitalism of both the NFL and the celebrity industrial complex that makes the cult of personality around his undoubtedly appealing Beast Mode persona profitable. Unless they confront and undo the underlying logics of copyright, patent, and trademark law, performative engagements with creatorship and citizenship can fall prey to the anti-affiliative and anti-intersectional labor sentiments that Brandzel critiques as problematic. Combating such problems requires addressing the *humanness* of people of color, their knowledge, and their rights to liveable and sustainable economic realities.

Decolonial theory, like CRT, foregrounds the need to make intellectual property's racial politics visible and confronts the exclusionary effects of inclusionary politics, through histories of modernity as well as the histories of Americanism and citizenship highlighted in this book. For decolonial theorists such as Walter Mignolo and Anibal Quijano, the colonial is always already in opposition with modernity, with the latter category associated with universal norms of "development" and "progress."

Decolonial thought, accordingly, breaks with the fundamental "myth of modernity,"[26] embracing instead practices of "epistemic delinking"[27] from the binary of coloniality/modernity created by the political and economic systems that originated in Europe and spread to the colonies. More specifically, "[d]e-coloniality turns the plate around and shifts the ethics and politics of knowledge. Critical theories emerge from the ruins of languages, categories of thoughts and subjectivities (Arab, Aymara, Hindi, French and English Creole in the Caribbean, Afrikaans, etc.) that had been consistently negated by the rhetoric of modernity and in the imperial implementation of the logic of coloniality."[28] Through this emphasis on centering marginalized categories of thought, decoloniality provides a useful theoretical frame for thinking across racial and national identity categories, in ways that aid in undoing anti-Blackness, anti-Indigeneity, and anti-Asianness, among others. As José David Saldívar explains, decolonial theory is a useful tool for thinking the politics of "becoming minor,"[29] and the epistemic marginalization that accompanies them.

In the context of intellectual property law, decoloniality is useful in advancing critiques of the area of law's consistent inability and refusal to recognize the full personhood, therefore creatorship and citizenship, of people of color, and building models of engagement that recognize multiverses of knowledge production, knowledge making, and indigenous wisdom, apart from their commodity value. It is also useful in thinking about policymaking as a practice of working from the bottom up instead of the top down. Deconstructing the racial logics of intellectual property law creates space for new ideas that are grounded in Otherness. Such ideas are not, by definition, emancipatory ones. However, they are prerequisites to building knowledge futures that are emancipatory.

While Mignolo sketches the importance of epistemic delinking from modernity, the specifics of his project are not always clear. Given the embeddedness of the nation-state, including its management of normative citizenship, with (neo)coloniality certainly requires moving away from inclusionary politics as a strategy for gaining full intellectual property citizenship. As Mignolo writes, "The emergence of 'modern nation-states' in Europe, means two things: that the state became the new central authority of imperial/colonial domination and that the 'nation' in Europe was mainly constituted of one ethnicity, articulated as 'whiteness.'"[30] White colonial nation-states became the arbiters of citizenship, in part through the creation of hierarchies through which they deemed themselves superior to (neo)colonial states and in part through the legal manipulation of the category itself.[31] They also became arbiters of the legitimacy of knowledge, specifically who has and does not have the capacity to create.

The project of remaking intellectual property law, then, must address the centrality of the *state* and the centrality of *whiteness* in the formation of intellectual property policy and its underlying ideologies and cultural formations. This does not mean doing away with the nation-state or completely disempowering white people. Instead, it means confronting the role of the nation state in epistemic violence and its complicity in white supremacy. Decoloniality, as a tool of a larger, interdisciplinary Critical Race IP agenda, "creates space for a complex and multifaceted engagement with race and, (neo)coloniality that addresses the fundamental historical power dynamics that shaped laws of knowledge production."[32] For instance, decolonizing intellectual property law requires undoing the state's oligopoly on defining and enforcing conceptions of infringement and the public domain. It also requires pushing back against the implicit whiteness in state and cultural conceptions of creativity, innovation, progress, and A2K. Both of these are necessary but not sufficient for intellectual property justice.

Darrel Wanzer-Serrano writes: "Decoloniality is an alternative accent—one marked by pluriversal commitments, geo-historical attentiveness, and bio-graphical considerations."[33] In order to get to a place in the context of intellectual property law where that trio of goals is possible, anti-racist and anti-colonial activists must persuade lawmakers that knowledge production comes in a variety of forms, not of all of which comport with notions of Romantic authorship. This project is an ongoing one, though it is sometimes impeded by commitments to incrementalism, inclusion, or capitalism. Approaching such issues from the vantage point of pluriversality, historicity, and contextual specificity forces engagement with intellectual property law's tendency to mark some people as less than human and prefigure solutions through racial capitalist lenses.

Important questions in building egalitarian copyright, patent, and trademark policies, then, include: "Whose labor is valuable? How is it valued? What systems underpin those definitions of labor? And how do we alter and remake the systems that undervalue the knowledge of people of color and maintain systems of white supremacy?"[34] Storytelling, protecting traditional knowledge, and A2K are important parts of the answers to those questions, as the three case studies in chapter 4 demonstrate. But they are necessary though not sufficient solutions to the circulation of racial scripts that this book traces.

Derrick Bell argues that making visible the racial non-neutrality of law is a central part of the project of CRT. Similarly, unveiling the nexus between coloniality/modernity is a core part of the project of decolonial theory—and one that is helpful in reimagining copyright, patent, and trademark law. Making visible intellectual property law's racial non-neutrality and investments in (neo)colonial flows of power has been a core aim of this project.

While scholars in a variety of disciplines have begun to work through the histories of intellectual property and race in particular instances, a great deal more work needs to be done in theorizing how copyrights, patents, and trademarks have played important roles in racial formation, how their racial scripts evolve and pervade public culture, in discursive and material ways, and how political economy is tied up with questions of race. Coming to grips with intellectual property law's stubborn doctrinal and discursive resistance to creating narrative space for non-white creators and their full personhood renders legible those discourses that subtly but persistently normalize Enlightenment views of creatorship, infringement, and concomitantly race. In the United States and globally, the struggle over creating equitable intellectual property law is a struggle about the ways in which Americans *imagine*, *feel*, and *commodify* knowledge in intersectionally raced and (neo)colonial ways.

Reimagining intellectual property through the lens of decoloniality is also a rhetorical project, one in which a developing theory of Critical Race IP can assist. The examples of Prince's name change, Lynch's Beast Mode®, decolonial vernacular in the Yoga Wars, and dewesternization through the TKDL demonstrate the broad spectrum of resistive performances and practices through which people of color remake notions of creatorship, citizenship, and personhood. They also concretize decoloniality in ways that are helpful for thinking about praxis in all its material realities.

Decolonial theory posits, as a core practice of decolonization, the idea of delinking. Decolonizing intellectual property requires delinking it from the epistemological foundations of modernity/coloniality, particularly with respect to the category of creatorship and, relatedly, its articulations with citizenship and personhood. Darrel Wanzer-Serrano explains the practice of delinking decolonially as:

> any practice, discursive or otherwise, that facilitates a divestment from modernity/coloniality and invents openings through which decolonial epistemics can emerge. . . . Delinking requires changes in both content and form . . . It requires being oriented toward shifts in our genealogies of thought, including drawing authority from colonized spaces/voices and resisting latent imperialisms—even when such resistance may not be exclusively oppositional.[35]

In this way, decolonial theory and praxis conceive of "epistemological re-constitution,"[36] in order to facilitate the making of "another rationality which may legitimately pretend to some universality."[37]

From this understanding of decolonial delinking, we can move between theory and practice to imagine how it might look to delink intellectual property law from its modern/colonial investments in creatorship/infringement. We can also imagine ways of undoing creatorship as it forms racial assemblages with national identity and citizenship, two categories that must also be decolonized. The praxis of decolonial delinking is far more complicated than the conceptualization of that which must be done, however. For instance, Prince and Lynch succeed in decolonial delinking even as they work to build space for Black capitalism to thrive. Similarly, the dewesternizing restructuring and spectacular nationalism that the TKDL prompts, even while encouraging the development of decolonial vernacular, is a move toward decolonial intellectual property. Yet both of these examples point to the tendency of resistance to be embedded within unsustainable systems and ideologies of racial capitalism and racial liberalism. Anti-racist and anti-colonial scholars ought to contemplate how to take decolonization even further, past beyond existing imaginaries.

From Phillis Wheatley to Alice Randall, from 2 Live Crew to Simon Tam, intellectual property discourses in the United States have repeatedly questioned whether people of color possess adequate creativity, inventiveness, and capacity to create specifically in ways that fit within the racialized ideals of Americanness, citizenship, and personhood. All too often, the answer to this question has been a resounding "no." Person of color creatorship continues to be coded as always already unoriginal or infringing as well as an inappropriate subject for court intervention. In *A Dying Colonialism*, Frantz Fanon observes: "An underdeveloped people must prove, by its fighting power, its ability to set itself up as a nation, and by the purity of every one of its acts, that it is, even to the smallest detail, the most lucid, the most self-controlled people."[38] The politics of people of color creation, including sampling, parody, and piracy, are repeatedly categorized as examples of the failure to live up to the politics of purity that Fanon describes as part of colonialism.

The failure to live up to impossible standards of purity is not the only factor that keeps people of color from occupying the category of creatorship.

So too does the connection of those perceived failures with discourses, feelings, and practices of race and capitalism. I do not intend to suggest that a pure politics of resisting intellectual property discourses is required—or even exists. As Lawrence Grossberg reminds us, "impure politics"[39] is bound to be the only path to revolution. Those who are against the racializing tendencies of intellectual property law must name and refuse the ways that people of color creatorship is held to different standards and accused of an impure politics of making that tautologically demonstrates an unfitness to create in the first place.

That fundamental double bind of white supremacy is one that ties together (neo)colonialism and internal colonialism oppressions. As Quijano explains: "European or Western culture imposed its paradigmatic image and its principal cognitive elements as the norm of orientation on all cultural development, particularly the intellectual and the artistic. That relationship consequently became a constitutive part of the conditions of reproduction of those societies and cultures that were pushed into Europeanization of everything or in part."[40] The "Europeanization of everything" can be undone through decolonial refusals of white supremacy.

Here, I come full circle, back to Hasian's notion of character within law. Rhetorical cultures, per his understanding of legal decision making, both enable and constrain legal and racial narratives. One important function that each moment of resistance performs is the creation of new character arcs for people of color in the overarching mythos of American creatorship. Characters build the rhetorical cultures and narrative roles that people of color can occupy, even with respect to knowledge production. While it is tempting to dismiss extralegal interventions as "mere rhetoric," those rhetorical interventions make possible the policy ones through which people of color can become creators, citizens, and persons who can transform racial capitalism.

INTELLECTUAL PROPERTY FUGITIVITY

The Color of Creatorship began with a look at "Blurred Lines" and the complicated and contradictory resolution that resulted from Robin Thicke's initial lawsuit against Marvin Gaye's estate. In part, *Williams* was a so-called "hard case" because it pitted people of color against one another in a manner that required the erasure of one or more forms of systematic discrimination while also refusing to take a critical look at the persistent problems of racial capitalism.

The amicus brief that sided with Gaye addressed only part of the problem of the case. Though it produced important counterscripts to the racial scripts and racial feelings that had disenfranchised Black creators before the 1970s, it also oversimplified the political economy of the situation in which copyright law—and indeed all intellectual property law—operates.

Williams offers a starting/ending point for imagining where anti-racist and anti-colonial activists should commit their energies. For instance, the racial dynamics of the conflicts between R&B and hip hop and Gaye and Pharrell may have justified advocating for neither or both parties in an amicus brief, by critiquing the divide-and-conquer ethos of the situation and the case and by critiquing the capitalist model around which victory was built. Advocating for intellectual property egalitarianism in a way that is legally and politically leg-ible requires pushing back against accepted (intellectual) property doctrines, which conceal racial logics. The Korematsu Center's amicus brief in *Tam*, for instance, performs such a task by grounding its opposition to trademarking the Slants' band name in the racial histories of the United States, specifically those that resulted in the internment and economic disenfranchisement of Japanese Americans during World War II. In many ways, merely creating counterscripts—i.e., advocating in an amicus brief even without attendant relief—accomplishes this end. Repeatedly engaging and refusing those myths that constrain creatorship, citizenship, and personhood pushes back against whiteness as property and shifts public cultural conversations.

One easy objection here is that an amicus brief that tells a just and com-pelling racial story does not have legal impact. However, this conclusion is both untrue and, at least in part, irrelevant. *The Color of Creatorship* has demonstrated how the unspoken desires that structure the economics of intellectual property law are based not in fact but in myths and feelings. Ra-cial scripts are about attachments to social constructions of race, property, nation, and person, not objective or rational conceptions of those terms.

As CRT scholars from Richard Delgado to Keith Aoki contend, telling stories in legal contexts shifts the purportedly race neutral language, rep-resentations, and emotions around which law is crafted, in ways that are invisible and seemingly unproductive but important. The Love Symbol, Beast Mode®, and the TKDL make claims of inclusion alongside radical claims to dignity and humanity, which are effective even though (intellec-tual) property law continues to be rigged against people of color. Telling legal stories about the personhood of people of color in intellectual property terms pushes back against the foundational racism and racial sentimentality of copyrights, patents, and trademarks.

These examples provide a useful starting point for thinking about how people of color can become intellectual property fugitives, thereby confronting the two-body problem that Stephen Best notes arose with the decoupling of physical labor and intangible labor. Such decoupling transformed people of color, particularly Black people, into commodity forms that, because they were the objects of property ownership, definitionally could not own their own intangible labor. The Love Symbol, Beast Mode, and the TKDL refuse this decoupling, by occupying and reclaiming the spirit of fugitivity. That occupation is a decolonizing move, which begins a long, arduous process of delinking intellectual property from modernity/coloniality and its implications.

Returning to Best's analysis of the relationship between the fugitive and embodiment—specifically that Fugitive Slave Laws gave rise to a two-body problem that allowed whites to treat Black people as "living property"—creates a bridge to a new and productive rereading of fugitivity, a concept that can be occupied to create a radical approach to intellectual property politics. Fred Moten, before defining the same term, asks, "How do we think the possibility and the law of outlawed, impossible things?"[41] He responds to that inquiry by writing on fugitivity as a resistive concept, practice, and mode of being:

> This fugitive movement is stolen life, and its relation is reducible neither to simple interdiction nor bare transgression. What can be attained in this zone of unattainability . . . is some sense of the fugitive law of movement of black social life ungovernable, that demands a para-ontological of the supposed connection between explanation and resistance.[42]

Harney and Moten's conception of fugitivity describes a "stolen life,"[43] in which anti-racist and anti-colonialist scholars and activists "do not come to pay their debts, to repair what has been broken, to fix what has come undone."[44] Harney and Moten continue:

> We cannot be satisfied with the recognition and acknowledgement generated by the very system that denies (a) that anything was ever broken and (b) that we deserved to be the broken part; so we refuse to ask for recognition and instead we want to take apart, dismantle, tear down

the structure that, right now, limits our ability to find each other, to see beyond it and to access the places that we know lie outside its walls . . . once we have torn shit down, we will inevitably see more and see differently and feel a new sense of wanting and being and becoming.[45]

The intellectual property fugitive, a figure I have sketched out through the examples in the previous chapter, engages law with the knowledge that intellectual property law can never be effectively reformed, even if it periodically benefits people of color, because it is too deeply intertwined with racism and racial capitalism to be redeemable. Moreover, the intellectual property fugitive performs radical resistance to copyright, patent, and trademark regimes that are mired in national identity, citizenship, and racial capitalism through consistent acts that "tear down the structure." The goal of the intellectual property fugitive is not only a series of policy proposals to tinker with intellectual property law but a hegemonic commitment to constant critique, particularly storytelling that rescripts racial formations, remakes racial feelings, and creates possibilities for more spacious conceptions of belonging, in knowledge and human cultures.

Mat Callahan, in an article titled "Why Intellectual Property? Why Now?" writes:

> Under these conditions, capitalist interests view IP not merely as an opportunity to seek profit, but more fundamentally as the underpinning of a global regime, especially the trade treaties and international agreements that dictate the flow of all goods and services be they material or intellectual. Indeed, the threat many movements pose . . . is not primarily one of piracy or "theft" of the intellectual property of one corporation or another; rather, the threat is to the foundation of private property and the ownership of ideas as a conceptual framework for law or governance of any kind. In other words, within any and every conflict revolving around IP are the core principles of capitalism: possessive individualism, private appropriation of public wealth—especially natural resources—and the despoiling or destruction of the commons. Thus, what makes IP a vital battlefront for our time is that the stakes are capitalist enslavement or human liberation.[46]

Though Callahan focuses on the issue of economics, he does not discuss the issue of race, which also underpins contemporary systems of intellectual property law. Specifically, race and economics are intertwined in ways that guarantee the valuation of *particular* kinds of ideas with *particular* kinds of owners. Reimagining creatorship, infringement, citizenship, nation, and personhood in intellectual property law requires answering fundamental and pressing questions about race and capitalism. Those questions will become increasingly important in coming years, as intellectual property becomes an even more central space for the negotiation of economics, politics, and humanness. For Harney and Moten, fugitivity as concept is adversarial toward state-based policy reforms as the ultimate mechanisms for producing equality. White supremacy guarantees failure as well as ontological collusion with a racist system invested in destroying people of color. Given that intellectual properties are legally constructed through domestic and international institutional action, the knee-jerk response is to intervene legally.

Unlike Harney and Moten, I do not conclude with the notion that individuals can never ask for inclusion or recognition within the state. Rather, I understand fugitivity, particularly when read alongside decoloniality, as metaphorical shorthand for the need for constant vigilance about the underlying racial investments of the state and publics as well as an epistemological break with the seductive forces of law, even when they seem appealing. Letting go of the illusion that, as Bell counsels, law can bring radical change and embracing, instead, that legal gains are frequently rolled back partially or completely, leaves space for committing to continuing anti-racist and anticolonial struggle. The legal and performative aspects of engaging in that struggle, which come in a variety of individual and institutional forms, are the path to treating people of color not as objects decoupled from their creativity and innovation, but as whole persons with dignity, humanity, and the capacity to occupy the category of creatorship in all its pluriversal forms.

NOTES

INTRODUCTION

1. See Thy Phu, *Picturing Model Citizens: Civility in Asian American Visual Culture* (Philadelphia: Temple University Press, 2012).

2. In order to narrow the scope of the project, I have largely left trade secret and right of publicity law unexamined. However, there is much to be said about race in those two areas of law as well.

3. Michel Foucault, *The Birth of Biopolitics: Lectures at the College de France, 1978–1979*, ed. Michel Senellart (New York: Palgrave Macmillan, 2008), 248.

4. Eduardo Bonilla-Silva, *White Supremacy and Racism in the Post–Civil Rights Era* (Boulder: Lynne Rienner Publishers, 2001), 73.

5. Natalia Molina, *How Race Is Made in America: Immigration, Citizenship, and the Historical Power of Racial Scripts* (Berkeley: University of California Press, 2014).

6. Michael Omi and Howard Winant, *Racial Formation in the United States: From the 1960s to the 1990s* (New York: Routledge, 1994), 55.

7. Ibid.

8. Derrick Bell, *Faces at the Bottom of the Well* (New York: Basic Books, 1992), 12.

9. See Keith Aoki, "(Intellectual) Property and Sovereignty: Notes toward a Cultural Geography of Authorship," *Stanford Law Review* 48, no. 5 (May 1996): 1293–1355; Rosemary Coombe, *The Cultural Life of Intellectual Properties: Authorship, Appropriation, and the Law* (Durham: Duke University Press, 1998); Margaret Chon, "Intellectual Property and the Development Divide," *Cardozo Law Review* 27, no. 6 (April 2006): 2821–2912; Boatema Boateng, *That Copyright Thing Doesn't Work Here: Adinkra and Kente Cloth and Intellectual Property in Ghana* (Minneapolis: University of Minnesota Press, 2011).

10. Alexander G. Weheliye, *Habeas Viscus: Racializing Assemblages, Biopolitics, and Black Feminist Theories of the Human* (Durham: Duke University Press, 2014), 28. Here and throughout his book, Weheliye draws on the work of Black feminist scholars Hortense Spillers and Sylvia Wynter.

11. For a general discussion of law as rhetorical and narrative practice, see James Boyd White, "Law as Rhetoric, Rhetoric as Law: The Arts of Cultural and Communal Life," *University of Chicago Law Review* 52, no. 3 (Summer 1985): 684–702.

12. 17 U.S.C.S. § 102 (2018).

13. Richard Stallman, "Did You Say 'Intellectual Property'? It's a Seductive Mirage," *GNU Project*, 2010, http://www.gnu.org/philosophy/not-ipr.html.

14. A number of scholars across Critical Race Theory, international relations, cultural studies, and rhetoric have written about citizenship as cultural and discursive construction. See Linda Bosniak, *The Citizen and the Alien: Dilemmas of Contemporary Membership* (Princeton: Princeton University Press, 2008); Ian Haney López, *White by Law: The Legal Construction of Race* (New York: New York University Press, 1996); Robert Asen, "A Discourse Theory of Citizenship," *Quarterly Journal of Speech* 90, no. 2 (May 2004): 189–211; Isaac West, *Transforming Citizenships: Transgender Articulations of the Law* (New York: New York University Press, 2014).

15. Jessica Silbey, "The Mythical Beginning of Intellectual Property," *George Mason Law Review* 15, no. 2 (Winter 2008): 319–81. See also Debora Halbert, Majid Yar, Tarleton Gillespie, John Logie, and Jessica Reyman, who explore the cultural and rhetorical constructions of creatorship/infringement. Debora Halbert, "Intellectual Property Piracy: The Narrative Construction of Deviance," *International Journal for the Semiotics of Law* 10, no. 1 (February 1997): 55–78; Majid Yar, "The Rhetorics and Myths of Antipiracy Campaigns: Criminalization, Moral Pedagogy, and Capitalist Property Relations in the Classroom," *New Media & Society* 10, no. 4 (2008): 605–23; Tarleton Gillespie, "Characterizing Copyright in the Classroom: The Cultural Work of Antipiracy Campaigns," *Communication, Culture & Critique* 2, no. 3 (September 2009): 274–318; John Logie, *Peers, Pirates, and Persuasion: Rhetoric in the Peer-to-Peer Debates* (West Lafayette: Parlor Press, 2006); Jessica Reyman, *The Rhetoric of Intellectual Property: Copyright Law and the Regulation of Digital Culture* (New York: Routledge, 2010), 16. James Boyle, *The Public Domain: Enclosing the Commons of the Mind* (New Haven: Yale University Press, 2008).

17. Silbey, "The Mythical Beginning of Intellectual Property," 321.

18. Intersectional analysis calls upon the Black feminist framework that Kimberlé Crenshaw originally articulated as a means of understanding how oppression is necessarily shaped by multiple identity categories, including race, gender, class, sexuality, age, disability, and so on. Kimberlé Crenshaw, "Mapping the Margins: Intersectionality, Identity Politics, and Violence against Women of Color," *Stanford Law Review* 43, no. 6 (July 1991): 1241–1299. Intellectual property's racial investments certainly call for intersectional analysis. See also Kimberlé Crenshaw, "Beyond Racism and Misogyny: Black Feminism and 2 Live Crew," *Boston Review*, December 1991, http://bostonreview.net/race-gender-sexuality/kimberle-w -crenshaw-beyond-racism-and-misogyny; Kevin J. Greene, "Intellectual Property at the Intersection of Race and Gender: Lady Sings the Blues," *American University Journal of Gender, Social Policy & the Law* 16, no. 3 (2008): 365–85. Though *The Color of Creatorship* does not centrally attend to intersectional axes around race, it engages them in as much depth as possible within the bounds of the project. The lack of consistent engagement with identity categories other than race is not intended to elide them but rather to center race and leave productive space for future scholarly works.

19. Haney López, *White by Law*, 113.

20. Coombe and Aoki lay the groundwork for exploration of this argument in their studies of the constitutive nature of intellectual property law, including with respect to

race. Rosemary J. Coombe, "Marking Difference in American Commerce: Trademarks and Alterity at Century's End," *PoLAR: Political and Legal Anthropology Review* 19, no. 1 (May 1996): 105–16; Coombe, *The Cultural Life of Intellectual Properties*; Aoki, "(Intellectual) Property and Sovereignty."

21. Haney López, *White by Law*, 163–69.

22. Raymond Williams, *Marxism and Literature* (Oxford: Oxford University Press, 2009), 127. For a discussion of the intersections of copyright and racial feelings, see Minh-Ha T. Pham, "Feeling Appropriately: On Fashion Copyright Talk and Copynorms," *Social Text* 34, no. 3 (2016): 51–74.

23. Foucault, *The Birth of Biopolitics*, 248.

24. Michel Foucault, *Power/Knowledge: Selected Interviews and Other Writings, 1972–1977*, ed. Colin Gordon (New York: Vintage, 1980), 197.

25. Thomas K. Nakayama and Robert L. Krizek, "Whiteness: A Strategic Rhetoric," *Quarterly Journal of Speech* 81, no. 3 (August 1995): 291–309.

26. Marouf Hasian, Jr., "Judicial Rhetoric in a Fragmentary World: 'Character' and Storytelling in the Leo Frank Case," *Communication Monographs* 64, no. 3 (September 1997): 254.

27. Ibid.

28. Ibid., 251.

29. Benedict Anderson, *Imagined Communities: Reflections on the Origin and Spread of Nationalism* (London: Verso, 1987), 21.

30. Ibid.

31. Molina, *How Race Is Made in America*, 6 (internal quotation marks omitted).

32. Vincent N. Pham, "Our Foreign President Barack Obama: The Racial Logics of Birther Discourses," *Journal of International and Intercultural Communication* 8, no. 2 (May 2015): 91.

33. Ibid.

34. Ibid.

35. Stuart Hall, "The Whites of Their Eyes," in *Gender, Race, and Class in Media: A Critical Reader*, ed. Gail Dines and Jean M. Humez (Los Angeles: SAGE Publications, 1995), 18–22.

36. Michael Lacy and Kent Ono contend that the rhetorical study of race must be a transdisciplinary practice. "Introduction" in *Critical Rhetorics of Race*, ed. Michael G. Lacy and Kent A. Ono (New York: New York University Press, 2011).

37. Ibid.

38. Raymie McKerrow, "Critical Rhetoric: Theory and Praxis," *Communication Monographs* 56, no. 2 (1989): 91–111.

39. Lacy and Ono, "Introduction", 6–7.

40. Haney López, *White by Law*.

41. Pham, "Our Foreign President Barack Obama," 93.

42. Imani Perry makes an argument for the necessity of drawing upon multiple disciplines in carrying out studies in CRT. Imani Perry, "Cultural Studies, Critical Race Theory, and Some Reflections on Methods," *Villanova Law Review* 50, no. 4 (2005): 915–24.

43. Anjali Vats and Deidré A. Keller, "Critical Race IP," *Cardozo Arts & Entertainment Law Journal* 36, no. 3 (2018): 740.

44. Stallman, "Did You Say 'Intellectual Property'?"

45. Silbey, "The Mythical Beginning of Intellectual Property," 326.

46. Jack Valenti, "Hollywood and the War against Terror," *New Perspectives Quarterly* 19, no. 2 (June 28, 2008): 69–72.

47. Stallman, "Did You Say 'Intellectual Property'?"

48. For her classic discussion of how white racial identity functions as property, see Cheryl I. Harris, "Whiteness as Property," *Harvard Law Review* 106, no. 8 (June 1993): 1707–91.

49. Zahr Said, "A Response to Madhavi Sunder's *From Goods to a Good Life*," *Concurring Opinions*, September 11, 2010, https://concurringopinions.com/archives/2012/09/a -response-to-madhavi-sunders-from-goods-to-a-good-life.html.

50. Mitu Gulati and Devon Carbado, "The Law and Economics of Critical Race Theory," *Yale Law Journal* 112, no. 7 (January 2003): 1757–1828.

51. Michael Mukasey, "Remarks Prepared for Delivery by Attorney General Michael B. Mukasey at the Tech Museum of Innovation," March 28, 2008, https://www.justice .gov/archive/ag/speeches/2008/ag_speech_080328.html.

52. Cedric J. Robinson, *Black Marxism: The Making of the Black Radical Tradition* (Chapel Hill: University of North Carolina Press, 2000). I invoke Robinson's theorization of Black Marxism, which scholars like R. D. G. Kelley and Jodi Melamed have taken up, instead of Nancy Leong's, for a variety of reasons, including that the work of the former is contextualized vis-à-vis a rich and long history of Black radicalism, one that Leong's suggestion of monetizing the contributions of people of color does not capture. See Nancy Leong, "Racial Capitalism," *Harvard Law Review* 126, no. 8 (June 2013): 2151–2226.

53. Jodi Melamed, "Racial Capitalism," *Critical Ethnic Studies* 1, no. 1 (Spring 2015): 76–77.

54. Ibid.

55. Ibid.

56. Ibid.

57. Greene, "Intellectual Property at the Intersection of Race and Gender."

58. Madhavi Sunder, "The Invention of Traditional Knowledge," *Law & Contemporary Problems* 70, no. 1 (Spring 2007): 97.

59. Coombe, "Marking Difference."

60. Dorian Lynskey, "Blurred Lines: The Most Controversial Song of the Decade," *The Guardian*, November 13, 2013, https://www.theguardian.com/music/2013/nov/13 /blurred-lines-most-controversial-song-decade.

61. *Williams v. Bridgeport Music, Inc.*, 2015 U.S. Dist. LEXIS 97262 (C.D. Cal. July 14, 2015).

62. Kristelia Garcia, "Fireside Chat" (Blurred v. Bright: The Changing Analysis of Copyright Infringement in Music, University of Colorado, Boulder, March 23, 2017).

63. *Williams v. Gaye*, 885 F.3d 1150 (9th Cir. March 21, 2018).

64. The idea-expression dichotomy is an important part of copyright law. It states that only the particular expression of ideas, not mere ideas, are copyrightable and thus protectable. See *Sheldon v. Metro-Goldwyn Pictures Corporation*, 81 F.2d 49 (2d Cir. January 17, 1936).

65. *Williams*, 2015 U.S. Dist. LEXIS 97262 at 31.

66. This issue is notable because it is intertwined with the history of racist copyright policy in the United States. Because Black artists like Gaye often could not read or write well enough to notate their own music as required under the Copyright Act of 1909, their works were either stolen by white musicians and industry executives or left without any copyright protection. The systematic disadvantage that this created for Black artists remained until

1971, when the Sound Recording Act extended copyright protection to sound recordings, not simply sheet music. Kevin J. Greene, "Intellectual Property at the Intersection of Race and Gender," Sound Recording Act, Pub. L. No. 92-140, 85 Stat. 39 (1971). Those who claim that the outcome of *Williams* was unfair largely do so by contending that the jury went beyond the scope of the sheet music in the case, turning to unprotectable elements of Gaye's sound recording as justification for protecting his music. Wendy Gordon, "How the Jury in the 'Blurred Lines' Case Was Misled," *The Conversation*, March 17, 2015, http://theconversation.com/how-the-jury-in-the-blurred-lines-case-was-misled-38751.

67. Lateef Mtima writes: "By allowing the jury to undertake the intrinsic infringement determination, the court's decision served copyright social justice by preventing musicological bias against aural traditions from improperly denying copyright protection to creative elements in 'Got to Give It Up.'" Lateef Mtima, "The Blurred Lines Controversy: Attaining IP Social Justice for African American Composers," Institute for Intellectual Property and Social Justice (2015), http://www.iipsj.org/index.php/resources/iipsj-scholarship. See also Toni Lester, "Blurred Lines—Where Copyright Ends and Cultural Appropriation Begins—The Case of Robin Thicke versus Bridgeport Music, and the Estate of Marvin Gaye," *Hastings Communications & Entertainment Law Journal* 36, no. 2 (November 2014): 217–42.

68. For one discussion of reparations in the intellectual property context, see Kevin J. Greene, "'Copynorms,' Black Cultural Production, and the Debate over African-American Reparations," *Cardozo Arts & Entertainment Law Journal* 25, no. 3 (2008): 1179–1227.

69. Lester, "Blurred Lines."

70. Gordon, "How the Jury in the 'Blurred Lines' Case Was Misled." Gordon, Professor of Law at Boston University, writes: "What's not lawful is to copy too much expression—that is, the details of the copied artist's aesthetic and organizational choices. At some point, as these details accumulate, enough expression might be copied to be considered 'substantial.' The difference between lawful copying of ideas and 'substantial' copying of expression is what the jury should have focused on in the Blurred Lines case—at least, if they were persuaded that copying occurred." Ibid.

71. Kal Raustiala and Chris Sprigman, "Squelching Creativity," *Slate.com*, March 12, 2015, http://www.slate.com/articles/news_and_politics/jurisprudence/2015/03/_blurred_lines_verdict_is_wrong_williams_and_thicke_did_not_infringe_on.html.

72. Jennifer Jenkins, "The 'Blurred Lines' of the Law," Center for the Study of the Public Domain, n.d., https://law.duke.edu/cspd/blurredlines/.

73. Gilbert B. Rodman, "Textual Stealing? Or (Williams and) Thicke as Thieves?: Copyright, Race, and Elusive Justice" (Paper Presentation at Race + IP 2017, Boston College, Chestnut Hill, MA, April 20–22, 2017).

74. Jody Rosen, "Robin Thicke on 'Blurred Lines' and Learning from His Mistakes," *New York Times*, July 1, 2015, https://www.nytimes.com/2015/07/05/arts/music/robin-thicke-on-blurred-lines-and-learning-from-his-mistakes.html.

75. "Robin Thicke and Pharrell Testify in Tense Blurred Lines Deposition Video," *The Guardian*, October 26, 2015, https://www.theguardian.com/music/2015/oct/26/blurred-lines-trial-video-shows-robin-thicke-testimony.

76. George Lipsitz, *The Possessive Investment in Whiteness: How White People Profit from Identity Politics*, (Philadelphia: Temple University Press, 2009).

77. Despite my qualms about siding with Gaye's estate, I signed on to the amicus brief that Lateef Mtima, Steven Jamar, and Sean O'Connor wrote in favor of Bridgeport Music. In addition to valuing the work that these three scholars have done in the interests of racial justice

in intellectual property law, I viewed (and still view) the brief as a productive rhetorical move to claim space for unprotectable elements of the work of any musician of color, in the interest of "access, inclusion, and empowerment." Brief Amicus Curiae of the Institute for Intellectual Property and Social Justice Musicians and Composers and Law, Music, and Business Professors in Support of Appellees at 2, *Williams et al. v. Gaye et al.* No. 13–cv-06004 JAK (AGRx) (9th Cir. 2016). Though the legal brief is an imperfect remedy, it performs important narrative work by highlighting racial justice as a concern of copyright law and confronting the racial scripts suggesting that Black artists lack sufficient imaginativeness to be creators. The amicus brief exemplifies how imperfect policy remedies can coexist with radical critiques of race.

78. Richard Dyer, *White* (New York: Routledge, 1997).

79. Gerald Lyn Early, *One Nation under a Groove: Motown and American Culture* (Ann Arbor: University of Michigan Press, 2004), 28.

80. Pharrell's rhetoric of the "new Black man," a phrase that he uses in a sense that is *very* different from the radical ways in which Mark Anthony Neal uses it to reimagine Black masculinity, embraces the postracial. Damon Young at *The Root* writes: "Between the G I R L cover color controversy and his remarks about the 'new Black,' Williams seems intent on being the executive producer for America's post-racial mixtape. And [naturally], this new Blackness went over about as well as a fart in a shared cubicle." Damon Young, "'New Black' Is the New Black," Very Smart Brothas, *The Root*, June 20, 2014, https://verysmartbrothas.theroot.com/new-black-is-the-new-black-1822521511. T.I., on the other hand, who was dismissed as a party to the case, has not been plagued by such negative publicity on questions of race and identity. Sheila Marikar, "Why T.I. Decided to Save His Old Atlanta Neighborhood (and How He's Doing It)," *Inc.com*, June 26, 2018, https://www.inc.com/magazine/201808/sheila-marikar/how-i-did-it-rapper-t-i-clifford-joseph-harris-jr-buy-back-the-block.html. He was, however, recently embroiled in a scandal about sexual "purity tests." Meagan Fredette, "The Internet is Disgusted by T.I. Checking His Daughter's Hymen," *Revelist.com*, November 7, 2019, https://www.revelist.com/celebrity/ti-rapper-daughter-hymen-virginity/16716.

81. Sherwin Siy, "On 'Blurred Lines,' Copyright Infringement, and 'Sample Trolls,'" *Public Knowledge*, August 20, 2013, https://www.publicknowledge.org/news-blog/blogs/blurred-lines-copyright-infringement-and-samp. See also Tim Wu, "Jay-Z versus the Sample Troll," *Slate*, November 16, 2006, http://www.slate.com/articles/arts/culturebox/2006/11/jayz_versus_the_sample_troll.html.

82. Kimberly C. Roberts, Entertainment Reporter, "'Blurred Lines' Decision Not 'Scary' for True Artists," *Philadelphia Tribune*, March 20, 2015, http://www.phillytrib.com/entertainment/blurred-lines-decision-not-scary-for-true-artists/article_3dfe5c89–0d21–5e29–97a0–8be94bf09241.html.

83. Ibid.

84. Mark A. Lemley, "Romantic Authorship and the Rhetoric of Property," *Texas Law Review* 75, no. 4 (1996): 873–906.

85. James Boyle and Jennifer Jenkins, *Theft! A History of Music* (Durham: CreateSpace, 2017).

86. Joycelyn A. Wilson, "Robin Thicke and the Art of Jacking for Beats," *The Root*, August 21, 2013, https://www.theroot.com/robin-thicke-and-the-art-of-jacking-for-beats-1790897794.

87. Ibid.

88. Alan David Freeman, "Legitimizing Racial Discrimination through Antidiscrimination Law: A Critical Review of Supreme Court Doctrine," *Minnesota Law Review* 62, no. 6 (1978): 1052.

89. Walter Mignolo, *The Darker Side of Western Modernity: Global Futures, Decolonial Options* (Durham: Duke University Press, 2011), 2.

90. Vats and Keller, "Critical Race IP," 789.

CHAPTER ONE

1. For a discussion of rhetorical inclusion and rhetorical exclusion, see Danielle Endres, "The Rhetoric of Nuclear Colonialism: Rhetorical Exclusion of American Indian Arguments in the Yucca Mountain Nuclear Waste Siting Decision," *Communication and Critical/Cultural Studies* 6, no. 1 (March 2009): 39–60; Anjali Vats, "(Dis)owning Bikram: Decolonizing Vernacular and Dewesternizing Restructuring in the Yoga Wars," *Communication and Critical/Cultural Studies*, 13, no. 4 (March 2016): 1–21.

2. Ian Haney López distinguishes between the "common sense" and the "scientific" approaches that courts took to categorizing races. Ian Haney López, *White by Law: The Legal Construction of Race* (New York: New York University Press, 1996), 4–5.

3. Michael Calvin McGee, "Text, Context, and the Fragmentation of Contemporary Culture," *Western Journal of Communication* 54, no. 3 (1990): 278.

4. Matthew Houdek, "Racial Sedimentation and the Common Sense of Racialized Violence: The Case of Black Church Burnings," *Quarterly Journal of Speech* 104, no. 3 (July 2018): 279–306.

5. Marouf Hasian, Jr., Michelle C. Condit, and John Luis Lucaites, "The Rhetorical Boundaries of 'The Law': A Consideration of the Rhetorical Culture of Legal Practice and the Case of the 'Separate but Equal' Doctrine," *Quarterly Journal of Speech* 82, no. 4 (November 1996): 323–42.

6. See *Stowe v. Thomas*, 23 F. Cas. 201 (E.D. Pa. 1853).

7. Stuart Hall, "The Whites of Their Eyes," in *Gender, Race, and Class in Media: A Critical Reader*, ed. Gail Dines and Jean M. Humez (Los Angeles: SAGE Publications, 1995), 18–22.

8. Charles W. Mills, *The Racial Contract* (Ithaca: Cornell University Press, 2011), 73. Mills writes:

Anthony Pagden suggests that a division of the European empires into their main temporal periods should recognize "two distinct, but interdependent histories: the colonization of the Americas, 1492 to the 1830s, and the occupation of Asia, Africa, and the Pacific, 1730s to the period after World War II. In the first period, it was, to begin with, the nature and moral status of the Native Americans that primarily had to be determined, and then that of the imported African slaves whose labor was required to build this 'New World.' In the second period, culminating in formal European colonial rule over most of the world by the early twentieth century, it was the character of colonial peoples that became crucial." Ibid., 21.

9. Eva Illouz, *Cold Intimacies: The Making of Emotional Capitalism* (Cambridge: Polity Press, 2007), 2.

10. Andrea Smith discusses anti-Blackness as one of three pillars of white supremacy. She contends that it is rooted in slaveability. Andrea Smith, "Indigeneity, Settler Colonialism, White Supremacy," *Global Dialogue* 12, no. 2 (2010), 1–13.

11. Frances L. Ansley, "Stirring the Ashes: Race, Class, and the Future of Civil Rights Scholarship," *Cornell Law Review* 74, no. 6 (1989): 1024n129.

12. Illouz, *Cold Intimacies*, 5.

13. Cheryl I. Harris, "Whiteness as Property," *Harvard Law Review* 106, no. 8 (June 1993): 1707.

14. 1 Stat. 124 (1790).

15. Kevin J. Greene, "Intellectual Property at the Intersection of Race and Gender: Lady Sings the Blues," *American University Journal of Gender, Social Policy, and the Law* 16 no. 3 (2008); Toni Lester, "Oprah, Beyoncé, and the Girls Who 'Run the World'—Are Black Female Cultural Producers Gaining Ground in Intellectual Property Law?" *Wake Forest Journal of Business and Intellectual Property Law* 15, no. 3 (2015): 537–62.

16. Karla Mari McKanders, "Sustaining Tiered Personhood: Jim Crow and Anti-Immigrant Laws," *Harvard Journal on Racial and Ethnic Justice* 26, no. 1 (2010): 163–210.

17. Ibid., 171.

18. 26 Stat. 1106 (1891).

19. Lauren Berlant, *The Female Complaint: The Unfinished Business of Sentimentality in American Culture* (Durham: Duke University Press, 2008), 145.

20. Sara Ahmed, "Affective Economies," *Social Text* 22, no. 2 (June 2004): 118 (italics omitted).

21. See George Lipsitz, *Dangerous Crossroads: Popular Music, Postmodernism, and the Poetics of Place* (London: Verso, 1994); Kembrew McLeod, *Freedom of Expression®: Resistance and Repression in the Age of Intellectual Property* (Minneapolis: University of Minnesota Press, 2007). Olufunmilayo Arewa and Brian Frye argue, for different reasons, that copyright's creativity requirement is deeply flawed. Olufunmilayo Arewa, "The Freedom to Copy: Copyright, Creation, and Context," *U.C. Davis Law Review* 41, no. 2 (December 2007): 477–558; Brian Frye, "Against Creativity," *New York University Journal of Law and Liberty* 11, no. 1 (2017): 426–54.

22. *Yuengling v. Schile*, 12 F. 97, 103 (S.D.N.Y. 1882).

23. Michael Perelman, "The Political Economy of Intellectual Property," *Socialism and Democracy* 28, no. 1 (2014): 24–33; Lateef Mtima, "What's Mine Is Mine but What's Yours Is Ours: IP Imperialism, the Right of Publicity, and Intellectual Property Social Justice in the Digital Information Age," *SMU Science & Technology Law Review* 15, no. 3 (Fall 2012): 323–88. For a detailed history of the move by authors to expand copyright protection, see Siva Vaidhyanathan, *Copyrights and Copywrongs: The Rise of Intellectual Property and How It Threatens Creativity* (New York: NYU Press, 2003).

24. Mtima, "What's Mine Is Mine but What's Yours Is Ours," 329.

25. Erika Lee, *The Making of Asian America: A History* (New York: Simon and Schuster, 2015), 89.

26. 1 Stat. 109 (1790). For a more detailed history of patent law's racial exclusions, see Brian L. Frye, "Invention of a Slave," *Syracuse Law Review* 68, no. 1 (2018): 181–230.

27. Kara W. Swanson, "Rubbing Elbows and Blowing Smoke: Gender, Class, and Science in the Nineteenth-Century Patent Office," *Isis* 108, no. 1 (March 2017): 40–61; Shontavia Johnson, "With Patents or Without, Black Inventors Reshaped American Industry," *Smithsonian Magazine*, February 16, 2017, https://www.smithsonianmag.com/innovation/with-patents-or-without-black-inventors-reshaped-american-industry-180962201/.

28. Patent Act of 1836, 5 Stat. 357 (1836). See also Gerald L. Neuman, "Back to Dred Scott?" *San Diego Law Review* 24, no. 2 (1987): 485–500, 495n40.

29. Rayvon Fouché and Sharra Vostral, "'Selling' Women: Lillian Gilbreth, Gender Translation, and Intellectual Property," *American University Journal of Gender, Social Policy & the Law* 19, no. 3 (January 2011): 827.

30. Dan L. Burk and Jessica Reyman, "Patents as Genre: A Prospectus," *Law and Literature* 26, no. 2 (2014): 163–90, 164.

31. Frye, "Invention of a Slave," 190.

32. Michael S. Burdett, *Eschatology and the Technological Future* (New York: Routledge, 2014), 25.

33. Brian Lee Pelanda, "Declarations of Cultural Independence: The Nationalistic Imperative behind the Passage of Early American Copyright Laws, 1783–1787, Part II: Articles," *Journal of the Copyright Society of the USA* 58 (2011), 432.

34. It is difficult to tease out racial scripts of anti-Blackness and anti-Indigeneity in this respect. On the one hand, Wheatley's case is a specific articulation of anti-Blackness in the United States. On the other hand, tropes of the noble savage that marginalized indigenous peoples were also prevalent and transported from settler colonial practices. My aim is not necessarily to identify an origin point for anti-Blackness/anti-Indigeneity but to note that both organized racial scripts in the United States.

35. Henry Louis Gates, Jr., *The Trials of Phillis Wheatley: America's First Black Poet and Her Encounters with the Founding Fathers* (New York: Basic Civitas Books, 2003), 22.

36. Ibid., 5.

37. Ibid., 66–68.

38. See Oren Bracha, "The Ideology of Authorship Revisited: Authors, Markets, and Liberal Values in Early American Copyright," *Yale Law Journal* 118, no. 2 (2008): 186–271.

39. Thomas Jefferson, *Notes on the State of Virginia* (New York: Penguin Books, 1998), 147 (emphasis added).

40. Ibid.

41. For a discussion of the racial scripts around Black masculinity, see Herman Gray, "Black Masculinity and Visual Culture," *Callaloo* 18, no. 2 (1995): 401–5.

42. Massachusetts Copyright Statute, Massachusetts (1783), *Primary Sources on Copyright (1450–1900)*, ed. Lionel Bently and Martin Kretschmer, n.d., http://www.copyrighthistory.org/cam/tools/request/showRecord.php?id=record_us_1783d.

43. Bracha, "The Ideology of Authorship Revisited."

44. Jefferson, *Notes on the State of Virginia*, 145.

45. Ibid.

46. Stephen Michael Best, *The Fugitive's Properties: Law and the Poetics of Possession* (Chicago: University of Chicago Press, 2004), 4.

47. Anthony Paul Farley, "The Apogee of the Commodity," *DePaul Law Review* 53, no. 3 (August 2005): 1229–46.

48. Best, *The Fugitive's Properties*. See also Anthea Kraut, *Choreographing Copyright: Race, Gender, and Intellectual Property Rights in American Dance* (Oxford: Oxford University Press, 2015). Kraut writes:

[Fred] Moten's opening pages are a direct response to Karl Marx, who introduces the counterfactual "Could commodities themselves speak" only to underscore their lack of any intrinsic value outside a system of exchange. Whereas the speaking commodity is an impossibility for Marx, Moten insists on not just the possibility but "the historical reality of commodities who spoke—of laborers who were commodities before, as it were, the abstraction of labor power from their bodies and who continue to pass on this material heritage across the divide that separates slavery and freedom." (95)

49. For an overview of justifications for granting intellectual property rights, including those based on the philosophy of John Locke that are implicated here, see Justin Hughes, "The Philosophy of Intellectual Property," *Georgetown Law Journal* 77, no. 2 (1988): 287–366.

50. Jessica Silbey, "The Mythical Beginning of Intellectual Property," *George Mason Law Review* 15, no. 2 (Winter 2008): 348n196. Here Silbey quotes Aoki to demonstrate the relationship between the Romantic author and national sovereignty.

51. Ibid., 350.

52. Ibid.

53. See Yuko Kawai, "Stereotyping Asian Americans: The Dialectic of the Model Minority and the Yellow Peril," *Howard Journal of Communications* 16, no. 2 (April 1, 2005): 109–30.

54. Ibid.

55. William Hearst, "Alien Competition Kills American Jobs—'Buy American' to End Bread Lines," *San Francisco Examiner*, December 30, 1932.

56. Ibid.

57. Silbey, "The Mythical Beginning of Intellectual Property," 350.

58. A Lexis Nexis search for "copyright w/50 imagin!" with a date range ending in 1952 produces twenty-eight cases. The three cases I have selected here are among the few that directly implicate race. They demonstrate how "imagination" was often a racialized concept.

59. Vaidhyanathan, *Copyrights and Copywrongs*. McLeod notes that imitation became a cause of action in the context of right of publicity in the 1980s. McLeod, *Freedom of Expression*®, 200–201. Cases like *Chaplin* and *Supreme Records* show the history of the expansion of such rights.

60. *Chaplin v. Amador*, 93 Cal. App. 358 (Cal. App., Div. I, July 30, 1928).

61. Ibid., 364. I have chosen to focus only on the precedential appellate decision here.

62. Ibid., 359–60.

63. Ibid.

64. Peter Decherney, *Hollywood's Copyright Wars: From Edison to the Internet* (New York: Columbia University Press, 2012), 70–73.

65. Ibid., 68. Bracha's argument about the narrowness of definitions of originality in the 1800s and early 1900s supports this reading. As he contends, Justice Joseph Story's articulation of originality in *Emerson v. Davies* (1845) set a high bar for creative genius, one that whites could attain more easily than people of color. Bracha, "The Ideology of Authorship Revisited," 230–31.

66. Decherney, *Hollywood's Copyright Wars*, 67–72.

67. Jason Borge, "Replaying Carlitos: Chaplin, Latin American Film Comedy, and the Paradigm of Imitation," *Journal of Latin American Cultural Studies* 22, no. 3 (2013): 271–86.

68. Vaidhyanathan, *Copyrights and* Copywrongs, 49–50.

69. Grier concedes "the genius and imagination of the author," even though she is a white woman. *Stowe*, 23 F. Cas. at 208.

70. The conversation about imitation more broadly is a complex interdisciplinary one that implicates who has the right to claim originality and propertize that originality. See Jason Richards, "Imitation Nation: Blackface Minstrelsy and the Making of African American Selfhood in *Uncle Tom's Cabin*," *NOVEL: A Forum on Fiction* 39, no. 2 (2006): 204–20.

71. Decherney, *Hollywood's Copyright Wars*, 68–69.

72. Ibid., 71.

73. Ibid., 75.

74. Ibid., 74.

75. Ibid., 72.

76. Steven W. Bender, *Greasers and Gringos: Latinos, Law, and the American Imagination* (New York: New York University Press, 2005), 32.

77. Peter Decherney, "Gag Orders: Comedy, Chaplin, and Copyright," in *Modernism and Copyright*, ed. Paul K. Saint-Amour and Peter Decherney (New York: Oxford University Press, 2010), 135–44.

78. Julian B. Carter persuasively argues that Chaplin's *Modern Times* is a commentary on the vulnerability of the family and thus whiteness in the Machine Age. He writes:

The preexisting chain of associations connecting machinery, modernity, and whiteness thus suggested not only the vulnerability of human bodies to mechanical forces but also the vulnerability of domestic ties . . . and . . . the vulnerability of whiteness as a set of consistent relational ideals that defined the nation and located it in the history of western civilization. (Julian B. Carter, *The Heart of Whiteness: Normal Sexuality and Race in America, 1880–1940* [Durham: Duke University Press, 2007], 86–87)

79. Olufunmilayo B. Arewa, "Blues Lives: Promise and Perils of Musical Copyright," *Cardozo Arts & Entertainment Law Journal* 27, no. 3 (2009): 573, 598–99 (emphasis added).

80. DeCherney, *Hollywood's Copyright Wars*, 75–76.

81. McLeod, *Freedom of Expression®*, 33–36.

82. Borge, "Replaying Carlitos," 272.

83. Ibid., 275.

84. *Supreme Records Inc. v. Decca Records Inc.*, 90 F. Supp. 904 (1950).

85. "Literary and Artistic Rights for Purposes of, and Their Infringement by or in Connection with, Motion Pictures, Radio, and Television," 23 A.L.R.2d 244.

86. *Supreme Records*, 90 F. Supp. at 908.

87. Ibid. at 906.

88. Philip Auslander, *Liveness: Performance in a Mediatized Culture* (New York: Routledge, 2008), 153–54n41.

89. *Supreme Records*, 90 F. Supp. 904 at 910.

90. Ibid. at 909.

91. Ibid. at 911.

92. Ibid.

93. Famed jazz musician Bo Diddley commented on the manner in which covers such as the one discussed here failed to protect innovative Black artists. Jennifer L. Hall, "Blues and the Public Domain—No More Dues to Pay? Part I," *Journal of the Copyright Society of the U.S.A.* 42, no. 3 (1994): 215–26. See also Kembrew McLeod and Peter DiCola, *Creative License: The Law and Culture of Digital Sampling* (Durham: Duke University Press, 2011).

94. *Supreme Records*, 90 F. Supp. at 912.

95. Ibid.

96. *Goldin v. Clarion Photoplays*, 202 A.D. 1, 7 (N.Y. App. Div. I July 14, 1922).

97. Leon R. Yankwich, "Legal Protection of Ideas: A Judge's Approach," *Virginia Law Review* 43, no. 3 (1957): 375–95.

98. Ibid.

99. Ibid., 382.

100. U.S. Const. art. I, § 8.

101. Kara Swanson, "Authoring an Invention: Patent Production in the Nineteenth Century," in *Making and Unmaking Intellectual Property: Creative Production in Legal and*

Cultural Perspective, ed. Mario Biagioli, Peter Jaszi, and Martha Woodmansee (Chicago: University of Chicago Press, 2011), 42.

102. Jefferson Morley, *Snow-Storm in August: The Struggle for American Freedom and Washington's Race Riot of 1935* (New York: Anchor, 2013).

103. Endres, "The Rhetoric of Nuclear Colonialism." See also Colin Dayan, *The Law Is a White Dog: How Legal Rituals Make and Unmake Persons*, reprint ed. (Princeton: Princeton University Press, 2013).

104. Edmund Burke, *Annual Report of the Commissioner of Patents* (Washington: Ritchie and Heiss, 1846) (emphasis added).

105. Johnson, "With Patents or Without, Black Inventors Reshaped American Industry."

106. *Men of Progress*, National Museum of American History, Smithsonian Institution, n.d., http://americanhistory.si.edu/american-enterprise-exhibition/videos/men-progress.

107. *Men of Progress* Text, http://npg.si.edu/object/npg_NPG.65.60.

108. Ibid.

109. See Rayvon Fouché, *Black Inventors in the Age of Segregation: Granville T. Woods, Lewis H. Latimer, and Shelby J. Davidson* (Baltimore: Johns Hopkins University Press, 2003). While there is considerably less research about the inventions of other groups of people of color, they likely fell prey to similar racial norms during the era.

110. E. Cram, "Queering Sexual Modernity in the Rocky Mountain West" (Paper Presentation at Public Address Conference: Embodying Justice, University of Colorado, Boulder, September 27–29, 2018.

111. United States Patent Office, *Official Gazette of the United States Patent Office* (Washington, 1878), 12.

112. David Punter, *A New Companion to the Gothic* (West Sussex: Wiley-Blackwell, 2015), 26.

113. Ibid.

114. James Boyle, *Shamans, Software, and Spleens: Law and the Construction of the Information Society* (Cambridge: Harvard University Press, 2009).

115. *Johnson v. M'Intosh*, 21 U.S. 543 (1823); Debora J. Halbert, *Resisting Intellectual Property* (New York: Routledge, 2005), 149–50.

116. Margaret Chon, "Law Professor as Artist: Themes and Variations in Keith Aoki's Intellectual Property Scholarship Symposium: (Un)Bound by Law: Keith Aoki Memorial Symposium: Tribute," *Oregon Law Review* 90, no. 5 (2012): 1251–64.

117. See Brewton Berry, "The Myth of the Vanishing Indian," *Phylon* 21, no. 1 (1960): 51–57.

118. Ibid.

119. Orlando Patterson, *Slavery and Social Death* (Cambridge: Harvard University Press, 1982).

120. Silbey, "The Mythical Beginning of Intellectual Property."

121. Jim Cullen, *The American Dream: A Short History of an Idea That Shaped a Nation* (New York: Oxford University Press, 2003), 4.

122. Ibid., 7.

123. Ibid., 10.

124. Robert C. Rowland and John M. Jones, "One Dream: Barack Obama, Race, and the American Dream," *Rhetoric & Public Affairs* 14, no. 1 (2011): 131.

125. Ibid.

126. George Lipsitz, *The Possessive Investment in Whiteness: How White People Profit from Identity Politics* (Philadelphia: Temple University Press, 2006).

127. Dana L. Cloud, "Hegemony or Concordance? The Rhetoric of Tokenism in 'Oprah' Winfrey's Rags to Riches Biography," *Critical Studies in Mass Communication* 13, no. 2 (1996): 115–37.

128. See generally Vandana Shiva, *Biopiracy: The Plunder of Nature and Knowledge* (Boston: South End Press, 1997).

129. See Reiland Rabaka, "The Souls of White Folk: W.E.B. Du Bois's Critique of White Supremacy and Contributions to Critical White Studies," *Journal of African American Studies* 11, no. 1 (2007): 1–15.

130. Cara A. Finnegan, "The Naturalistic Enthymeme and Visual Argument: Photographic Representation in the 'Skull Controversy,'" *Argumentation and Advocacy* 37, no. 3 (January 1, 2001): 143.

131. Because the racial identities of inventors of this period are frequently unknown, it is difficult to discern with certainty when and how the U.S. Patent Office was engaging in overt discrimination. Frye, "Invention of a Slave," 186. Reading the cultural texts of the era, however, provides important insight into the dominant ideological understandings of race and invention.

132. Zeynep Çelik, *Displaying the Orient: Architecture of Islam at Nineteenth-Century World's Fairs* (Berkeley: University of California Press, 1992), 1. See also Kara Swanson, "Patents and African American Civil Rights" (Paper Presentation at Race + IP 2017, Chestnut Hill, MA, April 21, 2017).

133. Çelik, *Displaying the Orient*, 5.

134. Robert W. Rydell, John E. Findling, and Kimberly Pelle, *Fair America: World's Fairs in the United States* (Washington: Smithsonian Institution, 2013); Robert W. Rydell, *All the World's a Fair: Visions of Empire at American International Expositions, 1876–1916* (Chicago: University of Chicago Press, 1987). For instance, while the 1876 Centennial Exposition in Philadelphia had a Women's Building to showcase the work of eighty female inventors, people of color were not offered a similar space ("Progress Made Visible: American World's Fairs and Expositions," University of Delaware Library, December 21, 2010, http://www .lib.udel.edu/ud/spec/exhibits/fairs/cent.htm). Instead, the event was meant to "carry the spectator through the successive steps of human progress," by representing Native Americans and Asians as threats to America's exceptionalism and advancement. Rydell, *All the World's a Fair*, 20. African Americans were largely excluded from the 1876 World's Fair. Ibid., 29–31.

135. "Negro Day, August 25, 1893, at the World's Columbian Exposition," Living History of Illinois and Chicago, http://livinghistoryofillinois.com/pdf_files/Negro%20 Day,%20August%2025,%201893%20at%20the%20Worlds%20Columbian%20Exposition.pdf; "The World's Columbian Exposition," Paul V. Galvin Library Digital History Collection, March 8, 1999, http://columbus.gl.iit.edu/reed2.html.

136. Ida B. Wells, Frederick Douglass, Irvine Garland Penn, and Ferdinand Lee Barnett, "The Reason Why the Colored American Is Not in the World's Columbian Exposition," University of Pennsylvania Digital Library, 1893, http://digital.library.upenn.edu/women /wells/exposition/exposition.html.

137. Indeed, in 1904, the United States responded to critiques of Empire by showing the purported willingness of Filipinos to work as American servants. "Interview with Robert Rydell," Race—The Power of an Illusion, 2003, http://www.pbs.org/race/000 _About/002_04–background-02-11.htm.

138. Cheryl Ganz, *The 1933 Chicago World's Fair: A Century of Progress* (Champaign: University of Illinois Press, 2008), 112.

139. Individual states offered trademark protection within their limited jurisdictions. Federal trademark legislation, however, became mired in the politics of constitutionality until the passage of the 1946 statute. See Kenneth L. Port, "The Congressional Expansion of American Trademark Law: A Civil Law System in the Making," *Wake Forest Law Review* 35, no. 4 (2000): 827–914.

140. 15 U.S.C. § 1051 et seq. (July 5, 1946).

141. See David Dante Troutt, "A Portrait of the Trademark as a Black Man: Intellectual Property, Commodification, and Redescription," *U.C. Davis Law Review* 38, no. 4 (2005): 1141–1208.

142. Berlant, *The Female Complaint*, 116.

143. Rosemary J. Coombe, "Marking Difference in American Commerce: Trademarks and Alterity at Century's End," *PoLAR: Political and Legal Anthropology Review* 19, no. 1 (May 1996): 106. (In an early commentary on the connections between trademark and race, Coombe also notes that "[s]uch legal forms always invite encounters with alterity.")

144. Richard Schur, "Legal Fictions: Trademark Discourse and Race," in *African American Culture and Legal Discourse*, ed. Lovalerie King and Richard Schur (New York: Palgrave Macmillan, 2009).

145. Lauren Berlant, *Cruel Optimism* (Durham: Duke University Press, 2011).

146. See *Groeneveld Transp. Efficiency, Inc. v. Lubecore Int'l, Inc.*, 730 F.3d 494 (6th Cir. September 12, 2013).

147. See *Abercrombie & Fitch Stores, Inc. v. American Eagle Outfitters*, 280 F.3d 619 (6th Cir. February 15, 2000).

148. See generally Laura Heymann, "The Reasonable Person in Trademark Law," *Faculty Publications*, Paper 194 (2008).

149. Christian Metz, *The Imaginary Signifier: Psychoanalysis and the Cinema* (Bloomington: Indiana University Press, 1982). The scopic regime, for Metz, refers to the production of a voyeuristic cinematic gaze around an absent or imagined object.

150. Judith Butler, "Endangered/Endangering: Schematic Racism and White Paranoia," in *Reading Rodney King/Reading Urban Uprising*, ed. Robert Gooding-Williams (New York: Routledge, 1993), 17.

151. See Laura Mulvey, "Visual Pleasure and Narrative Cinema," *Screen* 16, no. 3 (October 1975): 6–18.

152. See J. Allen Douglas, "The Most Valuable Sort of Property: Constructing White Identity in American Law, 1880–1940," *San Diego Law Review* 40, no. 3 (Fall 2003), 881.

153. bell hooks, *Black Looks: Race and Representation* (Boston: South End Press, 1992), 21.

154. See Kevin J. Greene, "Trademark Law and Racial Subordination: From Marketing of Stereotypes to Norms of Authorship," *Syracuse Law Review* 58, no. 3 (2008): 431–46; Malte Hinrichsen, *Racist Trademarks: Slavery, Orient, Colonialism, and Commodity Culture* (Münster: LIT Verlag, 2012).

155. Patricia Hill Collins, *Black Feminist Thought* (New York: Routledge, 2008).

156. Ibid., 80.

157. Ibid., 80–81.

158. Kimberly Wallace Sanders, 59–63.

159. M. M. Manring, *Slave in a Box: The Strange Career of Aunt Jemima* (Charlottesville: University Press of Virginia, 1998), 68.

160. Eric Lott, *Love and Theft: Blackface Minstrelsy and the American Working Class* (New York: Oxford University Press, 1993).

161. Manring, *Slave in a Box*, 77.

162. "Our History," Aunt Jemima, 2016, http://www.auntjemima.com/aj_history/.

163. Anjali Vats, "Marking Disidentification: Race, Corporeality, and Resistance in Trademark Law," *Southern Communication Journal* 81, no. 4 (August 2016): 237–51.

164. *Aunt Jemima Mills Co. v. Rigney & Co.*, 247 F. 407 (2d Cir. 1917).

165. Micki McEyla, *Clinging to Mammy: The Faithful Slave in Twentieth-Century America* (Cambridge: Harvard University Press, 2007), 223–27.

166. The same story repeated itself in 2014 when Harrington's family sued Quaker Oats for a percentage of the royalties derived from use of her image. The case was ultimately dismissed because the plaintiffs could not prove their relationship to Harrington. Claire Zillman, "Why It's So Hard for Aunt Jemima to Ditch Her Unsavory Past," *Fortune*, August 12, 2014, http://fortune.com/2014/08/12/aunt-jemima-racism/; Tim Kenneally, "Aunt Jemima Heirs' $3 Billion Lawsuit against Pepsi, Quaker Oats Tossed by Judge," *The Wrap*, February 18, 2015, https://www.thewrap.com/aunt-jemima-3–billion-lawsuit-against -pepsi-quaker-oats-tossed-by-judge/.

167. Marissa Fessenden, "Descendants of a Real Aunt Jemima Are Suing the Brand Bearing Her Name," https://www.smithsonianmag.com/smart-news/descendants -real-aunt-jemima-are-suing-brand-bearing-her-name-180952964/, *Smithsonian.com*, October 7, 2014.

168. "'Aunt Jemima' of Pancake Fame, Dead," *Sunday Morning Star*, September 9, 1923.

169. Ahmed, "Affective Economies."

170. *Gardella v. Log Cabin Products*, 89 F.2d 891, 895 (2d Cir. 1937).

171. Ibid.

172. Ibid.

173. Ibid.

174. Jane M. Gaines, *Contested Culture: The Image, the Voice, and the Law* (Chapel Hill: University of North Carolina Press, 1991), 125.

175. *Groeneveld Transp. Efficiency*, 730 F.3d 494 at 510.

176. *Abercrombie & Fitch*, 280 F.3d 619 at 628.

177. Schur, "Legal Fictions," 196.

178. Manning Marable, *How Capitalism Underdeveloped Black America: Problems in Race, Political Economy, and Society* (Cambridge: South End Press, 2015).

179. Heymann, "The Reasonable Person in Trademark Law." See also Ann Bartow, "Likelihood of Confusion," *San Diego Law Review* 41, no. 2 (2004), for a feminist critique of the trope of the so-called reasonable consumer.

180. The origin of this doctrinal standard is the Lanham Act of 1946, which provides in Section 2(d) that

[n]o trademark by which goods of the applicant may be distinguished from the goods of others shall be refused registration on the principal register on account of its nature unless it . . . (d) Consists of or comprises a mark which so resembles a mark registered in the Patent Office or a mark or trade name previously used in the United States by another and not abandoned as to be likely, when applied to the goods of the applicant, to cause confusion or mistake or to deceive purchasers. (15 U.S.C. § 1051 [July 5, 1946])

181. *Robertson v. Berry*, 50 Md. 591, 597 (Md. Ct. App. 1879).

182. Ibid. Other keywords that were unlikely to favor people of color include "unfair competition" or "unfair business competition." For a contemporary discussion of the double standards of business, see Kate Losse, "The Unbearable Whiteness of Breaking Things,"

Kate Losse (blog), August 19, 2013, https://medium.com/@katelosse/the-unbearable -whiteness-of-breaking-things-521cb394fda2.

183. *Hoyt v. Hoyt*, 1891 Pa. LEXIS 952, 14 (Pa. 1891).

184. Heymann, "The Reasonable Person in Trademark Law."

185. Melissa Milewski, *Litigating across the Color Line: Civil Cases between Black and White Southerners from the End of Slavery to Civil Rights* (Oxford: Oxford University Press, 2017).

186. Heymann, "The Reasonable Person in Trademark Law," 783.

CHAPTER TWO

1. Mary L. Dudziak, "Desegregation as a Cold War Imperative," *Stanford Law Review* 41, no. 1 (1988): 61–120.

2. Jodi Melamed, *Represent and Destroy* (Minneapolis: University of Minnesota Press, 2011), 9.

3. Ibid.

4. Ibid., 4.

5. Ibid. (quoting Nikhil Pal Singh).

6. Kimberlé Crenshaw, Neil Gotanda, Gary Peller, and Kendall Thomas, eds., introduction to *Critical Race Theory: The Key Writings That Formed the Movement* (New York: New Press, 1995), xiv (emphasis added).

7. David Nimmer, "Nation, Duration, Violation, Harmonization: An International Copyright Proposal for the United States," *Law and Contemporary Problems* 55, no. 2 (1992): 214.

8. See Margot E. Kaminski, "The Capture of International Intellectual Property Law through the U.S. Trade Regime," *Southern California Law Review* 87, no. 4 (2015): 977–1052.

9. Robert Asen, "A Discourse Theory of Citizenship," *Quarterly Journal of Speech* 90, no. 2 (May 2004): 191.

10. J. L. Austin, *How to Do Things with Words*, 2nd ed. (Cambridge: Harvard University Press, 1975).

11. Stuart Hall, "The Whites of Their Eyes," in *Gender, Race, and Class in Media: A Critical Reader*, ed. Gail Dines and Jean M. Humez, 4th ed. (Los Angeles: SAGE Publications, 1995), 21.

12. For instance, *In re Ah Yup* (1889), the first of the Prerequisite Cases, uses a combination of racial common sense, scientific classification, and legislative history to conclude that the Chinese petitioner, Ah Yup, is ineligible for naturalization. 1 F. Cas. 223, 223 (D. Cal. 1878).

13. Nils Gilman, "The Collapse of Racial Liberalism," *American Interest*, March 2, 2018, https://www.the-american-interest.com/2018/03/02/collapse-racial-liberalism/.

14. Lani Guinier writes that "[p]ost–World War II racial liberalism rejected scientific racism and discredited its postulate of inherent black inferiority. At the same time, racial liberalism positioned the peculiarly American race 'problem' as a psychological and interpersonal challenge rather than a structural problem rooted in our economic and political system." Lani Guinier, "From Racial Liberalism to Racial Literacy: *Brown v. Board of Education* and the Interest-Divergence Dilemma," *Journal of American History* 91, no. 1 (2004): 100.

15. Charles W. Mills, "Racial Liberalism," *PMLA* 123, no. 5 (2008): 1380–97.

16. John Locke, *Two Treatises of Government*, ed. Peter Laslett (Cambridge: Cambridge University Press, 1960), 285–302. For a critique of Locke's race and gender politics, see generally Martin Fredriksson, "Authors, Inventors and Entrepreneurs: Intellectual Property

and Actors of Extraction," *Open Cultural Studies* 2, no. 1 (2018): 319–29.

17. Mills, "Racial Liberalism," 1381.

18. Tim Wise, *Colorblind: The Rise of Post-Racial Politics and the Retreat from Racial Equity* (San Francisco: City Lights Publishers, 2010), 27.

19. As Derrick Bell contends: "Black people will never gain full equality in this country. Even those herculean efforts we hail as successful will produce no more than temporary 'peaks of progress,' short-lived victories that slide into irrelevance as racial patterns adapt in ways that maintain white dominance." Derrick Bell, *Faces at the Bottom of the Well: The Permanence of Racism* (New York: Basic Books, 1992), 12.

20. Crenshaw, building on Bell, speaks of this in terms of cycles of reform/retrenchment. Kimberlé Crenshaw, "Race, Reform, and Retrenchment: Transformation and Legitimation in Antidiscrimination Law," *Harvard Law Review* 101, no. 7 (1988): 1331–87. The limited extent to which people of color have broadly benefited from modern evolutions in intellectual property law is a compelling response to work such as that of Justin Hughes and Robert P. Merges, who contend that distributive justice remedies the inequalities of intellectual property law. Justin Hughes and Robert P. Merges, "Copyright and Distributive Justice," *Notre Dame Law Review* 92, no. 2 (2017): 513–77.

21. E. Johanna Hartelius, *The Rhetoric of Expertise* (Lanham: Lexington Books, 2010).

22. Zoltan P. Majdik and William M. Keith, "The Problem of Pluralistic Expertise: A Wittgensteinian Approach to the Rhetorical Basis of Expertise," *Social Epistemology* 25, no. 3 (2011): 275–90.

23. Foster, for instance, describes how non-expertness became a marketing tool in its own right, allowing pharmaceutical companies to advertise drugs as both traditional knowledge and scientific innovation, with the former demonstrating the authenticity of the remedy. Laura A. Foster, *Reinventing Hoodia: Peoples, Plants, and Patents in South Africa* (Seattle: University of Washington Press, 2017), 4. See also Linda Tuhiwai Smith, *Decolonizing Methodologies: Research and Indigenous Peoples* (London: Zed Books, 2012).

24. See Dennis S. Karjala, "Biotech Patents and Indigenous Peoples," *Minnesota Journal of Law, Science & Technology* 7 (2006), 483–527.

25. Cheryl I. Harris, "Whiteness as Property," *Harvard Law Review* 106, no. 8 (June 1993): 1707.

26. Majdik and Keith, "The Problem of Pluralistic Expertise," 277.

27. Michel Foucault defines "episteme" as "the 'apparatus' which makes possible the separation, not of the true from the false, but of what may from what may not be characterized as scientific." Foucault, *Power/Knowledge: Selected Interviews and Other Writings, 1972–1977*, ed. Colin Gordon (New York: Vintage, 1980), 197.

28. See generally Vandana Shiva, *Biopiracy: The Plunder of Nature and Knowledge* (Boston: South End Press, 1997). In the interest of space, I have cited those who write about the extractive nature of biopiracy throughout the book as the topic unfolds instead of condensing them into one note. I return to the topic in detail in chapter 4, in the discussion of yoga piracy.

29. *Diamond v. Chakrabarty*, 447 U.S. 303, 306 (1980).

30. Ibid. at 309.

31. Ibid. at 310.

32. Ibid.

33. Ibid. at 308.

34. Ibid. at 310.

35. Ibid. at 309.

36. Danielle Endres, "The Rhetoric of Nuclear Colonialism: Rhetorical Exclusion of American Indian Arguments in the Yucca Mountain Nuclear Waste Siting Decision," *Communication and Critical/Cultural Studies* 6, no. 1 (March 2009): 46.

37. Shobita Parthasarathy, "Whose Knowledge? What Values? The Comparative Politics of Patenting Life Forms in the United States and Europe," *Policy Sciences* 44, no. 3 (September 2011): 273.

38. It is worth noting that scholars and activists across disciplines and cultural spaces are working to create non-exploitative theories and practices around traditional knowledge. See e.g. Ruth Okediji, "Traditional Knowledge and the Public Domain in Intellectual Property," in *Intellectual Property and Development: Understanding the Interfaces,* ed. Carlos Corea and Xavier Seuba (Singapore: Springer, 2019), 249–76; Graham Dutfield, "TK Unlimited, The Emerging but Incoherent International Law of Traditional Knowledge Protection," *Journal of World Intellectual Property* 20, nos. 5–6 (2017): 144–59.

39. Brief Amicus Curiae of the Pharmaceutical Manufacturers Association in Support of Respondent at 1, *Diamond v. Chakrabarty,* 447 U.S. 303 (1980) (No. 79-136).

40. Ibid.

41. Ibid.

42. Brief Amicus Curiae of Genentech in Support of Respondent at 5, *Diamond v. Chakrabarty,* 447 U.S. 303 (1980) (No. 79-136).

43. Ibid. at *14.

44. There is a large body of literature on TRIPS and the exploitation of traditional knowledge. Vandana Shiva and Olufunmilayo Arewa are two of many thought leaders in that area. See Vandana Shiva, "TRIPS, Human Rights and the Public Domain," *Journal of World Intellectual Property* 7, no. 5 (September 2004): 665–73; Olufunmilayo B. Arewa, "TRIPS and Traditional Knowledge: Local Communities, Local Knowledge, and Global Intellectual Property Frameworks," *Marquette Intellectual Property Law Review* 10 (2006): 155–80.

45. Geoffrey C. Bowker and Susan Leigh Star, *Sorting Things Out: Classification and Its Consequences* (Cambridge: MIT Press, 2000), 45.

46. Sandra G. Harding, *Is Science Multicultural?: Postcolonialisms, Feminisms, and Epistemologies* (Bloomington: Indiana University Press, 1998), 84. See also Keith Aoki, "Weeds, Seeds & Deeds: Recent Skirmishes in the Seed Wars," *Cardozo Journal of International & Comparative Law* 11, no. 2 (2003), 253.

47. *Chakrabarty,* 447 U.S. 303 at 316.

48. Richard Slotkin, *Regeneration through Violence: The Mythology of the American Frontier, 1600–1860* (Norman: University of Oklahoma Press, 2000).

49. Wendy Brown, *Edgework: Critical Essays on Knowledge and Politics* (Princeton: Princeton University Press, 2009), 33–34.

50. Leah Ceccarelli, *On the Frontier of Science: An American Rhetoric of Exploration and Exploitation, Rhetoric and Public Affairs* (East Lansing: Michigan State University Press, 2013), 23.

51. Linda Greenhouse, "Science May Patent New Forms of Life, Justices Rule 5 to 4," *New York Times,* June 17, 1980.

52. Ibid.

53. Ceccarelli, *On the Frontier of Science.*

54. Hall, "The Whites of Their Eyes," 21.

55. Lisa Ikemoto, "Discovery + Race: From 'Savages' to HeLa" (Paper Presentation at Race + IP 2017, Boston College, Chestnut Hill, MA, April 20–22, 2018).

56. Parthasarathy, "Whose Knowledge? What Values?," 268.

57. *Moore v. Regents of the University of California*, 51 Cal. 3d 120, 126 (Cal. 1990).

58. Ibid.

59. Ibid., 130.

60. Ibid., 141–42.

61. See generally Marlon Rachquel Moore, "Opposed to the Being of Henrietta: Bioslavery, Pop Culture, and the Third Life of HeLa Cells," *Medical Humanities* 43, no. 1 (March 2017): 55–61.

62. For contextualization of this argument, see Margaret Lock, "The Alienation of Body Tissue and the Biopolitics of Immortalized Cell Lines," *Body and Society* 7, nos. 2–3 (2001): 63–91; David J. Jefferson, "Biosociality, Reimagined: A Global Distributive Justice Framework for Ownership of Human Genetic Material," *Chicago-Kent Journal of Intellectual Property* 14, no. 2 (2015): 357–78; Brenna Bhandar, *Colonial Lives of Property: Law, Land, and Racial Regimes of Ownership* (Durham: Duke University Press, 2018).

63. Laura A. Foster, "Patents, Biopolitics, and Feminisms: Locating Patent Law Struggles over Breast Cancer Genes and the Hoodia Plant," *International Journal of Cultural Property* 19, no. 3 (August 2012), 376.

64. The Lacks Family, "Henrietta Lacks," *thelacksfamily.net*, 2012, http://www.lacksfamily.net/henrietta.php.

65. Andrea K. McDaniels, "Henrietta Lacks's Family Wants Compensation for Her Cells," *Washington Post*, February 14, 2017, https://www.washingtonpost.com/local/henrietta-lackss-family-wants-compensation-for-her-cells/2017/02/14/816481ba-f302-11e6-b9c9-e83fce42fb61_story.html?utm_term=.cc49481d5ob9.

66. See generally Harriet A. Washington, *Medical Apartheid: The Dark History of Medical Experimentation on Black Americans from Colonial Times to the Present* (New York: Harlem Moon, 2008).

67. Dorothy Roberts, "What's Race Got to Do with Medicine?" *NPR.com*, February 10, 2017, https://www.npr.org/2017/02/10/514150399/what-s-race-got-to-do-with-medicine.

68. Walter V. Reid, Sarah A. Laird, Carrie A. Meyer, Rodrigo Gámez, Ana Sittenfeld, Daniel H. Janzen, Michael A. Gollin, and Calestous Juma, eds., *Biodiversity Prospecting: Using Genetic Resources for Sustainable Development* (Washington: World Resources Institute, 1993).

69. Cori Hayden, *When Nature Goes Public: The Making and Unmaking of Bioprospecting in Mexico* (Princeton: Princeton University Press, 2003), 1.

70. Vandana Shiva, "Bioprospecting as Sophisticated Biopiracy," *Signs* 32, no. 2 (2007): 309.

71. Ibid., 308.

72. See Bernard O'Connor, "Protecting Traditional Knowledge," *Journal of World Intellectual Property* 6, no. 5 (September 2003): 677–98.

73. Susan K. Sell, *Private Power, Public Law: The Globalization of Intellectual Property Rights* (Cambridge: Cambridge University Press, 2003).

74. Ikechi Mgbeoji, *Global Biopiracy: Patents, Plants, and Indigenous Knowledge* (Vancouver: UBC Press, 2006), 33.

75. Dan L. Burk and Jessica Reyman, "Patents as Genre: A Prospectus," *Law and Literature* 26, no. 2 (2014): 164.

76. Foster, *Reinventing Hoodia*, 37.

77. Ibid., 13.

78. Melamed, *Represent and Destroy*, ix.

79. Firouzeh Nahavandi, *Commodification of Body Parts in the Global South: Transnational*

Inequalities and Development Challenges (London: Palgrave Macmillan, 2016), 76–77.

80. Ibid.

81. Ibid.

82. Sanjay Dalmia, "India Lacks Risk-takers, Not Creativity: Sanjay Dalmia on Steve Wozniak's Comment," *Medium.com*, March 27, 2018, https://medium.com/@sanjaydalmiagroup/india-lacks-risk-takers-not-creativity-sanjay-dalmia-on-steve-wozniaks-comment-e9fe0897066c.

83. *Hearings on the Home Recording of Copyrighted Works before the Subcommittee on Courts, Civil Liberties, and the Administration of Justice*, 97 Cong. (1982) (Testimony of Jack Valenti) (emphasis added).

84. Ibid.

85. Ibid.

86. Ibid. For a discussion of the flaws in piracy doomsaying arguments, see e.g. Aram Sinnreich, *The Piracy Crusade: How the Music Industry's War on Sharing Destroys Markets and Erodes Civil Liberties* (Amherst: University of Massachusetts Press, 2013).

87. Thomas K. Nakayama and Robert L. Krizek, "Whiteness: A Strategic Rhetoric," *Quarterly Journal of Speech* 81, no. 3 (August 1995): 291–309.

88. Kaushik Sunder Rajan, "Some Initial Thoughts before a Trump Presidency," *opendemocracy.net*, January 7, 2017, https://www.opendemocracy.net/kaushik-sunder-rajan/some-initial-thoughts-before-trump-presidency. Agency capture occurs when governmental agencies tasked with acting in the public interest actually come to protect special-interest groups. Kaminski, "The Capture of International Intellectual Property Law through the U.S. Trade Regime." Patrick Burkart has written extensively about how oligopoly is a cyclic feature of the music industry. Patrick Burkart, "Loose Integration in the Popular Music Industry," *Popular Music and Society* 28, no. 4 (2005): 489–500; see also Ronald Bettig, *Copyrighting Culture: The Political Economy of Intellectual Property* (New York: Routledge, 2018). The argument I am making here emphasizes the political, cultural, and rhetorical links between individuals as proof of agency capture through mafia capitalism.

89. Zach Schonfeld, "An Oral History of the PMRC's War on Explicit Lyrics," *Newsweek*, September 19, 2015, http://www.newsweek.com/2015/10/09/oral-history-tipper-gores-war-explicit-rock-lyrics-dee-snider-373103.html. While the initial fifteen songs included the work of only two artists of color—Prince's "Darling Nikki" and the Mary Jane Girls' "In My House"—the organization turned its attention to rap music shortly thereafter. See generally Kory Grow, "PMRC's 'Filthy 15': Where Are They Now?," *Rolling Stone*, September 17, 2015, https://www.rollingstone.com/music/lists/pmrcs-filthy-15-where-are-they-now-20150917/black-sabbath-trashed-20150917.

90. Brock Cardiner, "The First 'Parental Advisory' Hip-Hop Album," *Highsnobiety*, August 13, 2015, https://www.highsnobiety.com/2015/08/13/ice-t-rhyme-pays-first-hip-hop-album-parental-advisory/.

91. David Mills, "Q & A: Ice Cube (Pt. 2)," *Undercover Black Man* (blog), June 26, 2007, http://undercoverblackman.blogspot.com/2007/06/q-ice-cube-pt-2.html.

92. Ibid.

93. Ibid.

94. Sara Rimer, Special to the *New York Times*, "Obscenity or Art? Trial on Rap Lyrics Opens," *New York Times*, October 17, 1990, http://www.nytimes.com/1990/10/17/us/obscenity-or-art-trial-on-rap-lyrics-opens.html. For an overview of attempts to censor rap and hip hop, see "A Decade in Rap Censorship (1990–1999)," *Spin.Com* (blog), August

2013, https://www.spin.com/2013/08/the-worst-moments-of-the-90s-worst-band-names-worst-lyrics-worst-video/130809–worst-of-the-90s-c-delores/.

95. John Broder, "Quayle Calls for Pulling Rap Album Tied to Murder Case," *Los Angeles Times*, September 23, 1992; Sheila Rule, "The 1992 Campaign: Racial Issues, Rapper, Chided by Clinton, Calls Him a Hypocrite," *New York Times*, June 17, 1992, https://www.nytimes.com/1992/06/17/us/the-1992–campaign-racial-issues-rapper-chided-by-clinton-calls-him-a-hypocrite.html.

96. Orlando Patterson, *Slavery and Social Death* (Cambridge: Harvard University Press, 1982). Patterson first used the term "social death" to describe how slaves could be both alive and unrecognized as full humans. Michael P. Jeffries argues that hip hop and rap are threatening because they operate as critiques and catalogs of the social death that white supremacy produced in post–civil rights inner cities. Michael P. Jeffries, *Thug Life: Race, Gender, and the Meaning of Hip-Hop* (Chicago: University of Chicago Press, 2011), 88.

97. Lee Edelman, *No Future: Queer Theory and the Death Drive* (Durham: Duke University Press, 2004). Edelman uses the term "reproductive futurism" to describe anti-queer cultural investments in children and their potentials as good and necessary. In the context of Napster, (white) teenagers were cast in the role of "youth as inventor-hero," a trope that was and continues to be deeply racialized. David Spitz and Starling D. Hunter, "Contested Codes: The Social Construction of Napster," *Information Society* 21, no. 3 (July 2005): 174. Notably, Spitz and Hunter contend that the young, heroic inventor was ultimately criminalized. Ibid., 174–75. However, there was considerably more space for white teenagers to occupy a heroic space than there was for Black youths.

98. David J. Leonard, "The Real Color of Money: Controlling Black Bodies in the NBA," *Journal of Sport and Social Issues* 30, no. 2 (May 2006): 158–79.

99. John Logie's study of the peer-to-peer debates implicitly examines some of their racial contours. John Logie, *Peers, Pirates, and Persuasion: Rhetoric in the Peer-to-Peer Debates* (Lafayette: Parlor Press, 2006).

100. For a discussion of how Black people were framed in technology, see Mark Dery, "Black to the Future: Interviews with Samuel R. Delany, Greg Tate, and Tricia Rose," *Flame Wars: The Discourse of Cyberculture* (1994): 179–222; Tricia Rose, *Black Noise: Rap Music and Black Culture in Contemporary America* (Middletown: Wesleyan University Press, 1994).

101. *Grand Upright Music, Ltd. v. Warner Bros. Records, Inc.*, 780 F. Supp. 182, 183 (S.D.N.Y. 1991).

102. Ibid. at 185.

103. Ibid.

104. A number of cases before *Grand Upright Music*, many of which pitted Black plaintiffs against white defendants, did *not* end in the kind of public trial or harsh language that Biz Markie faced. See Jordan Runtagh, "Songs on Trial: 12 Landmark Music Copyright Cases," *Rolling Stone*, June 8, 2016, https://www.rollingstone.com/politics/politics-lists/songs-on-trial-12–landmark-music-copyright-cases-166396/the-beach-boys-vs-chuck-berry-1963–65098/. Most cases before *Grand Upright Music* settled out of court, with shared authorship credits. Ibid.

105. Kembrew McLeod and Michael DiCola make a compelling case for the fundamental creativity of sampling in hip hop and rap music. See generally Kembrew McLeod and Peter DiCola, *Creative License: The Law and Culture of Digital Sampling* (Durham: Duke University Press, 2011).

106. *Grand Upright Music*, 780 F. Supp. at 184.

107. Lovalerie King, *Race, Theft, and Ethics: Property Matters in African American Literature* (Baton Rouge: Louisiana State University Press, 2007), 7.

108. *Grand Upright Music*, 780 F. Supp. at 185.

109. Benjamin Franzen and Kembrew McLeod, *Copyright Criminals* (Indiepix Films, 2010).

110. Aimé J. Ellis, *If We Must Die: From Bigger Thomas to Biggie Smalls* (Detroit: Wayne State University Press, 2011), 116.

111. *Campbell v. Acuff-Rose Music*, 510 U.S. 569, 579 (1994).

112. In determining whether fair use exists, courts consider four factors: (1) the purpose and character of the use; (2) the nature of the copyrighted work; (3) the amount and substantiality of the use; and (4) the effect of the use on the potential market for the work. Ibid. at 578–79.

113. Ibid. at 579.

114. Recent fair use cases have suggested that courts are becoming more accepting of sampling. While it is not clear how far this liberalization of fair use will go, the turn is notable. See *Estate of James Oscar Smith v. Cash Money Records*, 253 F. Supp. 3d 737 (S.D.N.Y. 2017). Nonetheless, licensing requirements still significantly limit possibilities for sampling. See Peter S. Menell, "Adapting Copyright for the Mashup Generation," *University of Pennsylvania Law Review* 164, no. 2 (2016): 441–512; Kayla Mullen, "Applying the *De Minimus* Exception to Sound Recordings: Digital Samplers Are Neither Thieves nor Infringers," *Journal of the Patent & Trademark Office Society* 99, no. 4 (2017): 731–760.

115. *Campbell*, 510 U.S. at 579.

116. Ibid., 582.

117. Robert Hariman, "Political Parody and Public Culture," *Quarterly Journal of Speech* 94, no. 3 (2008): 250.

118. *Campbell*, 510 U.S. at 588.

119. Ibid. at 599 (Kennedy, J., concurring).

120. Ibid.

121. Henry Louis Gates, Jr., "2 Live Crew, Decoded," *New York Times*, June 19, 1990.

122. McLeod and DiCola, *Creative License*, 159.

123. *Suntrust Bank v. Houghton Mifflin*, 268 F.3d 1257, 1280–81 (11th Cir. 2001).

124. Ibid.

125. Ibid. at 1276–77.

126. Ibid. at 1280.

127. Edward Schiappa, *Defining Reality: Definitions and the Politics of Meaning* (Carbondale: Southern Illinois University Press, 2003), xi.

128. Sunder Rajan, "Some Initial Thoughts before a Trump Presidency."

129. Franzen and McLeod, *Copyright Criminals*.

130. Bryan J. McCann, *The Mark of Criminality: Rhetoric, Race, and Gangsta Rap in the War-on-Crime Era* (Tuscaloosa: University of Alabama Press, 2017).

131. Davarian L. Baldwin, "Black Empires, White Desires: The Spatial Politics of Identity in the Age of Hip-Hop," in *That's the Joint! The Hip-Hop Studies Reader*, ed. Murray Forman and Mark Anthony Neal (New York: Routledge, 2004), 170.

132. Ibid.

133. Sunder Rajan, "Some Initial Thoughts before a Trump Presidency."

134. Rosemary J. Coombe and Andrew Herman, "Culture Wars on the Net: Trademarks, Consumer Politics, and Corporate Accountability on the World Wide Web," *South Atlantic*

Quarterly 100, no. 4 (October 2001): 919–47; Steven M. Cordero, "Cocaine-Cola, the Velvet Elvis, and Anti-Barbie: Defending the Trademark and Publicity Rights to Cultural Icons Note," *Fordham Intellectual Property, Media & Entertainment Law Journal* 8, no. 2 (1998): 599–654.

135. In this sense, the theory behind dilution law resembles the theory behind *Citizens United v. FEC* (2010). In the same way that corporations can be protected as persons, trademarks can be protected as persons in dilution law vis-à-vis the implicit notion that their reputations can be confused or tarnished. Sandra L. Rierson, "The Myth and Reality of Dilution," *Duke Law and Technology Review* 11, no. 2 (2013): 214.

136. Though an ideological resonance exists between dilution law and anti-miscegenation law, there is little explicit evidence to support a formal connection.

137. Frank I. Schechter, "The Rational Basis of Trademark Protection," *Harvard Law Review* 40, no. 6 (1927): 813.

138. Ibid.

139. Ibid., 825.

140. For an overview of dilution law in practice, see Jerre Swann, "The Evolution of Dilution in the United States from 1927–2013," *Trademark Reporter* 103, no. 4 (2013).

141. *Moseley v. V Secret Catalogue, Inc.*, 537 U.S. 418 (2003).

142. See Jonathan Stempel, "Ben & Jerry's, Porn Producer Settle Lawsuit over DVD Titles," *Reuters*, July 30, 2013, https://www.reuters.com/article/us-unilever-benandjerrys-porn/ben-jerrys-porn-producer-settle-lawsuit-over-dvd-titles-idUSBRE96T13T20130730.

143. Richard Schur, "Legal Fictions: Trademark Discourse and Race," in *African American Culture and Legal Discourse*, ed. Lovalerie King and Richard Schur (New York: Palgrave Macmillan, 2009), 198–200.

144. Ibid., 201.

145. *Congressional Globe*, January 16, 1866.

146. Ibid.

147. Todd Samuel Presner, *Muscular Judaism: The Jewish Body and the Politics of Regeneration* (New York: Routledge, 2007), 49.

148. Sander Gilman, "The Mad Man as Artist: Medicine, History, and Degenerate Art," *Journal of Contemporary History* 20, no. 4 (1985): 575–97.

149. Stephanie Barron, *Degenerate Art: The Fate of the Avant-Garde in Nazi Germany* (Los Angeles: Harry N. Abrams, 1991), 9. The 1937 *Entartete Kunst* was the largest exhibit of avant garde art in Nazi Germany, but similar shows, on a smaller scale, were held as early as 1933. Bruce J. Altshuler, *The Avant-Garde in Exhibition: New Art in the 20th Century* (Berkeley: University of California Press, 1998), 139–41.

150. Peter Selz, *Beyond the Mainstream: Essays on Modern and Contemporary Art* (Cambridge: Cambridge University Press, 1998), 108–9.

151. Altshuler, *The Avant-Garde in Exhibition*, 142–43.

152. Selz, *Beyond the Mainstream*, 108.

153. Barron, *Degenerate Art*, 11.

154. Altshuler, *The Avant-Garde in Exhibition*, 141.

155. James Douglas, *English Etymology* (London: Simpkin, Marshall, 1872), 71.

156. Hensleigh Wedgwood, *A Dictionary of English Etymology* (New York: Macmillan, 1878), 558.

157. William Chambers, *Etymological Dictionary of the English Language* (London: W. & R. Chambers, 1904), 46.

158. Ibid., 510.

159. James Stormonth and William Bayne, *Etymological and Pronouncing Dictionary of the English Language* (London: William Blackwell and Sons, 1904), 894.

160. Schechter, "The Rational Basis of Trademark Protection," 831.

161. Swann, "The Evolution of Dilution in the United States from 1927–2013."

162. Richard Dyer, *White* (New York: Routledge, 1997), 45.

163. Mary Douglas, *Purity and Danger: An Analysis of Concepts of Pollution and Taboo* (London: Routledge, 2003), 138.

164. Rima L. Vesely-Flad, *Racial Purity and Dangerous Bodies: Moral Pollution, Black Lives, and the Struggle for Justice* (Minneapolis: Augsburg Fortress Press, 2017), xxv–xxvii.

165. Ibid.

166. *Coca-Cola Co. v. Gemini Rising, Inc.*, 346 F. Supp. 1183 (E.D.N.Y. 1972).

167. Michael M. Cohen, "Jim Crow's Drug War: Race, Coca Cola, and the Southern Origins of Drug Prohibition," *Southern Cultures* 12, no. 3 (August 2006): 56.

168. Ibid., 57.

169. *Moseley* 537 U.S. at 422.

170. Ibid.

171. Jasbir K. Puar, *Terrorist Assemblages: Homonationalism in Queer Times* (Durham: Duke University Press, 2017), 113.

172. *Moseley*, 537 U.S. at 434.

173. Trademark Dilution Revision Act of 2006, 120 Stat. 1730 (October 6, 2006).

CHAPTER THREE

1. Kristen Hoerl, "Selective Amnesia and Racial Transcendence in News Coverage of President Obama's Inauguration," *Quarterly Journal of Speech* 98, no. 2 (2012): 178–202.

2. Marouf Hasian, Jr., "Judicial Rhetoric in a Fragmentary World: 'Character' and Storytelling in the Leo Frank Case," *Communication Monographs* 64, no. 3 (September 1997): 255.

3. J. David Cisneros and Thomas K. Nakayama, "New Media, Old Racisms: Twitter, Miss America, and Cultural Logics of Race," *Journal of International and Intercultural Communication* 8, no. 2 (2015): 111.

4. As a recent book on the subject notes, "DIY—do-it-yourself—no longer just describes the weekend warrior struggling to install their own bathroom tiles or build their own deck. Instead DIY increasingly constitutes our lived, daily experiences, in particular those that involve media and communication systems." Matt Ratto and Megan Boler, introduction to *DIY Citizenship*, ed. Matt Ratto and Megan Boler (Cambridge: MIT Press, 2014), 1.

5. Ralina Joseph, "'Tyra Banks Is Fat': Reading (Post-)Racism and (Post-)Feminism in the New Millennium," *Critical Studies in Media Communication* 26, no. 3 (2009): 249.

6. Catherine R. Squires, *The Post-Racial Mystique: Media and Race in the Twenty-First Century* (New York: New York University Press, 2014), 6.

7. Michael Ortiz, "The Age of Hyper-Racism: White Supremacy as the White Knight of Capitalism," Truthout, September 20, 2013, http://www.truth-out.org/news/item/18780-the-age-of-hyper-racism-white-supremacy-as-the-white-knight-of-capitalism.

8. B. Zorina Khan, *The Democratization of Invention: Patents and Copyrights in American Economic Development, 1790–1920* (Cambridge: Cambridge University Press, 2009).

9. Danny Marti, "Celebrating American Ingenuity and Innovation on World Intellectual

Property Day," whitehouse.gov, April 26, 2016, https://obamawhitehouse.archives.gov /blog/2016/04/26/celebrating-american-ingenuity-and-innovation-world-intellectual -property-day.

10. Ibid.

11. Michael B. Mukasey, "Remarks Prepared for Delivery by Attorney General Michael B. Mukasey at the Tech Museum of Innovation," San Jose, CA, March 28, 2008.

12. Barack Obama, "Remarks by the President at Signing of the America Invents Act," whitehouse.gov, September 16, 2011, https://obamawhitehouse.archives.gov/the-press- office/2011/09/16/remarks-president-signing-america-invents-act.

13. Other pro-creatorship narratives of the era in popular culture support this reading. For instance, shows such as *The Men Who Built America* and *Everyday Edisons* demonstrate the prevalence of the myth of the postracial creator. See Jeff Pantages, "Shaky History behind 'Men Who Built America,'" *Real Clear History*, November 9, 2012, http://www .realclearhistory.com/articles/2012/11/09/who_are_the_men_who_built_america_40 .html; Michael Cable, "Patents and Pitfalls," *Everyday Edisons* (PBS, 2007).

14. Obama, "Remarks by the President at Signing of the the America Invents Act."

15. While there is no consensus on the effects of the America Invents Act, many argue that the legislation was not good for the individual inventor. See Nathan Hurst, "How the America Invents Act Will Change Patenting Forever," *WIRED*, https://www .wired.com/2013/03/america-invents-act/; Adrian Pelkus, "The America Invents Act Was Wrong from the Start," *IPWatchdog.com* (blog), January 9, 2017, http://www.ipwatchdog .com/2017/01/09/america-invents-act-wrong-start/id=76646/.

16. Obama, "Remarks by the President at Signing of the America Invents Act."

17. See Robert Rowland and John M. Jones, "One Dream: Barack Obama, Race, and the American Dream," *Rhetoric and Public Affairs* 14, no. 1 (2011). Rowland and Jones discuss the manner in which Obama recasts the American Dream, making it attainable to all of the nation's citizens.

18. See Kate Losse, "The Unbearable Whiteness of Breaking Things," *Kate Losse* (blog), August 19, 2013, https://medium.com/@katelosse/the-unbearable-whiteness-of-breaking -things-521cb394fda2, for a discussion of the whiteness of entrepreneurship and innovation. Such an argument, of course, is consistent with the racial liberalism of the Napster era and its reproductive futurist understanding of (white) teenage techies.

19. "Startup America | The White House," *whitehouse.gov*, https://www.whitehouse. gov/economy/business/startup-america.

20. Ibid.

21. Deirdre N. McCloskey, "The Rhetoric of Law and Economics," *Michigan Law Review* 86, no. 4 (1988): 759.

22. Ibid., 758.

23. Angela Harris, "Where Is Race in Law and Political Economy?" *Law and Political Economy*, November 30, 2017, https://lpeblog.org/2017/11/30/where-is-race-in-law -and-political-economy/.

24. Joe Biden, "Economy, Intellectual Property, and Piracy" May 2, 2014, https:// www.c-span.org/video/?319155-1/vice-president-biden-addresses-mpaa.

25. Ibid.

26. Ibid.

27. While I have not gone into detail about Biden's anti-Chinese rhetoric here, he has repeatedly named the Chinese as lacking creative capacity. Amy Li, "Chinese Students

Demand Biden Apologise for 'Insensitive' Comments," *South China Morning Post*, May 22, 2013, https://www.scmp.com/news/china/article/1243330/chinese-demand-apology-biden-insensitive-commencement-speech.

28. Ernesto, "'Piracy Is Theft, Clean and Simple,' US Vice President Says," *Torrent Freak*, June 22, 2010, https://torrentfreak.com/piracy-is-theft-clean-and-simple-us-vice-president-says-100622/.

29. Rajeswari Sunder Rajan, *The Scandal of the State: Women, Law, and Citizenship in Postcolonial India* (Durham: Duke University Press, 2003), 1.

30. Ibid.

31. For contemporary critiques of whiteness and deregulation in the free speech context, see Charlotte Garden, "The Deregulatory First Amendment at Work," *Harvard Civil Rights–Civil Liberties Law Journal* 51 (2016); and Justin Hansford, "The First Amendment Freedom of Assembly as a Racial Project," *Yale Law Journal* 127, no. 3 (2018): 685–714.

32. *Matal v. Tam*, 137 S. Ct. 1744, 1754 (June 19, 2017).

33. Ibid. Tam originally appealed the denial of the trademark to the Trademark Trial and Appeal Board (TTAB), which refused to register the name "the Slants."

34. 15 U.S.C. § 1052(a) (2006).

35. *Tam*, 137 S. Ct. at 1751.

36. Eugene Volokh, "The Slants (and the Redskins) Win: The Government Can't Deny Full Trademark Protection to Allegedly Racially Offensive Marks," *Washington Post*, June 19, 1981, https://www.washingtonpost.com/news/volokh-conspiracy/wp/2017/06/19/the-slants-and-the-redskins-win-the-government-cant-deny-full-trademark-protection-to-allegedly-racially-offensive-marks/?utm_term=.ebaf7c7ef4aa.

37. Lisa P. Ramsey, "Increasing First Amendment Scrutiny of Trademark Law after *Matal v. Tam*," *SCOTUSblog*, June 20, 2017, http://www.scotusblog.com/2017/06/symposium-increasing-first-amendment-scrutiny-trademark-law-matal-v-tam/.

38. Volokh, "The Slants (and the Redskins) Win."

39. Joseph Lowndes, "William F. Buckley Jr.: Anti-Blackness as Anti-Democracy," *American Political Thought* 6, no. 4 (October 2017): 639.

40. Ibid., 636.

41. Ibid., 635.

42. Sara Shariari, Abby Ivory-Ganja, and Elena Rivera, "Intersection—Author Junot Díaz on Immigration, Empire and White Supremacy," *KBIA.com*, February 6, 2018, http://kbia.org/post/intersection-author-junot-d-az-immigration-empire-and-white-supremacy.

43. See generally Brian W. Dippie, *The Vanishing American: White Attitudes and U.S. Indian Policy* (Lawrence: University Press of Kansas, 1991).

44. A Lexis Nexis search for "trademark w/100 disparag!" yielded fifteen cases between 1890 and 1953. I have surveyed those cases in drawing conclusions here.

45. See *Brothers v. Journeymen Tailors' Union*, 1890 Ohio Misc. LEXIS 180 (1890) (describing "the oral utterance of slander, which disparages the business of another"); *Cleveland Stone Co. v. Wallace*, 52 F. 431 (E.D. Mich. May 2, 1892)(writing "he disparages the exclusive right to that company to the names and labels as trademarks"); see also *H.E. Allen Mfg. Co. v. Smith*, 224 A.D. 187 (June 29, 1928) (holding that "[t]he defendant may be restrained from fraudulently disparaging plaintiff's product").

46. *Lee v. Tam*, 2016 U.S. S. Ct. Briefs LEXIS 4551, *25 (2016).

47. A Lexis Nexis search for "trademark w/100 disparag!" yielded 657 cases between 1953 and 2008.

48. *Bromberg et al. v. Carmel Self Service, Inc.*, 1978 T.T.A.B. LEXIS 24, *1 (March 28, 1978).

49. Derrick Bell, *Faces at the Bottom of the Well: The Permanence of Racism* (New York: Basic Books, 1992).

50. *Harjo v. Pro-Football, Inc.*, 50 U.S.P.Q.2d 1705, 1740 (T.T.A.B. April 2, 1999).

51. Ibid. at 112.

52. See *Blackhorse v. Pro-Football, Inc.*, 111 U.S.P.Q.2d 1080 (T.T.A.B. June 18, 2014), aff'd, 112 F. Supp. 3d 439, 115 U.S.P.Q.2d 1524 (E.D. Va. July 8, 2015).

53. See Mari J. Matsuda, ed., *Words That Wound: Critical Race Theory, Assaultive Speech, and the First Amendment* (Boulder: Westview Press, 1993); Richard Delgado and Jean Stefancic, *Must We Defend Nazis?: Hate Speech, Pornography, and the New First Amendment* (New York: New York University Press, 1999).

54. The Federal Circuit asked, sua sponte, "Does the bar on registration of disparaging marks in 15 U.S.C. § 1052(a) violate the First Amendment?" *In re Tam*, 808 F.3d 1321, 1334 (Fed. Cir. December 22, 2015). See generally *In re McGinley*, 660 F.2d 481 (October 1, 1981).

55. *In re McGinley*, 660 F.2d at 484.

56. *In re Tam*, 808 F.3d at 1328.

57. Angela R. Riley and Kristen A. Carpenter, "Owning Red: A Theory of Indian (Cultural) Appropriation," *Texas Law Review* 94, no. 5 (April 2016): 859–932.

58. *In re Tam*, 808 F.3d at 1328.

59. Ibid.

60. The Slants arguably perform radical Asian American masculinity. After all, their Chinese Dance Rock style is unexpected for Asians, who are stereotyped as quiet, deferential, weak, and feminine. Dressed in black shirts and black jackets with dark jeans or black pants, unsmiling and looking directly at the camera, the Slants urge the audience to question their assumptions about Asian men as well as their professions. Unlike oft forgotten and backgrounded characters, the Slants are not your Asian (American) sidekicks. Tam reportedly selected the name for the band after a friend, when asked, named "slanted eyes" as a common stereotype for Asians (though it is also worth noting that Tam may not have intended to reclaim the term; he has previously described it in interviews as descriptive and not derogatory), stating that "['Slants'] sounded like this '80s new wave band that maybe Debbie Harry or someone would front. . . . But [I thought] maybe we could use it in a way to engage people, to drive conversation and talk about it from our perspective." Teta Alim, "Why This Band Is Fighting for Its Right to Have an 'Offensive' Name | Bandwidth," *WAMU 88.5* (blog), September 18, 2015, http://bandwidth.wamu.org/why-this-band-is-fighting-for-its-right-to-have-an-offensive-name/. In this sense, the Slants actively remake Asian American masculinities in ways that can be read as stereotype breaking. Yet such resistance must always be understood in relation to the harm that it causes Native Americans and other people of color.

61. *In re Tam*, 808 F.3d at 1331.

62. Ibid. at 1332.

63. Ibid.

64. For a discussion about the workings of injurious speech, particularly in the context of the First Amendment debate, see Judith Butler, *Excitable Speech: A Politics of the Performative* (New York: Routledge, 2013). In this way, Tam highlights central tentions in "community activism" and "consumer citizenship." See e.g. Roopali Mukherjee and Sarah Bannet-Weiser, "Introduction: Community Activism in Neoliberal Times," in *Community Activism: Cultural Resistance in Neoliberal Times*, ed. Roopali Mukherjee and Sarah Banet Weiser (New York, NYU Press, 2012.)

65. Danielle Endres, "The Rhetoric of Nuclear Colonialism: Rhetorical Exclusion of American Indian Arguments in the Yucca Mountain Nuclear Waste Siting Decision," *Communication and Critical/Cultural Studies* 6, no. 1 (March 2009): 46.

66. Ibid.

67. *In re Tam*, 808 F.3d at 1336.

68. Matsuda, *Words That Wound.*

69. *Ass'n for Molecular Pathology v. Myriad Genetics, Inc.*, 133 S. Ct. 2107, 2118–19 (June 13, 2013). I have not detailed the complex procedural history of *Myriad* here. For a thorough discussion of that aspect of the case and its implications, see Dan L. Burk, "The Curious Incident of the Supreme Court in *Myriad Genetics*," *Notre Dame Law Review* 90, no. 2 (2014): 505–42.

70. Laura Foster, "Privatizing Knowledge: Patent Ownership, Benefit Sharing, and Indigenous Knowledge in South Africa," in *Privatization, Vulnerability, and Social Responsibility: A Comparative Perspective*, ed. Martha Fineman, Ulrika Andersson, and Titti Mattsson (New York: Routledge, 2017).

71. *Chakrabarty*, 447 U.S. at 310.

72. John Conley, "Myriad, Finally: Supreme Court Surprises by Not Surprising," *Genomics Law Report* (blog), https://www.genomicslawreport.com/index.php/2013/06/18/myriad-finally-supreme-court-surprises-by-not-surprising/. While a number of critiques have been leveled against *Myriad*, the consensus is that the case was *not* an overwhelming loss for biotechnology firms. See Christopher M. Holman, "Do Biotech Patent Lawsuits Really 'Overwhelmingly Lose?': A Response to *Our Divided Patent System*," *Biotechnology Law Report* 34, no. 2 (April 2015): 59–67. Holman writes: "Significantly, the patent claims targeted by the plaintiffs were not the most relevant to genetic diagnostic testing, which is Myriad's business, and were not representative of the patent claims Myriad would have asserted if it had chosen to bring a lawsuit. This is clearly illustrated by the number of lawsuits filed by Myriad against competitors alleging infringement of patent claims that were left unaffected by the Supreme Court's decision." Ibid. A number of scholars have critiqued the racial implications of genetic testing. See Ruha Benjamin, "Informed Refusal: Toward a Justice-Based Bioethics," *Science, Technology & Human Values* 41, no. 6 (November 2016): 967–90; Dorothy E. Roberts, *Fatal Invention: How Science, Politics, and Big Business Re-create Race in the Twenty-First Century* (New York: New Press, 2011); Keith Wailoo and Stephen Gregory Pemberton, *The Troubled Dream of Genetic Medicine: Ethnicity and Innovation in Tay-Sachs, Cystic Fibrosis, and Sickle Cell Disease* (Baltimore: Johns Hopkins University Press, 2006); Bita Amani and Rosemary J. Coombe, "The Human Genome Diversity Project: The Politics of Patents at the Intersection of Race, Religion, and Research Ethics," *Law & Policy* 27, no. 1 (January 2005): 152–88.

73. See generally Jonathan Kahn, "Race-ing Patents/Patenting Race: An Emerging Political Geography of Intellectual Property in Biotechnology," *Iowa Law Review* 92, no. 2 (February 2007): 353–416.

74. Sandra Park, "VICTORY! Supreme Court Decides: Our Genes Belong to Us, Not Companies," American Civil Liberties Union, https://www.aclu.org/blog/free-speech/victory-supreme-court-decides-our-genes-belong-us-not-companies.

75. *Bowman v. Monsanto* (2013) is similarly problematic. That case involved consideration of the subject of patent exhaustion, specifically in the context of seed patents. Monsanto sued a farmer, Vernon Hugh Bowman, for saving and replanting Roundup Ready soybean seeds that he purchased from a local grain elevator. *Bowman v. Monsanto Co.*, 133 S. Ct. 1761, 1765 (2013) (hereinafter *Bowman*). Bowman argued that because he replanted seeds that he had

saved after a sale consistent with Monsanto's patent and he planted them late in the season in a manner he considered risky, he had not infringed on the company's patent. He further argued that the doctrine of patent exhaustion applied to him. Ibid. The Supreme Court reasoned that the purpose of the patent exhaustion doctrine is to prevent patent holders from restricting the uses of patented products that it has sold. Bowman, however, the Supreme Court reasoned, created additional copies of the patented Roundup Ready soybean seeds; he did not use already purchased products in a manner that Monsanto unlawfully attempted to restrict. The Court reasoned in a manner that, I contend, prioritized the economic concern of compensating the inventor and erased the fundamental racial capitalism of Monsanto's patents.

Creating monocultures, preventing farmers in developing countries from accessing expensive seeds, and destroying culturally significant crops are just a few of the reasons that environmentalists as well as antiracist and anticolonial activists have pushed against Monsanto's zealous enforcement of its seed patents for decades. See Vandana Shiva, *Monocultures of the Mind: Perspectives on Biodiversity and Biotechnology* (London: Zed Books, 1993); Lara E. Ewens, "Seed Wars: Biotechnology, Intellectual Property, and the Quest for High Yield Seeds," *Boston College International & Comparative Law Review* 23, no. 2 (Spring 2000): 285–310; Keith Aoki, "Free Seeds, Not Free Beer: Participatory Plant Breeding, Open Source Seeds, and Acknowledging User Innovation in Agriculture," *Fordham Law Review* 77, no. 5 (April 2009): 2275–2310. Moreover, the Court's maximalist ruling makes a rhetorical choice to read patent exhaustion broadly and liberally, not narrowly and conservatively. In *Bowman*, the Court addressed none of those concerns, despite their being raised in amicus briefs. The Court chose instead to focus on the economic harm to the inventor and the inviolability of the patent. Brief for Amici Curiae Center for Food Safety and Save Our Seeds in Support of Petitioner, *Bowman v. Monsanto*, 133 S. Ct. 1761 (December 10, 2012). The Supreme Court's ruling found that Bowman was asking for an "unprecedented exception" despite a litany of scholars claiming that the courts have gone too far in protecting seed patents. *Bowman*, 133 S. Ct. at 1768.

76. "Free seeds, not free beer," Aoki cheekily declared in a reworking of the Free Software Foundation's most well-known catchphrase in 2009. See generally Aoki, "Free Seeds, Not Free Beer"; Daryl Lim, "Rebooting the Bean," *ABA Section of Antitrust Law, Agriculture and Food Committee Bulletin* 3, no. 2 (Fall 2012), https://papers.ssrn.com/abstract=2163220. As in *Myriad*, the Supreme Court retains the Romantic mythology of the inventor, here as inviolable subject, in a manner that not only disproportionately harms people of color but also reinforces the racial scripts of the Western maker, often a corporate entity, as holding unassailable (intellectual) property rights that must be protected against countervailing concerns.

77. Homi K. Bhabha, *The Location of Culture* (New York: Routledge, 1994), 122.

78. For instance, in a seemingly respectful speech at the Mumbai Stock Exchange in 2013, Joe Biden attempted to coax India into compliance with international legal regimes, using compliments, criticism, and shame. "Joe Biden: Remarks by the Vice President on the U.S.-India Partnership at the Bombay Stock Exchange in Mumbai, India," *The American Presidency Project*, July 24, 2013, http://www.presidency.ucsb.edu/ws/index.php?pid=121023.

79. See Lawrence Liang, "Porous Legalities and Avenues of Participation," in *Sarai Reader 2005: Bare Acts*, ed. Monica Narula et al. (New Delhi: Sarai, 2005), 6–17.

80. Aihwa Ong, *Neoliberalism as Exception: Mutations in Citizenship and Sovereignty* (Durham: Duke University Press, 2006), 4.

81. United Nations Office of Drugs and Crime, "Counterfeit: Don't Buy into Organized Crime," Vienna, Austria, 2014, https://www.unodc.org/documents/counterfeit/FocusSheet/Counterfeit _focussheet_EN_HIRES.pdf.

82. Edward W. Said, *Orientalism* (New York: Vintage Books, 1979).

83. Yahya Sadowski, "The New Orientalism and the Democracy Debate," *Middle East Report*, no. 183 (1993): 14.

84. Dag Tuastad, "Neo-Orientalism and the New Barbarism Thesis: Aspects of Symbolic Violence in the Middle East Conflict(s)," *Third World Quarterly* 24, no. 4 (August 2003): 591–99.

85. Ibid.

86. Sheldon Pollock, "Deep Orientalism? Notes on Sanskrit and Power beyond the Raj," in *Orientalism and the Postcolonial Predicament: Perspectives on South Asia*, ed. Carol Breckenridge and Peter van der Veer (Philadelphia: University of Pennsylvania Press, 1993).

87. Stanley Kurtz, "Democratic Imperialism: A Blueprint," *Hoover Institution*, May 2003, http://www.hoover.org/research/democratic-imperialism-blueprint.

88. Elizabeth Littlefield, "Democracy and Progress in India," *whitehouse.gov*, January 28, 2015, https://obamawhitehouse.archives.gov/blog/2015/01/28/democracy-and-progress-india.

89. Dinesh C. Sharma, "'Pharmacy of the World' Is in Peril," *Hindu Business Line*, January 23, 2018, https://www.thehindubusinessline.com/news/science/pharmacy-of-the-world-is-in-peril/article10048324.ece.

90. T. Prashant Reddy and Sumathi Chandrashekaran, *Create, Copy, Disrupt: India's Intellectual Property Dilemmas* (New Delhi: Oxford University Press, 2017) 95–105.

91. See generally Roger Collier, "Drug Patents: The Evergreening Problem," *CMAJ?: Canadian Medical Association Journal* 185, no. 9 (June 11, 2013): E385–86.

92. Thomas Blom Hansen, *The Saffron Wave: Democracy and Hindu Nationalism in Modern India* (Princeton: Princeton University Press, 1999), 9.

93. Ibid., 5.

94. Kavita Philip, "What Is a Technological Author? The Pirate Function and Intellectual Property," *Postcolonial Studies* 8, no. 2 (2005): 216.

95. James Fredal, "The Language of Delivery and the Presentation of Character: Rhetorical Action in Demosthenes' Against Meidias," *Rhetoric Review* 20, no. 3–4 (October 2001): 259.

96. Ibid., 261.

97. Ibid.

98. Ibid., 265.

99. Ibid.,

100. Ibid.,

101. William E. Wiethoff, "The Nature and Limits of Slave Insolence in the American South," *Quarterly Journal of Speech* 87, no. 2 (May 1, 2001): 199.

102. Allison K. Shutt, "'The Natives Are Getting Out of Hand': Legislating Manners, Insolence, and Contemptuous Behaviour in Southern Rhodesia, c. 1910–1963," *Journal of Southern African Studies* 33, no. 3 (September 2007): 654.

103. Ibid.

104. Ibid., 655.

105. Biden, http://www.presidency.ucsb.edu/ws/index.php?pid=121023.

106. Office of the United States Trade Representative, *Special 301 Report*, 2013.

107. The Patents Act, 1970, Act No. 39 of 1970, 27 India A.I.R. Manual 450, http://www.wipo.int/clea/docs-new/pdf/en/in/in004en.pdf.

108. *Novartis v. Union of India & Others*, Civil Appeal No. 2706–2716 of 2013 (April 2013). For a detailed discussion on the passage and evolution of Section 3(d) of the Indian Patents Act, 2005, see Reddy and Chandrashekaran, *Create, Copy, Disrupt*, 55–114.

109. Reddy and Chandrashekaran, *Create, Copy, Disrupt*, 55–114.

110. *Novartis*, Civil Appeal No. 2706–2716 of 2013.

111. John Bringardner, "Poorly Waged Patent Battle Becomes International Controversy; Novartis Hoped India's New Patent Laws Would Protect the Company's Breakthrough Cancer Treatment. But Such Was Not the Case," *National Law Journal*, October 3, 2007.

112. Reddy and Chandrashekaran, *Create, Copy, Disrupt*, 36.

113. For a critique of *Novartis*, see Dorothy Du, "*Novartis AG v. Union of India*: 'Evergreening,' TRIPS, and 'Enhanced Efficacy' Under Section 3(d)," *Journal of Intellectual Property Law* 21, no. 2 (2014): 225–63. For a defense of *Novartis*, see Yogesh Pai, "Promoting Diversity in Pharmaceutical Innovation and Access: India's Experience in the Post-TRIPS World," in *Diversity in Intellectual Property: Identities, Interests, Intersections*, ed. Irene Calboli and Srividhya Ragavan (Oxford: Cambridge University Press, 2015): 77–101; Saby Ghoshray, "3(d) View of India's Patent Law: Social Justice Aspiration Meets Property Rights in *Novartis v. Union of India & Others*," *John Marshall Review of Intellectual Property* 13, no. 4 (2014): 721–60.

114. Office of the United States Trade Representative, *Special 301 Report*, 2013.

115. John and Jean Comaroff offer important insight into the manner in which such power politics work in the (neo)colonial context, between the Global North and the Global South. They write:

> All of this points to something much larger: to the fact that postcolonies are quite literally associated with a counterfeit modernity, a modernity of counterfeit . . . In the postcolonial era, copies declare independence as commodities and circulate autonomously . . . These brazen simulacra, like counterfeit money, expose a conceit at the core of the culture of Western capitalism: that its signifiers can be fixed, that its editions can be limited, that it can franchise the platonic essence of its mass-produced modernity." John Comaroff and Jean Comaroff, *Law and Disorder in the Postcolony: An Introduction* (Chicago: University of Chicago Press, 2006), 13.

The licitness and lawfulness of the developed world is evidence not of the existence of an a priori governmental functionality or morality, but rather of the ability to control the definitions of illicitness and lawlessness. Comaroff and Comaroff demonstrate the fundamental premise that the legal definition is "in and of itself" a site for social and political negotiation, particularly with respect to the contestation of race.

116. Gardiner Harris, "President Obama and India's Modi Forge and Unlikely Friendship," *New York Times*, June 2016.

117. Ed Silverman, "India's New Patent Policy Spurs Debate over Implications for Pharma," *Stat News*, May 2016.

118. Mari Korepela, "A Postcolonial Imagination? Westerners Searching for Authenticity in India," *Journal of Ethnic and Migration Studies* 31, no. 3 (2010), 1299.

119. Lawrence Liang, "Piracy, Creativity, and Infrastructure: Rethinking Access to Culture," July 20, 2009, https://papers.ssrn.com/sol3/papers.cfm?abstract_id=1436229. Philip's critique of Lawrence Lessig is also notable here. She contends that his *Free Culture* presents Asian piracy as an "alibi for the saving of bourgeois law. Global capitalist free markets and liberal law are the best we have, he wants us to conclude—abandon those lifelines and we fall into the pit of Asian sameness." Philip, "What Is a Technological Author?" 212.

120. Ibid.

121. Office of the United States Trade Representative, *Special 301 Report*, 2016.

122. Partha Chatterjee, *Lineages of Political Society*, (New York: Columbia University Press, 2011), ix.

123. The recent Delhi University copyright case, in which the Indian Supreme Court held that photocopying academic materials for students is fair use, not copyright infringement, is another parallel example of this purported insolence. Radhika Oberoi, "DU Photocopy

Case: What Happened and Why It's Important," *The Wire*, October 26, 2016, https://thewire.in/education/du-photocopy-case.

124. Shampa Biswas, "'Nuclear Apartheid' as Political Position: Race as a Postcolonial Resource?," *Alternatives: Global, Local, Political* 26, no. 4 (October 2001): 507.

125. Ibid.

126. Raka Shome, "Race and Popular Cinema: The Rhetorical Strategies of Whiteness in City of Joy," *Communication Quarterly* 44, no. 4 (1996): 502–518.

127. Kavita Philip, "Keep on Copyin' in the Free World? Genealogies of the Postcolonial Pirate Figure," in *Postcolonial Piracy: Media Distribution and Cultural Production in the Global South*, ed. Lars Eckstein and Anja Schwarz (London: Bloomsbury, 2014), 174.

128. Ibid., 168.

129. Copyright restoration revives copyright in previously unprotected foreign works.

130. *Golan v. Holder*, 565 U.S. 302, 302 (January 18, 2012).

131. Ibid.

132. Ibid. at 317.

133. Ibid. at 330.

134. Derrick A. Bell, Jr., "Brown v. Board of Education and the Interest-Convergence Dilemma," *Harvard Law Review* 93, no. 3 (January 1980): 518.

135. Ibid.

136. *Golan*, 565 U.S. at 327–28.

137. Wendy Brown, "Wounded Attachments," *Political Theory* 21, no. 3 (1993): 400.

138. "A Brief History of the Berne Convention," WIPO, 2017, /about-wipo/en/history.html. See also Berne Convention for the Protection of Literary and Artistic Works, September 9, 1886, revised at Paris, July 24, 1971, 25 U.S.T. 1341.

139. David Nimmer, "Nation, Duration, Violation, Harmonization: An International Copyright Proposal for the United States," *Law and Contemporary Problems* 55, no. 2 (Spring 1992): 211–40.

140. Ibid. The United States chose the Universal Copyright Convention instead, which allowed for adherence to copyright formalities.

141. David Nimmer, "The Impact of Berne on United States Copyright Law," *Cardozo Arts & Entertainment Law Journal* 8, no. 2 (1990): 27–46, 28. Nimmer speaks to the U.S. minimalist approach in implementing the treaty.

142. Berne Convention for the Protection of Literary and Artistic Works, September 9, 1886, as revised at Paris on July 24, 1971, and amended in 1979, S. Treaty Doc. No. 99–27 (1986).

143. Lateef Mtima, "What's Mine Is Mine but What's Yours Is Ours: IP Imperialism, the Right of Publicity, and Intellectual Property Social Justice in the Digital Information Age," *SMU Science & Technology Law Review* 15, no. 3 (Fall 2012): 329.

144. Ruth L. Okediji, "The International Relations of Intellectual Property: Narratives of Developing Country Participation in the Global Intellectual Property System," *Singapore Journal of International & Comparative Law* 7 no. 2 (2003): 315.

145. Peter Drahos, "Developing Countries and International Intellectual Property Standard-Setting," *Journal of World Intellectual Property* 5, no. 5 (2005): 767.

146. Angelie Thomas, "The Costs of Harmonization: The Embrace of an International Copyright Regime in *Golan v. Holder*," St. John's *Journal of International and Comparative Law* 3, no. 2 (2013): 253–63.

147. Drahos, "Developing Countries and International Intellectual Property Standard-Setting." Drahos comments on the structural bargaining inequalities between the United States and Europe and the developing world.

148. *The Chancellor, Masters & Scholars of the University of Oxford and Ors. v. Rameshwari Photocopy Services & Ors.* (High Court of Delhi, December 7, 2016).

149. See generally Reddy and Chandrashekaran, *Create, Copy, Disrupt.*

150. *Golan,* 565 U.S at 303.

151. Ibid. at 307.

152. Ibid. at 309.

153. Ibid.

154. Ibid. at 311.

155. Ibid.

156. Ibid. at 320.

157. Ibid.

158. Ibid. at 326.

159. Ibid. at 332.

160. Ibid. at 333–34. See also John J. Sierotnik, "*Golan v. Holder,* the Copyright Clause, and the Changing Public Policy Underlying Copyright Law in the United States," *Notre Dame Journal of Law, Ethics & Public Policy* 28, no. 1 (2014): 411–31.

161. Laura A. Foster, "Situating Feminism, Patent Law, and the Public Domain," *Columbia Journal of Gender and Law* 20, no. 1 (2011).

162. Carol Rose contends that European and American theories of property rights are invested *not* in granting property rights to individuals but rather in defining, managing, and allocating property rights in a manner that maintains peace, justice, and economic stability. *Golan* is consistent with this principle, that property rights are always contingent. Carol M. Rose, "Property as the Keystone Right," *Notre Dame Law Review* 71, no. 3 (1995): 329–69.

163. *Golan,* 565 U.S. at 335.

164. *Golan,* 565 U.S. at 349 (Breyer, J., dissenting).

165. Ibid. at 350.

166. Ibid. at 353.

167. Anupam Chander and Madhavi Sunder, "The Romance of the Public Domain," *California Law Review* 92, no. 5 (2004): 1331–73.

168. Rose critiques the overemphasis on property rights, in a manner that is implicated here. Rose, "Property as the Keystone Right," 356.

169. *Golan,* 565 U.S. at 353 (Breyer, J., dissenting).

170. Madhavi Sunder, *From Goods to a Good Life: Intellectual Property and Global Justice* (New Haven: Yale University Press, 2012), 4–8.

171. *Golan,* 565 U.S. at 356 (Breyer, J., dissenting).

172. Ibid.

173. See Brianna Dahlberg, "The Orphan Works Problem: Preserving Access to the Cultural History of Disadvantaged Groups Note," *Southern California Review of Law and Social Justice* 20 (2011): 275–316.

174. *Golan,* 565 U.S. 302 at 364.

175. Corynne McSherry, "Supreme Court Gets It Wrong in *Golan v. Holder,* Public Domain Mourns," Electronic Frontier Foundation, January 23, 2012, https://www.eff.org/deeplinks/2012/01/supreme-court-gets-it-wrong-golan-v-holder-public-domain-mourns. As Tarleton Gillespie argues in *Wired Shut,* battles such as the one that the EFF is fighting here are

relatively minor with respect to protecting the public domain. Tarleton Gillespie, *Wired Shut: Copyright and the Shape of Digital Culture* (Cambridge: MIT Press, 2009). While the EFF's commitment to a broad public domain is understandable, the struggle here seems to miss the forest for the trees.

176. Ibid.

177. For a critique of zombie discourse and its links to capitalism, see generally Jean Comaroff and John L. Comaroff, "Alien-Nation: Zombies, Immigrants, and Millennial Capitalism," *South Atlantic Quarterly* 101, no. 4 (2002): 779–805.

CHAPTER FOUR

1. Debora J. Halbert, *Resisting Intellectual Property* (New York: Routledge, 2006), 5.

2. Lawrence Liang, "Porous Legalities and Avenues of Participation," in *Sarai Reader 2005: Bare Acts*, ed. Monica Narula et al. (New Delhi: Sarai, 2005), 6–17. Liang explicitly builds upon the work of the Raqs Media Collective.

3. Ibid., 14.

4. Ibid.

5. Ibid.

6. Ibid., 15.

7. Ibid.

8. Isaac West, *Transforming Citizenships: Transgender Articulations of the Law* (New York: New York University Press, 2014), 37.

9. Halbert, *Resisting Intellectual Property*, 6.

10. Brittney Cooper, "America's 'Prince' Problem: How Black People—and Art—Became 'Devalued,'" *Salon.com*, April 4, 2016, http://www.salon.com/2016/04/21/americas_prince _problem_how_Black_people_and_art_became_devalued/.

11. Kevin Fallon, "Why You Can't Listen to Prince's Music after His Death," *Daily Beast*, April 21, 2016, http://www.thedailybeast.com/articles/2016/04/21/why-you -can-t-listen-to-prince-s-music-after-his-death.html; Emily Blake, "Prince Videos Probably Coming Down Soon, Because That's What He'd Want," *Mashable*, April 28, 2016, http:// mashable.com/2016/04/28/prince-youtube-performance-videos/.

12. Keith Caulfield, "Prince Sets Record with Five Albums in Top 10 of Billboard 200 Chart," *Billboard.com*, May 3, 2016, https://www.billboard.com/articles/columns/chart -beat/7356812/prince-sets-record-five-albums-top-10–billboard-200.

13. Parker Higgins, "Prince Inducted into Takedown Hall of Shame with New Lifetime Aggrievement Award," Electronic Frontier Foundation, May 7, 2013, https:// www.eff.org/deeplinks/2013/05/prince-inducted-takedown-hall-shame-new-lifetime- aggrievement-award.

14. Touré, *I Would Die 4 U: Why Prince Became an Icon* (New York: Atria Books, 2013), 17.

15. CapnOfCrunch, "Prince Shows Love 4 Baltimore during 'Purple Rain' Solo at Rally" *4 Peace*, 2015, https://www.youtube.com/watch?v=4m6dOjM44Zc.

16. Kim Taylor Bennet, "Owen Husney: The Man Who Discovered Prince," *Noisey*, May 24, 2016, https://noisey.vice.com/en_us/article/689pwv/the-man-who-discovered -prince-owen-husney.

17. Ibid.

18. Alan Light, *Let's Go Crazy: Prince and the Making of Purple Rain* (New York: Atria Books, 2014), 231. It is worth noting here that Prince's bandmates were not particularly fond of him during this period of time, in which he was, according to them, detached

from politics and self-absorbed. That may not have hurt his career, but it did affect his relationships. Ibid., 231–33.

19. Julie Baumgold, "Why Prince Became a Symbol. (Literally.)," *Esquire*, April 11, 2016, http://www.esquire.com/entertainment/music/a44218/prince-1995-esquire-gentleman/.

20. As with most things Prince, there are conflicting reports about whether and how he intended to call upon histories of slavery. See Zack Stiegler, "'Slave 2 the System': Prince and the Strategic Performance of Slavery," *Journal of Popular Music Studies* 21, no. 2 (June 2009): 213–39; Anil Dash, "Message from the Artist," *Medium*, May 16, 2016, https://medium.com/@anildash/message-from-the-artist-c611535da21c.

21. Twila Perry, "'Let's Work!' The Racial and the Universal in Prince's Fight for Artists' Rights," Prince from MPLS, University of Minnesota, Minneapolis, April 16–18, 2018.

22. Kevin Bales, "Expendable People: Slavery in the Age of Globalization," *Journal of International Affairs* 53, no. 2 (2000): 463.

23. Cynthia J. Fuchs, "'I Wanna Be Your Fantasy': Sex, Death, and the Artist Formerly Known as Prince," *Women & Performance: A Journal of Feminist Theory* 8, no. 2 (1996): 140.

24. Terrence W. Epperson, "Race and the Disciplines of the Plantation," *Historical Archaeology* 24, no. 4 (1990): 30. Epperson is one of many scholars who have written on the importance of naming practices for African Americans. See also Kimberly W. Benston, "'I Yam What I Am': Naming and Unnaming in Afro-American Literature," *Black American Literature Forum* 16, no. 1 (1982); Sigrid King, "Naming and Power in Zora Neale Hurston's *Their Eyes Were Watching God*," *Black American Literature Forum* 24, no. 4 (Winter 1990): 683–96; Ben L. Martin, "From Negro to Black to African American: The Power of Names and Naming," *Political Science Quarterly* 106, no. 1 (1991): 83–107; Jerome S. Handler and JoAnn Jacoby, "Slave Names and Naming in Barbados, 1650–1830," *William and Mary Quarterly* 53, no. 4 (1996): 685–728.

25. Danielle Endres, "The Rhetoric of Nuclear Colonialism: Rhetorical Exclusion of American Indian Arguments in the Yucca Mountain Nuclear Waste Siting Decision," *Communication and Critical/Cultural Studies* 6, no. 1 (March 2009): 49.

26. Fuchs, "'I Wanna Be Your Fantasy,'" 145.

27. Homi Bhabha, "Of Mimicry and Man: The Ambivalence of Colonial Discourse," *October* 28 (1984): 125–33.

28. Dash, "Message from the Artist."

29. Anthony DeCurtis, "O(+> Free at Last," *Rolling Stone*, November 28, 1996, https://sites.google.com/site/prninterviews/home/rolling-stone-748-28-november-1996.

30. Judith Butler, *Excitable Speech: A Politics of the Performative* (New York: Routledge, 2013), 2.

31. Kevin J. Greene, "Intellectual Property at the Intersection of Race and Gender: Lady Sings the Blues," *American University Journal of Gender, Social Policy & the Law* 16, no. 3 (2008), 370.

32. "National Assessment of Adult Literacy (NAAL)," https://nces.ed.gov/naal/lit_history.asp.

33. Judy G. Russell, "X (or W) Marks the Spot," *Legal Genealogist*, April 5, 2012, https://www.legalgenealogist.com/2012/04/05/x-or-w-marks-the-spot/.

34. Christopher Hooton, "Prince Dead: When Prince Changed His Name to a Symbol Warner Bros Had to Mail Floppy Disks with a Custom Font," *Independent*, April 21, 2016, http://www.independent.co.uk/arts-entertainment/music/news/prince-dead-when-prince-changed-his-name-to-a-symbol-warner-bros-had-to-mass-mail-floppy-disks-with-a6995196.html.

35. Benston, "'I Yam What I Am,'" 3.

36. Tom Breihan, "Prince Explains Why Tidal Will Win the Streaming Wars," *Stereogum*, December 23, 2015, https://www.stereogum.com/1850356/prince-explains-why-tidal -will-win-the-streaming-wars/news/.

37. "Prince's Troubled Relationship with Copyright," *Tedium: The Dull Side of the Internet*, April 22, 2016, http://tedium.co/2016/04/21/prince-troubled-relationship -with-copyright/.

38. Breihan, "Prince Explains Why Tidal Will Win the Streaming Wars"; Daniel Kreps, "Tidal, Prince Estate Agree to Release New Prince Album," *Rolling Stone*, May 11, 2018, https://www.rollingstone.com/music/music-news/tidal-prince-estate-agree-to-release -new-prince-album-628669/.

39. Fallon, "Why You Can't Listen to Prince's Music after His Death."

40. Prince, Twitter post, June 25, 2015, 4:25 p.m. https://twitter.com/prince/status /614212927709577216?lang=en.

41. Dorian Lynskey, "Prince: 'I'm a Musician. And I Am Music,'" *The Guardian*, June 23, 2011, https://www.theguardian.com/music/2011/jun/23/prince-interview-adele-internet.

42. See Anjali Vats, "Prince of Intellectual Property: On Creatorship, Copyright, and Black Capitalism in the Life/Afterlives of the Purple One," *Howard Journal of Communications* 30, no. 2 (2019).

43. Julianne Escobedo Shepherd, "Prince Spent His Life Elevating and Mentoring Women," *The Muse*, April 22, 2016, https://themuse.jezebel.com/prince-spent-his-life -elevating-and-mentoring-women-1772479454.

44. Kembrew McLeod notes that only people in white lab coats, not indigenous peoples, can produce patentable knowledge. Patents are built on "the fiction of individualistic scientific innovation." Kembrew McLeod, *Freedom of Expression®: Resistance and Repression in the Age of Intellectual Property* (Minneapolis: University of Minnesota Press, 2007), 53–54.

45. "India Makes Moves to Reclaim Heritage from 'Yoga Piracy,'" *Washington Times*, September 22, 2005, https://www.washingtontimes.com/news/2005/sep/22/20050922 -114821-4035r/. For a detailed discussion of Bikram Yoga in relation to the Yoga Wars, see Anjali Vats, "(Dis)owning Bikram: Decolonizing Vernacular and Dewesternizing Restructuring in the Yoga Wars," *Communication and Critical/Cultural Studies* 13, no. 4 (2016), 1–21.

46. Kent A. Ono and John M. Sloop, "The Critique of Vernacular Discourse," *Communication Monographs* 62, no. 1 (1995): 20.

47. I use "layperson" to describe non-intellectual property lawyers here, i.e., non-experts.

48. Vats, "(Dis)owning Bikram," 2–3.

49. Daniel Robinson, *Confronting Biopiracy: Challenges, Cases, and International Debates* (London: Earthscan, 2016), 3. Here, Robinson offers a succinct and contextualized definition of bioprospecting/biopiracy.

50. Vandana Shiva, *Biopiracy: The Plunder of Nature and Knowledge* (Boston: South End Press, 1997), 5.

51. Ibid.

52. Lawrence Lessig, *Remix: Making Art and Commerce Thrive in the Hybrid Economy* (New York: Penguin, 2008).

53. Nona Walia, "Kissa Copyright Ka," *Times of India*, July 9, 2004, http://timesofindia .indiatimes.com/city/delhi-times/Kissa-copyright-ka/articleshow/771448.cms?

54. See *Bikram's Yoga College of India, L.P. v. Evolation Yoga, LLC*, 803 F.3d 1032 (9th Cir. October 8, 2015).

55. Kruttika Vijay, "SpicyIP Tidbit: Yoga Asanas Soon to Be Protected by the TKDL," *Spicy IP*, June 7, 2010, https://spicyip.com/2010/06/spicyip-tidbit-yoga-asanas-soon-to-be.html.

56. Shwetasree Majumder, "A Dash of Yoga and a Whole Lot of Confusion," *Spicy IP*, May 25, 2007, https://spicyip.com/2007/05/dash-of-yoga-and-whole-lot-of-confusion.html.

57. Laura A. Foster, "Situating Feminism, Patent Law, and the Public Domain," *Columbia Journal of Gender and Law* 20, no. 1 (2011).

58. Halbert, *Resisting Intellectual Property.*

59. Endres, "The Rhetoric of Nuclear Colonialism."

60. Walia, "Kissa Copyright Ka."

61. Ibid.

62. Ibid.

63. Gerard A. Hauser, *Vernacular Voices: The Rhetoric of Publics and Public Spheres* (Columbia: University of South Carolina Press, 2008).

64. Christopher Mattison, "Delinking, Decoloniality & Dewesternization: Interview with Walter Mignolo (Part II)," *Critical Legal Thinking*, May 2, 2012, http://criticallegalthinking.com/2012/05/02/delinking-decoloniality-dewesternization-interview-with-walter-mignolo-part-ii/.

65. This is not to say that the TKDL is a perfect solution to the issues presented here. Many scholars have pointed to its difficulties and deficiencies. See Seemantani Sharma, "Traditional Knowledge Digital Library: 'A Silver Bullet' in the War against Biopiracy?," *John Marshall Review of Intellectual Property Law* 17, no. 2 (2017).

66. Marouf Hasian, Jr., and Fernando Delgado, "The Trials and Tribulations of Racialized Critical Rhetorical Theory: Understanding the Rhetorical Ambiguities of Proposition 187," *Communication Theory* 8, no. 3 (August 1998): 245–70.

67. Lawrence Liang, "Piracy, Creativity, and Infrastructure: Rethinking Access to Culture," SSRN Working Papers, 2009, http://www.ssrn.com/abstract=1436229.

68. Patrick Burkart, *Pirate Politics: The New Information Policy Contests*, The Information Society Series (Cambridge: MIT Press, 2014).

69. Martin Fredriksson, "Copyright Culture and Pirate Politics," *Cultural Studies* 28, no. 5–6 (September 2014): 1022–47.

70. Vinod K. Gupta, "The Functioning of the TKDL, Cooperation with International Patent Offices & Security & Access Considerations" (International Conference "Utilization of the Traditional Knowledge Digital Library [TKDL] as a Model for the Protection of Traditional Knowledge," New Delhi, India, 2011), http://www.kipo.ke.wipo.net/export/sites/www/meetings/en/2009/ip_gc_ge/presentations/gupta.pdf).

71. Ibid.

72. Laura A. Foster, "Situating Feminism, Patent Law, and the Public Domain," *Columbia Journal of Gender and Law* 20, no. 1 (2011).

73. James Boyle, *The Public Domain: Enclosing the Commons of the Mind* (New Haven: Yale University Press, 2008).

74. Laura A. Foster, "Patents, Biopolitics, and Feminisms: Locating Patent Law Struggles over Breast Cancer Genes and the Hoodia Plant," *International Journal of Cultural Property* 19, no. 3 (August 2012): 379.

75. Vats, "(Dis)Owning Bikram."

76. Mangala Hirwade, "Protecting Traditional Knowledge Digitally: A Case Study of TKDL," National Workshop on Digitization Initiatives & Applications in Indian Context,

Nagpur, India, 2010, http://hdl.handle.net/10760/14020.

77. Susanne Hiller, "Hottest Yoga in Town: At 100 Degrees You Feel the 'Bikram Glow.' It's Not Pretty," *National Post*, March 12, 2003.

78. Walter Mignolo, "Geopolitics of Sensing and Knowing," European Institute for Progressive Cultural Policies, September 2011, http://eipcp.net/transversal/0112/mignolo/en.

79. Walter Mignolo, "Delinking," *Cultural Studies* 21, no. 2 (March 2007): 449–514.

80. Mattison, "Delinking, Decoloniality, and Dewesternization."

81. Traditional Knowledge Digital Library, "TK Resource Classification," 2013, http://www.tkdl.res.in/tkdl/langdefault/common/TKRC.asp?GL=Eng.

82. Strasbourg Agreement Concerning the International Patent Classification, World Intellectual Property Organization, http://www.wipo.int/treaties/en/classification/strasbourg/.

83. Traditional Knowledge Digital Library, "TK Resource Classification."

84. Chidi Oguamanam, "Patents and Traditional Medicine: Digital Capture, Creative Legal Interventions, and the Dialectics of Knowledge Transformation," *Indiana Journal of Global Legal Studies* 15, no. 2 (Summer 2008): 489–528.

85. Darrel Wanzer-Serrano, *The New York Young Lords and the Struggle for Liberation* (Philadelphia: Temple University Press, 2015), 25.

86. European Patent Office, "India's Traditional Knowledge Digital Library (TKDL): A Powerful Tool for Patent Examiners," September 6, 2010.

87. See Drahos, "Developing Countries and International Intellectual Property Standard-Setting." *Journal of World Intellectual Property* 5, no. 5 (2005): 767.

88. Oguamanam, "Patents and Traditional Medicine."

89. Ibid., 497.

90. Ibid., 502.

91. Michael Shamburger, "Marshawn Lynch's Nickname, Beast Mode, Has Become a Fan Favorite," *thebiglead*, January 20, 2015, http://thebiglead.com/2015/01/20/marshawn-lynchs-nickname-beast-mode-has-become-afan-favorite/.

92. Ibid.

93. Jenn M. Jackson, "Slavery Much? On Racism in the NFL, Richard Sherman, and Hypocrisy," *Water Cooler Convos*, January 22, 2014, http://watercoolerconvos.com/2014/01/22/slavery-much-on-racism-in-the-nflrichard-sherman-and-hypocrisy/.

94. Robin Boylorn, "What Marshawn Lynch and Richard Sherman Teach Us about Respectability and Black Masculinity," *Crunk Feminist Collective*, February 3, 2015, http://www.crunkfeministcollective.com/2015/02/03/what-marshawn-lynch-and-richard-sherman-teach-us-about-respectability-black-masculinity/.

95. José Esteban Muñoz, *Disidentifications: Queers of Color and the Performance of Politics*, Cultural Studies of the Americas (Minneapolis: University of Minnesota Press, 1999), 11–12.

96. Matt Kolsky, "Marshawn Lynch Does More for Oakland Than Raiders Could Ever Hope," *San Francisco Examiner*, August 1, 2017, http://www.sfexaminer.com/marshawn-lynch-does-more-for-oakland-than-raiders-could-ever-hope/.

97. Andrew B. Leiter, *In the Shadow of the Black Beast: African American Masculinity in the Harlem and Southern Renaissances* (Baton Rouge: Louisiana State University Press, 2010), 2–3.

98. Calvin John Smiley and David Fakunle, "From 'Brute' to 'Thug': The Demonization and Criminalization of Unarmed Black Male Victims in America," *Journal of Human*

Behavior in the Social Environment 26, no. 3–4 (2016): 350–66.

99. Suzanne Marie Enck-Wanzer, "All's Fair in Love and Sport: Black Masculinity and Domestic Violence in the News," *Communication and Critical/Cultural Studies* 6, no. 1 (March 2009): 9.

100. Thomas P. Oates, "The Erotic Gaze in the NFL Draft," *Communication and Critical/Cultural Studies* 4, no. 1 (March 1, 2007): 74–90.

101. Smiley and Fakunle, "From 'Brute' to 'Thug.'"

102. Boylorn, "What Marshawn Lynch and Richard Sherman Teach Us about Respectability and Black Masculinity."

103. As I have previously shown, authors of the Harlem Renaissance and the Southern Renaissance used the figure of the Black beast as a site for redefining Black masculinity. Anjali Vats, "Marking Disidentification: Race, Corporeality, and Resistance in Trademark Law," *Southern Communication Journal* 81, no. 4 (August 2016): 245–47.

104. Tony Drovetto, "The Top 10 Quotes of Marshawn Lynch's Seahawks Career," Seattle Seahawks, February 2, 2016, http://www.seahawks.com/news/2016/02/08/top-10-quotes-marshawn-lynchs-seahawks-career.

105. Vats, "Marking Disidentification," 244.

106. Muñoz, *Disidentifications*, 44.

107. "Marshawn Lynch: Beast Mode," *E:60*, *ESPN.com*, December 2, 2013, http://espn.go.com/video/clip?id=9927540.

108. Peter Odell Campbell, "Marshawn Lynch's Labor Actions" (Paper Presentation at Race and Media Conference, Albuquerque, New Mexico, September 2015), http://www.peterodellcampbell.com/marshawn-lynch-labor-action/.

109. Herman Gray, "Black Masculinity and Visual Culture," *Callaloo* 18, no. 2 (1995): 401–5.

110. Oates, "The Erotic Gaze in the NFL Draft," 75.

111. Ashraf H. A. Rushdy, "Exquisite Corpse," *Transition* 9, no. 3 (2000): 70–77.

112. Anjali Vats, "Racechange Is the New Black: Racial Accessorizing and Racial Tourism in High Fashion as Constraints on Rhetorical Agency," *Communication, Culture & Critique* 7, no. 1 (2014): 119.

113. See Brittney Cooper and Treva Lindsey, "Love in a Time of Scandal," *Feminist Wire*, February 11, 2013, http://www.thefeministwire.com/2013/02/10180/ for a discussion of the politics of pleasure.

114. Enck-Wanzer, "All's Fair in Love and Sport," 9.

115. Gray, "Black Masculinity and Visual Culture," 403.

116. Ad Age Studio 30, "Beast Mode's Business Empire," *Ad Age*, January 24, 2018, http://adage.com/article/special-report-building-brand/beast-mode-business-empire/312052/.

117. Cheryl I. Harris, "Whiteness as Property," *Harvard Law Review* 106, no. 8 (June 1993): 1761.

CONCLUSION

1. Amy L. Brandzel, *Against Citizenship: The Violence of the Normative* (Urbana: University of Illinois Press, 2016), x.

2. Ibid., 3.

3. Ibid., x.

4. Ibid., xv.

5. Ravi Sunder Rajan, *Pharmocracy*: Value, Politics, and Knowledge in Global Biomedicine

(Durham: Duke University Press 2017), 238.

6. Robert Chang and Neil Gotanda trace how vying for political rights and entitlements can lead to destructive racial triangulation. Robert S. Chang and Neil Gotanda, "The Race Question in LatCrit and Asian American Jurisprudence," *Nevada Law Journal* 7, no. 3 (2007).

7. Walter Mignolo, *The Darker Side of Western Modernity: Global Futures, Decolonial Options* (Durham: Duke University Press, 2011), 2. Significantly, decoloniality emerged conceptually after the Bandung Conference, as a means of situating Latinx nations in a globalizing world.

8. Ramón Grosfoguel, "The Epistemic Decolonial Turn," *Cultural Studies* 21, no. 2–3 (March 2007): 211–23.

9. Georg Wilhelm Friedrich Hegel and John Sibree, *The Philosophy of History* (Buffalo: Prometheus Books, 1991), 110–11.

10. David Hume, *Essays Moral, Political, and Literary (Life of the Author, Etc.).* (London: J. B. Bebbington, 1862), 178.

11. Ibid.

12. Ruth L. Okediji, "The International Relations of Intellectual Property: Narratives of Developing Country Participation in the Global Intellectual Property System," *Singapore Journal of International and Comparative Law* 7 (2003): 324.

13. Edward W. Said, *Orientalism* (New York: Vintage Books, 1979), 49.

14. Leigh Boucher, "'Whiteness,' Geopolitics, and the Settler Empire," in *Re-Orienting Whiteness*, ed. Katherine Ellinghaus, Jane Carey, and Leigh Boucher (New York: Palgrave-Macmillan, 2009), 53–54.

15. James Boyle, *Shamans, Software, and Spleens: Law and the Construction of the Information Society* (Cambridge: Harvard University Press, 2009), 195.

16. Rudyard Kipling, *The White Man's Burden* (New York: Doubleday and McClure Company, 1899).

17. Boyle, *Shamans, Software, and Spleens*, 355. See also Zaheer Baber, *The Science of Empire: Scientific Knowledge, Civilization, and Colonial Rule in India* (Albany: State University of New York Press, 1996). Baber argues that though colonialism did not result in the complete erasure of traditional knowledge practices and sometimes even led to cross-cultural exchange—but it was nonetheless predominantly a tool for expanding the reach of colonial regimes.

18. Martha Woodmansee, "On the Author Effect: Recovering Collectivity," *Cardozo Arts & Entertainment Law Journal* 10, no. 2 (1991): 279–92.

19. Grosfoguel, "The Epistemic Decolonial Turn," 214.

20. Mignolo, *The Darker Side of Western Modernity*, 45.

21. Ibid., 45.

22. Alexander G. Weheliye, *Habeas Viscus: Racializing Assemblages, Biopolitics, and Black Feminist Theories of the Human* (Durham: Duke University Press, 2014), 77.

23. Nelson Maldonado Torres, "The Topology of Being and the Geopolitics of Knowledge: Modernity, Empire, Coloniality," *City* 8, no. 1 (April 2004): 42.

24. Brandzel, *Against Citizenship*, 4.

25. Suhag Shukla, "Yoga Won't Wreck Your Body but May Make You More Hindu," *Huffington Post*, January 10, 2012, http://www.huffingtonpost.com/suhag-a-shukla-esq /yoga-wont-wreck-your-body_b_1195754.html.

26. Walter Mignolo, "Delinking," *Cultural Studies* 21, no. 2 (March 2007): 454.

27. Ibid.

28. Ibid., 457.

29. Ibid.

30. Walter Mignolo, Introduction, *Cultural Studies* 21, no. 2 (2007): 157.

31. Javier Sanjinés C., "Mestizaje Upside Down: Subaltern Knowledges and the Known," *Nepantla: Views from South* 3, no. 1 (March 2002): 39–60.

32. Anjali Vats and Deidre A. Keller, "Critical Race IP," *Cardozo Arts & Entertainment Law Journal* 36 no. 3 (2018): 788.

33. Wanzer-Serrano, *The New York Young Lords and the Struggle for Liberation* 22.

34. Vats and Keller, "Critical Race IP," 765.

35. Wanzer-Serrano, *The New York Young Lords and the Struggle for Liberation*, 22.

36. Anibal Quijano, "Coloniality and Modernity/Rationality," *Cultural Studies* 21, no. 2–3 (2007), 176.

37. Ibid. at 177.

38. Frantz Fanon and Adolfo Gilly, *A Dying Colonialism*, trans. Haakon Chevalier (New York: Grove Press, 1994), 24.

39. Lawrence Grossberg, *We Gotta Get Out of This Place: Popular Conservatism and Postmodern Culture* (New York: Routledge, 2014), 388. See also Phaedra C. Pezzullo, "Contextualizing Boycotts and Buycotts: The Impure Politics of Consumer-Based Advocacy in an Age of Global Ecological Crises," *Communication and Critical/Cultural Studies* 8, no. 2 (June 2011): 124–45; Isaac West, *Transforming Citizenships: Transgender Articulations of the Law* (New York: New York University Press, 2014.

40. Quijano, "Coloniality and Modernity/Rationality," 170.

41. Fred Moten, "The Case of Blackness," *Criticism* 50, no. 2 (2008): 178.

42. Ibid.

43. Stefano Harney and Fred Moten, *The Undercommons: Fugitive Planning & Black Study* (Wivenhoe: Minor Compositions, 2013), 28.

44. Ibid., 6.

45. Ibid.

46. Mat Callahan, "Why Intellectual Property? Why Now?" *Socialism and Democracy* 28, no. 1 (January 2014): 5. In a fitting way to end these Notes, Ted Striphas and Kembrew McLeod remind us that "intellectual property disturbs material and epistemological boundaries, recodes existing significations and patterns of information flows, and helps to actualize nascent modes of thought, conduct, affect, expression and embodiment. Ted Striphas and Kembrew McLeod, "Strategic Improprieties: Cultural Studies, the Everyday, and the Politics of Intellectual Properties," *Cultural Studies* 20, no. 2–3 (2006): 122.

INDEX

Access to Knowledge (A2K), 83, 113, 134, 140, 145, 148–50, 154, 201. *See also* cultural appropriation

Adams, James Truslow, 52

affect, 1, 7, 30, 31, 38, 55–57, 61, 75, 91, 99, 105, 106, 167, 187, 205, 216n19, 223n169, 249n46. *See also* public feelings

Africans and African Americans: Aunt Jemima stereotype and, 57–63; bestiality ascribed to, 25, 37, 157, 180–87, 190, 247n103; civility and respectability and, 135; criminality ascribed to, 107; copyright and, 35 inferiority ascribed to, 135, 162; histories of, 215n73; literacy rates and, 166; medical exploitation of, 82; music industry and, 85–95, 97–100, 158–69; naming and, 162; personhood of, 30, 32, 34, 36, 54, 158–59, 162–64, 179–81, 186, 190; treated as property, 157, 161, 184, 206; and publishing, 35. *See also* anti-

Blackness; Blackness, as racial category; citizenship, enslaved persons and slavery; intellectual property citizenship; personhood; racial categories; racial scripts

Afropessimism. *See* social death

Agreement on Trade-Related Aspects of Intellectual Property Rights (TRIPS), 76, 83, 130, 133, 136–42, 148, 174, 197

Ahmed, Sara, 31, 61

Amador, Charles (Charlie Aplin), *The Race Track* (film) 39–44

America Invents Act. *See* Leahy-Smith America Invents Act (2011)

American Civil Liberties Union, 131

American Dream: agency and free will and, 52; Asian piracy as antithetical to, 140–41; attributes associated with, 10, 51; authorship/invention linked to, 20, 33, 51–53, 75, 79, 111–12, 115–17, 140; Black criminality contrasted with, 91; bootstraps and, 114; definition of, 52; colorblindness

251

The authorized representative in the EU for product safety and compliance is:
Mare Nostrum Group
B.V Doelen 72
4831 GR Breda
The Netherlands

www.ingramcontent.com/pod-product-compliance
Lightning Source LLC
Chambersburg PA
CBHW020841270326
41928CB00006B/502